SOUTH-WESTERN

Working Smart

2nd Edition

Madelyn Schulman, Ph.D.
Assistant Director
Office of Career and Occupational Education
Board of Education of the City of New York
Brooklyn, New York

Bonnie F. Kowadlo
Formerly of Seward Park High School
New York, New York

VISIT US ON THE INTERNET
www.swep.com
www.thomsonlearning.com

South-Western
EDUCATIONAL PUBLISHING
Thomson Learning™

Australia • Canada • Denmark • Japan • Mexico • New Zealand • Philippines
Puerto Rico • Singapore • South Africa • Spain • United Kingdom • United States

Business Unit Director: Peter McBride
Executive Editor: Eve Lewis
Acquisitions Editor: Susan Carson
Project Manager/Editor: Alan Biondi
Production, Art/Design Coordinator: Patricia Matthews Boies
Marketing Manager: Mark Linton
Internal Design: Lou Ann Thesing
Cover Design: Ann Small-Wills/a small design studio, Inc.
Manufacturing Coordinator: Kathy Hampton
Electronic Prepress: A.W. Kingston Publishing Services

Photos on pages 51 and 183 © 1998 Corbis Corp. Digital Stock
All other photos © PhotoDisc, Inc.

ISBN: 0-538-69144-1

1 2 3 4 5 6 7 8 9 0   WV   05 04 03 02 01 00 99

Printed in the United States of America

Preface

American businesses and workers strive to provide quality products and services in an increasingly complex, rapidly changing marketplace where competition is global in scope. The ability of a person to work productively and keep a job has always been important.

As the world becomes smaller, the work becomes more technologically complex and the people in the workplace more diverse, a broader range of skills is needed to achieve success on the job. Business needs employees who can think critically; communicate effectively both verbally and in writing; interact well with staff, the public, and customers; and use the available resources optimally. *Working Smart* addresses the skills that are needed in the high-performance workplace of the twenty-first century.

Purpose

Working Smart helps the user learn how to be successful and gain rewards and satisfaction on the job. This is a user-friendly text-workbook that will take the user through a large number of hands-on exercises as they learn to navigate through the many obstacles that may hinder success on the job.

Features

Working Smart, as a text-workbook, is simple and direct. The main topics of the text—orientation to a new job, expectations of employers and employees, communication skills, interpersonal relationships, evaluations, and future planning—are of vital importance for newcomers as they enter the workforce. Workplace competencies and foundation skills that are formulated in the U.S. Department of Labor's *A Scans Report for America 2000 (SCANS SKILLS)* have been integrated into every chapter.

Working Smart has many salient features that encourage learning and allow for applied learning and diverse assessment methods:

- Activities and case studies are interspersed within the text to encourage immediate practice and reinforcement.
- Additional activities appear at the end of each chapter and unit.
- All activities stress writing, critical thinking, and problem solving.
- A practice simulation affords an opportunity to apply learning to new situations.
- The creation of portfolios is guided and encouraged.
- There is opportunity to refine computer and Internet skills.
- Each chapter has team activities that lead to the creation of a finished product.

Although each chapter stands alone, skills build on each other and what is learned and practiced in earlier sections will be applied later in the text. All activities and exercises deal with self-management, interpersonal skills, decision-making and critical thinking, and ethics. The emphasis is on verbal communication through the expression of ideas, concepts, and knowledge. All exercises require written answers using complete sentences, thereby giving the user an opportunity to develop writing skills. Critical thinking is encouraged as the user is asked to make substantive choices.

The authors have paid particular attention to breaking down gender stereotypes with regard to various careers by recognizing the right of each individual to work in any type of job that best suits his or her interest and abilities. Respect for others, regardless of background or cultural orientation, is encouraged. The increasingly multicultural global environment demands our understanding and acceptance of others with whom we work and live.

The authors wish all who use this text success on the job and attaining the goals they set for the future.

Acknowledgments

Sincere thanks are extended to the reviewers whose advice and constructive suggestions helped shape this second edition of *Working Smart:*

Audie Cline
California High School
Jefferson City, Missouri

Julia Harper
Cabell County Vocational-Tech Center
Huntington, West Virginia

Julie Ann Jachne
University of Houston
Houston, Texas

Ann Jordan
Great Oaks Institute of Technology and Career Development
Cincinnati, Ohio

Jerry O'Bryan
Danville Area Community College
Danville, Illinois

Sue Walter
Loveland High School
Douglas, Colorado

Enjoy Success with *Working Smart*

As you can see, this dynamic new text-workbook concentrates on essential job-keeping skills. Hands-on activities, group projects, and case studies deal with contemporary issues like self-management, interpersonal skills, diversity, decision-making, ethics, responsibility, and working in teams.

In today's workplace, *Working Smart* is the key to success.

Madelyn Schulman
Bonnie F. Kowadlo

Table of Contents

Unit 2 **Smart Communications on the Job** 83

Unit 1

Starting Your New Job

Chapter 1

Getting Ready for the First Day on the Job

Skills OBJECTIVES

After completing this chapter you will be able to:

1. Develop a list of important information required on the first day at a new job.

2. Recognize important information presented during the orientation process at work.

3. Make personal decisions relating to your preparation for the first day on a job.

4. Learn from analyzing and discussing typical problems arising on the first day of a new job.

Jenna could not sleep at all last night. She found the job she has always dreamed of having and today is the first day of what, she hopes, will be a long and successful career. She knows that first impressions are important, but what should she do to make that impression? Nerves have made her mouth dry, tension is causing her stomach to rebel at the thought of food. Jenna plans to wear the outfit she used for job hunting, as it is businesslike and looks good on her. She checks to make sure that she has all the necessary papers in her purse, three times, just to make sure. Leaving for the short drive, she runs back to have a last look in the mirror. Jenna knows she has plenty of time to arrive at work, but is afraid that she will encounter a traffic delay, she will get lost, her car will break down, or all sorts of other calamities will befall her.

It is 5:30 A.M. and Aaron is awake and excited about starting his new job as a clerical assistant at the offices of a daily newspaper. He is up earlier than usual because this is his first full-time job. Although Aaron is prepared for the day, he is nervous about meeting new people. Still, he is determined to make a good impression when meeting his new supervisor and coworkers. Aaron knows the importance of getting off to a good start on the very first day of his new job. His business clothes are cleaned and pressed, his shoes are shined, and he knows he must catch the 7:30 A.M. bus. All the items Aaron has to take with him to work are lined up on his dresser and he looks them over as he heads for the shower.

Congratulations! Like Aaron and Jenna, you have completed your job search successfully and are starting your new job. You are excited, nervous, and unsure about what to expect. Chapter 1 will acquaint you with what you need to prepare for that all-important first day.

Learn about the Company

Familiarize yourself with the company before you start your new job. Knowing the products or services the company provides, its competition, and some company history will make you feel more at home once you start to work. Your employer might provide you with written information such as an annual report or published articles about the company. Ask the Human Resources Department or the person who interviews you for information.

To find out more about your company's business, you can read articles in newsletters produced by the company for in-house distribution, plus business and consumer magazines and newspapers. Ask friends, neighbors, or contact the Chamber of Commerce. You can also visit your local library. Three good library and Internet sources of company information are the *Standard & Poor's Directory*, the *Dun and Bradstreet Directory*, and the *Fortune 500 Directory*. Additionally, you can ask the librarian for more sources.

Smart **TIP**

Learn all you can about your firm.

Smart **TIP**

Planning ahead helps make good first impressions.

First Impressions Affect Your Job

When Pauline Chung was introduced to her new supervisor, she smiled and gave a firm handshake as she said, "I'm so pleased to meet you, Ms. Garner. I am looking forward to working in the data entry department." Ms. Garner was delighted to welcome Pauline. First impressions affect everyone you meet as you interact with your boss and coworkers.

A summary of *Do's* and *Don'ts* can be found in Figure 1-2.

How Do You Make a Good Impression?

Do
- Smile.
- Be polite.
- Give a firm handshake.
- Accept others who are different from you.
- Listen carefully.
- Be aware of your surroundings.
- Ask questions about work if you do not understand.
- Be friendly.
- Dress appropriately for the job.

Don't
- Tell everyone you know how to do the job.
- Tell anyone how he or she should do his or her job.
- Talk too much about yourself.
- Talk about how things were done at your previous job.
- Talk about previous supervisors.
- Smoke.
- Chew gum.

Figure 1-2: Do's and Don'ts for a Good First Impression

How do first impressions affect your supervisor? When you have made a positive first impression, your supervisor is more likely to make an extra effort to help you adjust to your new job. In the example above, Ms. Garner's introduction of Pauline to department members will be upbeat and welcoming, a reflection of the positive impression Pauline made on her. If she had formed a negative first impression, Ms. Garner probably would be more likely to criticize or have low expectations of Pauline's work. Once a supervisor has negative feelings about you, you will have a hard time changing those feelings.

How do first impressions affect your coworkers? Imagine you are the newcomer in a company where everyone knows each other and has worked together for a long time. In those first few moments, your coworkers will react to you and begin forming an opinion about you. A positive impression will prompt them to make you feel welcome. They might ask you to join them for lunch or participate in social activities. You will find they are eager to answer your questions and help you learn company routines. If you leave them with an unfavorable impression, coworkers might ignore you, talk about you behind your back, pile extra work on you, not offer to help you, or exclude you from social activities.

Figure 1-1: Positive first impressions help pave the way to good relationships on the job.

How do first impressions influence your work expectations?

Your supervisor and coworkers will make a first impression on you, too. Your first impressions of your work place, supervisor, and colleagues will affect your expectations at work. A positive first impression helps you begin your job with confidence and expectations that you will be happy and successful there. The expectations of success and happiness are missing when you have a negative impression of your supervisor and coworkers. If you envision a negative work environment, you probably will not have high expectations of your ability to work well in your new job.

Being Nervous Is Natural

Being nervous means you feel apprehensive, upset, or worried. You might show your nervousness in physical ways like having shortness of breath, feeling jumpy or moody, getting a headache, experiencing "butterflies" in your stomach, or breaking out in hives. Talking in a loud voice, getting angry, interrupting, not paying attention, or crying are some of the ways extreme anxiety can show up in your behavior. Just the idea of starting something new is enough to make many people very nervous. Some new experiences that can make you nervous are:

1. A new job.
2. A new routine.
3. Using and learning new skills.
4. Accepting new responsibilities.
5. Learning new ways a company does things.

You are entering a new situation when you begin a new job. You are facing new challenges in an unfamiliar environment. You are interacting with supervisors and coworkers whom you do not know. You feel lost because:

1. Everyone seems to know the rules of the game.

2. You don't know what will be expected of you.

3. You will be meeting new people who know each other.

4. You have a fear of being rejected. Maybe your new supervisor and coworkers will not like you or will exclude you from their cliques.

5. You are afraid of not liking your supervisor or coworkers.

6. You have to prove yourself. During the job interview you said you could do many things; now you have to prove it.

7. _____

8. _____

ACTIVITY I

Griselda is entering a new situation at Power Plumbing Supply as an accounting clerk. She doesn't know what to expect and wants to make a good impression on her supervisor and coworkers. Griselda is afraid she will not fit in and she doesn't want to be treated like an outsider.

1. List four things Griselda can do to make a good impression.

_____

_____

_____

_____

2. Why should Griselda make a good impression on her new supervisor?

_____

_____

_____

_____

How to Prepare for Your First Day on the Job

Cassandra stood in front of her closet this morning trying to decide what to wear to her new job. "I can't wear my gray suit," she moaned, "because there's a spot on the jacket. And my plaid dress needs to be pressed. I'm going to be late for my first day on the job because I don't have anything to wear." With proper planning, Cassandra could have avoided this scenario.

Starting a new job as a plumber's assistant, Ashanti dressed in a flash at 6:00 A.M. He didn't have to make decisions about what to wear because Jim Magnus, the owner of Progressive Plumbing, told him to wear work clothes—jeans, tee shirt, work boots, and tool belt. He expects to be getting a work shirt with the company logo and a set of tools from his supervisor this morning.

Dress for the job you want.

Deciding What to Wear

Your **attire**, the clothes that you wear, is a key part of the first impression you make. In the preceding examples, Cassandra and Ashanti wore completely different types of clothing to work. They dressed according to the kind of work they will do. Current fashion trends, geographic location, climate, cultural requirements, and local customs are a few of the things you need to take into consideration when choosing your wardrobe for work. Suggestions for business clothing are shown in Checklist 1-1.

✓ Attire

Checklist 1-1

Males

- Business suit or slacks and sport coat. The material should be a natural fabric—cotton, wool, wool blend, or flannel. Shiny fabrics are frowned on and should be avoided, at least during your first days and months. Use subdued colors such as dark blue, black, gray, or brown. A pinstripe or tweed is acceptable, but avoid plaids, stripes, or patterns.
- Solid-color or striped shirt and a conservative striped or small-print tie.
- Leather shoes (not sneakers) and dark socks.
- Belt or suspenders.

Females

- Business suit, skirt and blouse, or dress made of daytime fabrics, such as cotton, rayon, silk, or wool. Avoid shiny or metallic fabrics, especially those with beads or rhinestones. Solid colors or conservative prints in dark or pastel shades are preferable. Avoid bold prints and loud colors.
- Knee-length or below-knee-length hems.
- Plain hosiery.
- Mid-heel pumps or flat shoes.
- Moderate use of small, simple jewelry and subdued accents like a scarf.

What about uniforms? Some jobs require employees to wear uniforms. Company policies about who supplies these uniforms and how they are paid for and maintained differ. It is important to discuss the company policy when you are interviewing for the job. The following careers and jobs require workers to wear uniforms. At the end of this list, add some other jobs that require uniforms, especially in your city or state.

- Construction, cleaning, and maintenance jobs.
- Fast-food businesses.
- Hospitals and medical-care facilities.
- Local government services such as police, post office, fire department, sanitation, and transportation.
- Military.
- Private service industries like United Parcel Service (UPS), Federal Express (FedEx), telephone companies, utility companies, and cable television service providers.
- Travel personnel such as ticket agents, flight attendants, pilots, and railroad conductors.
- Franchise businesses such as gas stations, florists, and auto rental agencies.

- _____
- _____
- _____

Prepare your wardrobe ahead of time. You can divide your clothes preparation into two phases: grooming and accessories. Checklists 1-2 and 1-3 will help you make decisions on what to wear. **Grooming** refers to making yourself look neat and tidy. In fact, an employee who arrives at work looking untidy and messy creates the impression that the work he or she produces might not meet the quality standards expected. **Accessories** are extra things you wear to enhance your appearance. Using accessories is a way to say something unique about yourself. In this category are all forms of jewelry; perfumes and scents; scarves and ties; hats; belts and suspenders; handbags, tote bags, and attachè cases; and footwear.

What items can you add to Checklists 1-2 and 1-3 that concern wardrobe issues where you live or work?

Smart **TIP**

Be prepared to work immediately.

Grooming   Checklist 1-2

- Are your clothes clean and pressed ahead of time?
- Did you make needed repairs, such as mending torn seams and hems, sewing on buttons, and fixing zippers?
- Do the clothes fit you properly? Are they too short and tight, or too long and baggy?
- Did you take a good look at yourself in the mirror or look at a photograph of yourself wearing these clothes to see whether you look good in them?

- _____
- _____

✔ Accessories

- Women should wear plain hosiery, preferably flesh-colored or off-black. Men should wear socks that match the color of their slacks and/or shoes.
- For men, a conservative tie is a necessity. A pocket handkerchief is optional, but only the tips should be showing. Limit jewelry to simple, small items; don't overdo it.
- Limit use of perfume, cologne, toilet water, and after-shave lotion because many people have allergies and asthma.
- _____
- _____

Being Prepared Making a good impression also requires you to come prepared to meet the needs of the job. First, you bring yourself, eager to learn and use the skills for which you were hired. Second, being prepared means that you must bring the tools of your trade, those items you will need in order to accomplish your assigned tasks successfully. Suggestions for what to bring on your first day are shown in Checklist 1-4. On the first day of a new job you will need to bring information about yourself and your family to complete all personnel forms thoroughly and accurately.

✔ Things to Take Along on the First Day

- Small notebook to jot down information.
- Pens, pencils, erasers, or easy-to-use white-out or correction tape.
- Identification: Social Security Card, Resident Alien Card, Work Permit, Driver's License.
- License required to work at this kind of job. Examples of jobs needing this kind of license include dental hygienist, pharmacy assistant, X-ray technician, bus driver, manicurist, hair stylist, RN, or practical nurse.
- Spouse and dependent data. Bring their Social Security numbers and dates of birth.
- Name, address, and phone number of person to contact in case of an emergency.
- Tools and equipment that you will need on the job.

Getting to Work on Time

Smart **TIP**

Being on time is vital.

Punctuality is part of making that first impression your first day on the job. Punctuality means getting to a job or appointment exactly on time, or a little ahead of time. It means arriving on or before the time you are to be at your workstation. Therefore, if you are to begin work at 8:00 A.M., you _must_ arrive at or before 8:00, not at 8:06 A.M. A 9:00 A.M. starting time means you cannot start at 9:06 A.M. Here, an 8:50 to 9:00 A.M. arrival is perfect. To ensure your punctuality, you will need to prepare ahead of time.

Figure 1-3: Don't get yourself into difficult situations. Prepare ahead of time.

Preparation Tips for Getting to Work on Time

Preparation Tip	Example
1. Know the exact **place** where you are to report.	1. Report to 650 East Marsh Street, 3rd floor, room 300B.
2. Know the exact **time** at which you are to report.	2. Report to room 300B at 9:30 A.M. to sign in. Orientation starts at 10:00 A.M.
3. Know the exact **person** to whom you should report.	3. Report to Mr. Soo Ling Park, room 300B to sign in and get instructions.

Prepare travel plans and how to get to your job. Plan your travel route a day or two ahead of time. Travel the route at rush hour to find out exactly how long getting to the job site takes. Nothing is more frustrating than getting lost or encountering an unexpected traffic jam on your way to a new job. You're nervous to start with and this just makes you more anxious.

*S**mart* **T I P**

Plan ahead to reduce tension and stress.

What should you do if you are delayed? Sometimes you will know before you leave home that you will be late. In this case, let your employer know what is happening. Sometimes emergencies happen while you are in transit, and here your employer should be informed as soon as possible. Checklist 1-5 can help you avoid problems if you are going to be late.

What to Do If You Are Going to be Late

Checklist 1-5

1. Call the company office.

2. Ask for the person to whom you are supposed to report.

3. Explain the delay.

4. Give an estimated time of arrival (ETA).

5. Leave a message if necessary.

6. Write down the name of the person who takes your message and note the time you called in case you need to verify the call.

Being Ready To Work

You will perform best in a new job if you had a good night's sleep and are rested. If you've partied all night, it shows, and will diminish the first impression you will make. Your new supervisor and coworkers will think that you aren't really taking your job seriously. Also be sure to set your alarm or clock radio so you get up on time. Leaving home in a mad rush will make you feel disorganized and anxious.

Usually you will be expected to complete some paperwork on the first day at work. To show your readiness to work, you should be prepared to fill in forms.

What Kinds of Information Will You Have to Provide?

You will be required to provide some additional information on your first day. Much of it will involve completing a variety of forms and documents. In large corporations, the Personnel or Human Resources Departments take care of this. In a small company, your supervisor or a payroll manager will probably handle these tasks. Be prepared to complete some or all of the following documents.

Employment Record

An employment record is a file containing your history with the company. It includes your hiring date, job title, salary, and any forms you completed when you applied for the job. Later, performance reviews, promotions, raises, and other data will be added. Information in the employment record is more detailed than the application you filled out when you applied for the job. Once you are employed, the company can ask you more questions—some of which are illegal to ask during a job interview—for insurance purposes or to satisfy government regulations. Figures 1-4 and 1-5 show some examples of questions that can be asked once you are employed and others that cannot be asked.

Kinds of Questions Companies CAN Ask Once You Are an Employee

1. What is your age?
2. How many dependents do you have? What are their names and dates of birth?
3. What is your marital status?
4. What is your health status? What illnesses or accidents have you had? Are you under the care of a doctor now? What for? What medications do you take? Why?
5. Do you have a physical handicap? What workplace adjustments will you need to make to do the job effectively?
6. Have you ever been convicted of a crime? What for? What was the sentence?

Figure 1-4: Kinds of Questions Companies Can Ask Once You Are an Employee

Kinds of Questions Companies CANNOT Ask You

1. What is your sexual orientation?
2. What is your religion?
3. What clubs or organizations do you belong to?
4. What is your arrest record? (Companies do have the right to ask you whether you have been convicted.)
5. What does your spouse or partner do for a living? (Companies can ask if a security clearance is required.)
6. What is your financial status? Have you ever filed for for bankruptcy? Do you have other sources of income?

Figure 1-5: Kinds of Questions Companies Cannot Ask You

Payroll Forms

To take the proper income tax deductions from your gross salary, the company must know how many dependents you are claiming. You might also have the option of participating in savings plans. A **dependent** is someone who relies on you for most of his or her financial support, usually a spouse or a child under age 18.

W-4 Form. This form (see Figure 1-6) is provided by the Internal Revenue Service (IRS) and lists the number of dependents you are claiming for income tax withholding purposes. Spouse and dependent data are required to substantiate the number of dependents you claim.

┄┄┄┄┄┄┄┄┄┄┄┄┄┄┄┄ **Cut here and give the certificate to your employer. Keep the top part for your records.** ┄┄┄┄┄┄┄┄┄┄

Form **W-4** Department of the Treasury Internal Revenue Service	**Employee's Withholding Allowance Certificate** ► **For Privacy Act and Paperwork Reduction Act Notice, See Page 2.**	OMB No. 1545-0010 20--

1 First name	Last name	**2** Your social security number

	3 ☐ Single ☐ Married ☐ Married, but withhold at higher Single rate. Note: *If married, but legally separated, or spouse is a nonresident alien, check the Single box.*
	4 If your last name differs from that on your social security card, check here and call 1-800-772-1213 for a new card ┄ ┄ ┄ ┄ ► ☐

5 Total number of allowances you are claiming (from line H above or from the worksheets on page 2 if they apply) **5**

6 Additional amount, if any, you want withheld from each paycheck ┄ ┄ ┄ ┄ ┄ ┄ ┄ ┄ **6** $

7 I claim exemption from withholding for 1998, and I certify that I meet **BOTH** of the following conditions for exemption:
- Last year I had a right to a refund of **ALL** Federal income tax withheld because I had **NO** tax liability **AND**
- This year I expect a refund of **ALL** Federal income tax withheld because I expect to have **NO** tax liability.

If you meet both conditions, enter "EXEMPT" here ┄ ┄ ┄ ┄ ┄ ┄ ┄ ┄ ┄ ► **7**

Under penalties of perjury, I certify that I am entitled to the number of withholding allowances claimed on this certificate or entitled to claim exempt status.

Employee's signature ►

Date ► , 20

8 Employer's name and address (Employer: Complete 8 and 10 only if sending to the IRS)	**9** Office code (optional)	**10** Employer identification number

Cat. No. 10220Q

Figure 1-6: W-4 Form

Automatic Savings. You designate some of your pay to be deducted and deposited directly into a savings plan set up by your employer.

Charitable Withholding. You designate some of your pay to be deducted by your employer and donated to a charity such as The United Way, Red Cross, or Disaster Relief.

Security and Fidelity Bonding

If your job requires that you handle large sums of cash, important documents, or sensitive information, your employer will want to guarantee your honesty. To do this, the employer will take out a security or fidelity bond, which is an insurance policy that reimburses your employer if you lose documents or steal from the company. A good security bond rating can enhance your reputation and provide you with a good reference in the future. To receive this bonding, you might be required to supply additional personal information.

Current Employer Practices

- **Background checks.** Investigation of court and government sources to verify an employee's "clean" record.
- **Random drug testing.** Unannounced tests of employees using sophisticated equipment that can disclose drug and/or alcohol use as long ago as six months.
- **Lie detector tests.** Legal or not, these are used for security reasons.

Lie Detector (Polygraph) Tests

Most private-sector employers are prohibited by federal and state law from requiring or requesting that employees submit to a lie detector test as a condition of employment. Even so, some employers do request that prospective or current employees do so. Many laws regulate the use of such tests. Your best bet is to seek legal advice in your own state. The Department of Labor for your county or city probably has a representative whom you can consult.

"Today we're going to talk about fall protection."

Insurance Coverage

Many firms provide employees with hospital, medical, and dental coverage, and life insurance. This coverage can be extended to cover an entire family, sometimes at an additional cost to the employee. A waiting period might be imposed before you are actually eligible for this coverage, perhaps 30-60 days. A deduction from your paycheck can be made to pay the premiums for the policy. To qualify, you will be asked to complete the required insurance enrollment forms.

Additional Information Required

Large businesses use a variety of identification and screening devices and might provide you with a photo identification badge or have you fingerprinted on your first day. This will require you to have your picture taken and to complete special security forms.

"Of all days to get up late!" Brent exclaimed. "Why did I have to oversleep the first day of my new office job at the broadcast studio? It's a good thing all my clothes are ready and I know the quickest way to get to work. I've got to get to work on time!"

1. Why must Brent make a good impression at the broadcast studio this morning?

_____
_____
_____
_____

2. How did Brent successfully prepare for his first day on the job?

_____
_____
_____
_____

3. Describe the clothes Brent should wear today.

_____
_____
_____
_____

4. Because he might be late to work, what should Brent do before he leaves his home?

_____
_____
_____
_____

A New Employee Has Much To Learn

A Day of Learning and Orientation

The first day of a job can be overwhelming. You might be nervous entering a new work situation. Once you are on the job, you will have much to learn, many people to meet, and new responsibilities to be assumed. Keep in mind the important things that you will be learning.

About the Company

Most large companies have formal orientation sessions for new employees. This might or might not be scheduled on your first day on the job. During a company orientation you can expect to be informed about a wide range of company subjects, such as benefits, safety and security regulations, managerial philosophy, and rules and regulations governing your employment.

Mid-size or small companies that do not have large numbers of new employees might handle orientation more informally. You might receive a booklet that explains company policies and benefits or your supervisor might provide you with the information you need. The following subjects are usually covered in the orientation:

1. Work hours, attendance, and time-keeping procedures
2. Lunch and breaks
3. Pay periods
4. Overtime
5. Benefits
6. Tryout period of employment (probationary period)
7. Evaluation, job performance review
8. Career paths
9. Rules regarding dismissal of employees
10. Security procedures

About Your Department

A department is a group of people in the company that handles specific duties and responsibilities vital to the company operation. For example, in a hospital, one department could be in charge of keeping all the medical records of clinic visits, while another department prepares all the billing of clinic patients and insurance companies.

Most small companies do not have enough personnel to divide the work into separate departments. Usually, staff members are responsible for completion of a variety of tasks. For example, in a single doctor medical practice, the office manager would be in charge of tasks such as billing patients and insurance companies, handling correspondence, making appointments, and maintaining the filing system.

What you must learn about your department. Some things you must learn about your department include answers to the following questions.

1. What is the relationship of your department to other departments and to the whole company?
2. Who is the head of the department and what is the person's title? Who is your immediate supervisor and what is the person's title?
3. What is the chain of command in the department? The chain of command is the hierarchy of who reports to whom. If you have a problem, who is the next person in the chain to whom you should

go for help? After that person, who is the next person to see? And so on up to the head of the department or president of the company.

4. What are the department policies and regulations? Overall, they generally follow company policies. What policies are particular to your department, such as work schedules, telephone usage, and interaction with coworkers?

5. Where is your workstation (the area where you do your job) located?

6. What are the time-keeping procedures to be followed? For example, do you need to clock in or sign in each day?

7. Where do you keep your valuables and outer wear? If you have to change clothing, where is your locker and the changing room?

8. Where are the lounges and rest rooms?

9. What keys or other security devices will you need and who will give them to you?

10. How do you get supplies? Where is the supply room located?

Meeting the members of your new department. Getting along with your coworkers is discussed fully in Chapter 5. Below, Checklist 1-6 provides a few tips to help you on your first few days.

Tips for Surviving the First Few Days Checklist 1-6

- Be friendly.
- Observe.
- Be polite.
- Listen.
- Take notes.
- Don't make snap judgements about others whom you meet.

- Accept others who are different from you.
- Take moderate teasing in your stride and with humor.
- Don't be upset if you are not accepted immediately.
- Be prepared to eat lunch on your own.
- Don't be pushy.

A Word about Training

What kind of training does your company provide? Training can be done in-house, at the company offices; off-site, at a training center outside company offices; or, through college tuition reimbursement, a refund of tuition and/or textbook expenses made directly to you when you successfully complete a course.

About Your Particular Job

During the application and interview process, you will have learned something about the specific job for which you were hired. Now you need to learn the details about your job duties and the tasks you are expected to perform. Learn about your particular job by being able to answer these questions.

1. What are your specific job duties and responsibilities? These could be listed in a job description, a list of all the duties you are expected to perform on the job.

2. Who is your direct supervisor? Your supervisor is the person who assigns you work to do. You need to know *specifically* what your supervisor expects of you.

3. Who are the people with whom you work? What should you expect of them?

4. If you have a problem, whom should you ask for help?

5. How does your job affect the department? What is your overall role in the department? Where do you fit in as part of the team?

6. Where is your workstation located? How do you operate the equipment in your work area?

7. Will you need to ask for structural changes in your work area, furniture, or equipment to accommodate your special physical needs?

8. Will you need any training? If so, when, where, and how will it take place?

9. What are the policies in your department regarding your job? A policy refers to the rules and procedures that management expects employees to follow. Policies can be both written and unwritten.

About Your Performance Review

A job performance review is an evaluation of your performance of the job for which you were hired. Your job orientation should include an explanation of the review process at your company. Most companies will evaluate your job performance at the end of a probationary period, a trial period of employment during which you have the status of a trainee. Each company is different, but probationary periods are usually three to six months long. The important things you should learn about your job performance review are shown in the following checklist.

Smart **TIP**

Plan ahead for your first job evaluation.

✔ **What You Should Know About Job Performance Reviews**   **Checklist 1-7**

- When will you be evaluated on job performance?
- Who will be evaluating you?
- What behaviors and job skills will be assessed in your review?
- What happens if you receive a poor review?
- What effect does the evaluation have on your employment status?
- What recommendations can you expect, such as additional training and formal courses?

Activity 1-1

Using Important Words and Information

A. **Important Words.** Your instructor will assign various projects to help you achieve the goal of adding these words to your business vocabulary.

1. Accessories	8. Employment record	16. Policy
2. Automatic savings	9. First impression	17. Probationary period
3. Chain of command	10. Grooming	18. Punctuality
4. Charitable withholding	11. In-house training	19. Security bond
5. College tuition reimbursement	12. Job description	20. Supervisor
6. Department	13. Job performance review	21. W-4 form
7. Dependent	14. Off-site training	22. Workstation
	15. Orientation	

B. **Learning Log.** Summarize what you have learned from the material in this chapter and what it means to you. How could you apply this information and insights you have gained from it to yourself or your employment situation?

Activity 1-2

Write answers to the questions in this section. Explain your answers completely using examples. Be prepared to discuss your answers with the class.

1. Why is a first impression important?

   _____

   _____

2. Why should you practice your travel route to your new job before your first day?

   _____

   _____

3. What things should you learn about your department on the first day?

   _____

   _____

4. What things should you learn about your job on the first day?

   _____

   _____

5. Describe a new situation you have encountered at school, home, or work.

   _____

   _____

6. What went particularly well for you in that situation?

   _____

   _____

7. How would you let other people at your new job know you are glad to be on their team?

   _____

   _____

8. Describe what you plan to wear on the first day on the job. What accessories will you use?

   _____

   _____

   _____

9. Discuss the statement: "You have 30 seconds to make a first impression."

   _____

   _____

   _____

   _____

Activity 1-3

A. Write complete answers to the questions asked in the case studies in this section. Be prepared to discuss and explain your responses with your classmates.

CASE 1: Alfred started a new job today in the mailroom at Barber and MacArthur, an advertising firm. You have worked there as a mailroom clerk for 18 months. Mr. Leung, the mailroom supervisor, introduced you to Alfred, then asked you to teach him the duties of the job. As Alfred shook your hand he said, "I am looking forward to working with you. I know I'll have a lot of questions to ask about the job and I'm sure you will be able to help me get used to working here. If you see that I have misunderstood your directions, have done things incorrectly, or forgot to do something, please tell me so I can make improvements."

1. Do you think you will like working with Alfred? Why or why not?

_____

_____

_____

_____

2. What things did Alfred do that made a good impression on you?

_____

_____

_____

_____

3. Write down two or three statements that you could make in reply to what Alfred said.

_____

_____

_____

_____

CASE 2: June is unhappy after her first day as a bookkeeper at the Color Printing Company. She worked at her previous job for five years, but the company went out of business last month. Her job at the Color Printing Company is not like her old job. She doesn't know anybody at work now, she shares a room with five other employees, and she has to learn a new computer system. June thinks her new coworkers were unfriendly towards her today. At lunch, they went out to a local coffee shop and did not ask her to join them. Although she is not an emotional person, June starts to cry as she leaves the office at 5:00 P.M.

1. Why is June unhappy on her first day at the Color Printing Company?

_____

_____

2. List several ways June can make adjusting to her new job easier.

_____

_____

3. If you were June's coworker and saw her crying at the end of the day, what would you do?

_____

_____

B. Choose an occupation or job in which you would like to work. Collect pictures from newspapers and magazines showing the proper attire for this kind of job. Cut out the pictures and create a collage or poster. You can also take photographs of people wearing the right kind of clothes for the job.

C. Patrice arrived at his new job on time today. The Human Resources representative, Ms. Barstow, remarked, "Welcome to Classic Construction, Patrice. We have some paperwork to complete and questions to answer today before we get you started." On the lines provided, write **LEGAL** or **ILLEGAL**, to indicate whether Ms. Barstow can ask Patrice these questions:

_____ 1. What is your age?

_____ 2. What is your marital status?

_____ 3. How many dependents do you have?

_____ 4. Are you a citizen of the United States?

_____ 5. What is the highest grade of school you completed?

_____ 6. What is your religion?

_____ 7. What is your sexual preference?

_____ 8. Have you ever been arrested?

_____ 9. Have you ever been convicted?

_____ 10. Do you have a physical disability?

Activity 1-4

Welcome to the Internet

Electronic resumes are the way of the future. You will be able to do job searches, contact prospective employers, and send your resume via e-mail. Doing so requires a special type of resume, however.

1. Search for samples of electronic resumes and download those that meet your needs.

2. Develop your own electronic resume.

Activity 1-5

The Team Approach

`team`

1. Working in a team, design a presentation illustrating proper business attire for a variety of different careers such as doctor, waitress, business executive, or chauffeur. This presentation should employ both visual (photos, computer graphics, drawings, actual samples) and audio (lecture, music, poetry) media.

2. Collect electronic resumes written by others within the group. Critique the resumes and make suggestions to help each resume be more effective.

Activity 1-6

What I Learned at Work Today

Directions: Take this worksheet with you to your new job. Fill in the blanks with all the important information you learned on your first few days.

1. What products or services does the company provide? _____

2. What is my supervisor's name? _____

3. What is my supervisor's title? _____

4. If I must reach my supervisor, what is the number I should call? _____

5. In what department do I work? _____

6. What does my department do? _____

7. What are my job responsibilities? _____

8. Where is my workstation? _____

9. What is my telephone number at work? _____

10. What is my e-mail address? _____

11. What is the company FAX number? _____

12. What is the company Web address? _____

13. What are my coworkers' names? _____

14. If I am going to be late or absent, what telephone number should I call (_____) and

    to whom should I speak? _____

15. When do I get paid? _____

16. When can I expect to get my first paycheck? _____

17. What is my salary or rate of pay? _____

18. When are my lunch and break times? _____

19. When will I get my first job performance review? _____

20. How long is my probation period? _____

Activity 1-7

Functional Resume

Directions: This is a resume worksheet for you to keep handy in your wallet or handbag. You can refer to it when you are completing an application form or other paperwork required on your first day at the job. Fill in all the information below.

Name: _____ Date of birth: _____

Address: _____ Phone: _____

Social Security number: _____ Driver's license? _____

U.S. citizen? [ ] Yes   [ ] No   Resident Alien Number: _____

Education: Presently enrolled at: _____

What grade are you in: _____ Major subject: _____

Cumulative GPA?_____ Year to graduate: _____

Extracurricular activities: _____

Honors and awards: _____

Hobbies and interests: _____

Employment Experience: List company name, address, phone number, dates of employment, job title, and reason for leaving for each job:

_____

_____

_____

_____

Equipment you can operate: _____

References:

Name: _____   Name: _____

Address: _____   Address: _____

Phone: Work _____   Phone: Work _____

        Home _____   Home _____

Relationship: _____   Relationship: _____

Name: _____   Name: _____

Address: _____   Address: _____

Phone: Work _____   Phone: Work _____

        Home _____   Home _____

Relationship: _____   Relationship: _____

Carry this with you. Refer to it as needed.

Chapter 2

What You Can Expect from Your Employer

Skills OBJECTIVES

After completing this chapter, you will be able to:

1. Differentiate between employee rights, expectations, and benefits.

2. Describe the components of a benefits package and recognize their added value to the basic salary.

3. Verbalize the similarities and differences between harassment and discrimination.

4. Describe the importance of each employer expectation of the employee.

The elevator door opens and Ian walks into the hallway, his footsteps dragging as he nears the doors to the company where he has a new job as a researcher assistant. This is a new beginning and he is nervous. Ian remembers the experiences of his last job and does not know what to expect, but hopes this one will be better.

Yvonne is starting her new job today and is really very nervous about what will happen. Everyone has told her such horror stories about their first day on the job and about those people called supervisors who take advantage of everyone who works for them. She doesn't know what she has a right to expect from her employer or her supervisor. What must be provided for her in the workplace?

Like Yvonne, you have the right to expect certain things from your employer. City, state, and federal laws guarantee some of these expectations; others are on the basis of standard practices and ethics.

Ian and Yvonne are experiencing many of the new job "jitters." In this chapter we will discuss what you can do to make your first days on the job a happy experience.

Basic Expectations

This chapter covers some of the basic things you can expect from your employer. Some of them, such as salary and benefits, should be discussed and clarified to your satisfaction before you accept a job. Once you are on the job, these things will become more real to you. The responsibility for making sure you are treated fairly will rest largely with you.

Salary

Smart TIP

Questions about salary should be clarified during the job interview.

How do you get paid? Your **salary** is the amount of money you earn doing your job. It can also be called wage or pay. Most companies pay employees by check, with only a few giving employees cash in an envelope.

Rate of Pay

The minimum wage is set by the federal government, but no governmental restrictions are placed on how much you can be paid for any given job. What you earn is between you and your employer and is based on the job to be performed and the skills you bring to the company. You must ask how much you will be paid for your work *before* you accept any job.

You have a right to be paid honestly, in a timely manner, and at specified times agreed upon by you and your employer. Most employers issue paychecks weekly or biweekly (every two weeks). This is your **pay period**, the time worked and covered by your pay. Your salary can be in the form of cash or check, based on company policy. When you are in the process of interviewing and accepting a new job, ask if you will be paid by check or cash.

The total amount of money you earn in a pay period is called your **gross pay**. Your salary can be calculated in a number of ways:

- **Hourly** This means you earn a given amount of money for each hour you work. For example, you say, "I earn $6.26 an hour." Most companies pay overtime if you work more than 40 hours in a week. Overtime rates vary from company to company, but are usually one-and-a half times the hourly rate of pay. Therefore, if you earn $6 per hour, overtime would be $6 plus $3, or $9 per overtime hour.

- **Weekly** This means you earn a given salary for each week you work. In this case, you would say, "I earn $325 per week." You can be an hourly employee and still be paid weekly. For example, if you earn $240 per week, you really are being paid $6 per hour for a 40-hour week. On the other hand, you could also be paid on the basis of a **straight salary**, meaning you earn the same weekly salary no matter how many hours you work.

- **Monthly** You earn a certain amount of money per month and say, "I make $2,000 per month at my job." Those who are paid monthly are usually straight-salary employees.

- **Annually** "I have a $28,000-a-year job." This rate of pay is expressed as the amount earned in one year and is almost always a straight-salary position.

- **Piecework** Salary is calculated on the basis of the number of items or amount of work you produce. Piecework is common in the garment industry. The sewers, for example, only get paid for each garment they complete. Therefore, a sewer who earns $2.00 per shirt and completes 30 shirts in a day will receive $60 for that day.

- **Commission** Income is computed as a percentage of the sales you generated for the company during a period of time. For example, Joel, a furniture salesperson, will get 10 percent of all the sales he makes during a given month. Therefore, if he sells a dining set for $600, he will earn $60. The more he sells, the more he earns.

Computing Your Pay

Multiply your rate of pay times the number of hours you worked during the pay period. For example, if you worked 40 hours last week at the rate of $6.50 per hour, your calculation would look like this:

$$\$6.50 \times 40 = \$260.00 \qquad \text{This is your gross pay.}$$

- **Deductions From Your Pay** Certain legal deductions are withheld from your pay each pay period. These are city, state, federal, and Social Security (FICA) taxes, and are based on the W-4 forms (shown in Chapter 1) you completed on your first day on the job. Other deductions can include insurance premiums for health, dental, disability, and life insurance, union dues, pension plan contributions, savings bond programs, and charitable donations. Your net pay is your gross pay minus deductions. This is also called take-home pay.

Computing Your Net Pay

Subtract the total of all deductions from gross pay to compute your net pay. For example, Clara's gross pay this week is $350.00. Her employer withheld the following from her pay:

Federal taxes	=	$ 45.90
State taxes	=	10.00
Local taxes	=	8.50
Social Security (FICA)	=	26.78
Health insurance	=	10.00
Total Deductions	=	$101.18

Now, do the following calculation:

Gross Pay	=	$350.00
Minus deductions	=	101.18
NET PAY	=	$248.82

Figure 2-1 shows an example of a paycheck and its pay stub. The pay stub shows your name, social security number, other identifying information, and contains an itemized listing of your gross pay, deductions, and your net pay. The amount of your net pay is the amount written on your paycheck. If you are paid in cash, your pay envelope should list all deductions, just like a check stub. Your employer is legally responsible for withholding taxes from your salary and submitting them to the Federal and local government agencies.

Keep the pay stubs in a file at home so you can check the accuracy of the *W-2 form* you will get from your employer at the end of the year. The W-2 form (see Figure 2-2) lists your total pay and taxes withheld for the previous calendar year. You need the W-2 form to file your income taxes every year. Report discrepancies to your payroll office so your employer can make the necessary corrections.

Smart **TIP**

Read your pay stub carefully.

McDermott Computer Supply Company

217 West 8th Avenue
Dubuque, IA 52099-0142

John T. Long
1830 4th St.
Clinton, IA 52732-6142

Check Number: 291337
Pay Period Ending: 12/27/--

HOURS & EARNINGS		TAXES & DEDUCTIONS		
DESCRIPTION	AMOUNT	DESCRIPTION	CURRENT AMOUNT	Y-T-D AMOUNT
Rate of Pay Reg.	7.00	FICA Tax	21.50	1,118.00
Rate of Pay O.T.	10.50	Federal Income Tax	79.33	4,125.50
Hours Worked Reg.	40	U.S. Savings Bonds	7.00	364.00
Hours Worked O.T.	10	United Fund	2.00	104.00
Net Pay	275.17			
Total Gross Pay	385.00	Total	109.83	5,711.50
Total Gross Y.T.D	20,020.00			

STATEMENT OF EARNINGS. DETACH AND KEEP FOR YOUR RECORDS

McDermott Computer Supply Company

217 West 8th Avenue
Dubuque, IA 52099-0142

LaGesse Savings & Loan
33 Katie Avenue, Suite 33
Clinton, IA 52736-3581

24-2/531

DATE: 12/27/--   291337

PAY
To the
Order of

TWO HUNDRED SEVENTY-FIVE AND 17/100 . . . . **DOLLARS**

$***275.17

JOHN T. LONG
1830 4TH ST.
CLINTON, IA 52732-6142

Edward D. McDermott

⑈291337⑈ ⑆153111123⑆ ⑈938540 2⑈

Figure 2-1: Sample Paycheck and Pay

a Control number		OMB No. 1545-0008		

b Employer's identification number	**1** Wages, tips, other compensation	**2** Federal income tax withheld
c Employer's name, address, and ZIP code	**3** Social security wages	**4** Social security tax withheld
	5 Medicare wages and tips	**6** Medicare tax withheld
	7 Social security tips	**8** Allocated tips
d Employee's social security number	**9** Advance EIC payment	**10** Dependent care benefits
e Employee's name, address, and ZIP code	**11** Nonqualified plans	**12** Benefits included in box 1
	13 See Instrs. for box 13	**14** Other

15 Statutory employee	Deceased	Pension plan	Legal rep.	Hshld. emp.	Subtotal	Deferred compensation
☐	☐	☐	☐	☐	☐	☐

16 State	Employer's state I.D. No.	**17** State wages, tips, etc.	**18** State income tax	**19** Locality name	**20** Local wages, tips, etc.	**21** Local income tax

Department of the Treasury—Internal Revenue Service

Form **W-2** Wage and Tax Statement **20 - -**

Copy B To Be Filed With Employee's FEDERAL Tax Return

This information is being furnished to the Internal Revenue Service.

Figure 2-2: Sample W-2 Form

ACTIVITY 1

Mark is earning $6.25 per hour as a clerk in a small store. He is working 18 hours a week while going to school. His deductions are $33.60 per week. Perform the following calculations. Please show your work.

1. What is his gross pay per week? _____

2. What is his net pay per week? _____

3. Mark is upset when he receives his paycheck because the amount is less than he was expecting. Why do you think his take-home pay was less than the total amount he earned?

_____

_____

_____

Work Environment

"Oh, sure. <u>Now</u> you want safety training."

Smart TIP

Know and follow all safety rules.

Safe Working Conditions

These are factors in the workplace protecting your physical safety and must be provided by your employer. Federal, state, and local law mandate safety regulations. The Occupational Safety and Health Agency (OSHA) administers these laws in local communities. Safe working conditions mean specific things.

✔ The Meaning of Safe Working Conditions
Checklist 2-1

- All safety rules must be posted and followed.
- All machinery and equipment should be kept in good working order and used properly.
- All employees who use the machinery and equipment are to be fully trained.
- Safety equipment should be provided when appropriate. This includes goggles, aprons, overalls, shoes, ear plugs, gloves, ultraviolet filters for computer screens, and other protective gear. In many instances, the company might require you to purchase personal items to meet safety standards, such as special work shoes.
- All exits and aisles must be kept clear and doors must be unlocked from the inside.

Safe Health Conditions

Your employer is responsible for providing and maintaining workplace conditions ensuring your health and preventing accidents. Safe health conditions include the following:

1. Your work site should be in a well-ventilated area free from noxious fumes.

2. Your work site should be well lit so you are not subject to insufficient light or undue glare, either of which can hurt your eyes, cause headaches, and hinder your productivity and accuracy.

3. Meal times must be provided when you are to be at your job for more than 5 or 6 hours, depending on the labor laws of the state concerned.

4. Rest breaks are required at appropriate times, especially for employees doing work requiring constant concentration, operating dangerous machinery, or needing great physical stamina.

5. Hazardous materials must be properly stored, transported, and used. Hazardous waste and fumes must be disposed of properly. The handling and disposal of hazardous materials are regulated by the Environmental Protection Agency (EPA).

*S*mart **T I P**

Hazardous materials are labeled; pay attention to EPA posters.

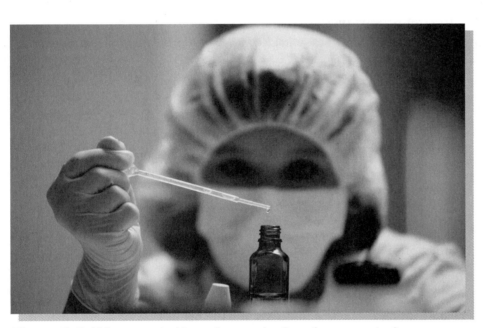

Figure 2-3: What items is this worker wearing for safety protection?

Harassment

*S*mart **T I P**

Do not suffer in silence, tell authorities about your problem.

Exactly what constitutes harassment on the job can be difficult to define. Harassment is the act of being harassed, meaning one is annoyed, plagued, pestered, teased, or tormented by others.

The person being harassed can find the situation upsetting to the point of not wanting to go to work or being unable to perform his or her work productively. People who indulge in harassment usually do not think of themselves as doing anything more than teasing or "having fun." Often harassment is used as a way for an individual to assume control of a situation or to exert power over another person. Harassment can take the form of offensive talk, items or pictures displayed prominently, or physical gestures.

Any unsolicited sexual advance considered offensive by another person is called **sexual harassment**. Sexual harassment can take the form of verbal descriptions or references, pictures, erotic items or gestures, or the demand for sexual favors in return for keeping a job or getting a promotion. Workers to whom this behavior is not directed, but who find the harassment creates a hostile work environment, can also claim to be sexually harassed. ***This kind of behavior is illegal.*** Companies are responsible for establishing training programs to enlighten all employees as to what constitutes sexual harassment, preventing it from occurring, and stopping it should it occur. Additionally, a complaint procedure must be established and publicized within the company. An employee who considers herself or himself sexually harassed should take steps to stop the unwanted harassment including, but not limited to the following:

Bothered by Sexual Harassment? Follow These Steps: Checklist 2-2

- Confront the individual or individuals responsible.
- Report the behavior to a supervisor, following the established grievance procedures.
- Make a formal charge of harassment with the US Equal Employment Opportunity Commission (EEOC).

Discrimination

Being denied an employment opportunity on the basis of factors such as race, ethnic background, religion, gender, or physical disability is called **discrimination**. This means you are treated worse than other people. Discrimination can mean you are not considered for promotion, are denied training opportunities, or are paid less than others doing the same work in the same company. For example, a female computer operator who is paid less than a male computer operator doing the *same work* is a victim of discrimination.

If you believe you are the victim of harassment, sexual harassment, or discrimination, you should discuss the problem with your supervisor first. If your supervisor is the problem, complain to the state Department of Labor or the EEOC. Although employers usually tell you to direct harassment problems to the Human Resources Department, remember that HR representatives are also employed by the company. You could find yourself being treated like a *complainer,* a *whistleblower,* or an *undesirable.* If you think, however, that you have been sexually harassed or discriminated against, lodging a complaint is better than continuing to be a victim of this undesirable behavior.

If you do not get relief from the harassing situation, you can take legal action by filing a formal complaint with your local Department of Civil and Human Rights or Equal Employment Opportunity Commission. You will be required to provide documentation of your charges, so keep a journal detailing each incident of harassment and noting the days on which they occurred. Keep originals of any pertinent documents, including correspondence, reports, and drawings, plus photographs and other relevant materials.

A. Hugh is the only male executive assistant at Barton, Grace, and MacArthur. His job description and tasks are the same as those of the other legal secretaries. Also, he has been employed at his job for 12 years, longer than any other legal secretary. When a job opening as Senior Legal Secretary was announced, Hugh, eager for the promotion, applied for it. The job was given to a secretary who has been with the firm for four years and has a history of excessive absence.

1. How do you think Hugh feels? Why?

_____

_____

2. Is Hugh a victim of harassment? If yes, what kind? Explain your answer.

_____

_____

3. What should Hugh do?

_____

_____

B. Fabian, a business executive, has a second career as a stand-up comic at a local nightclub and loves to try out his new material on coworkers during the work day. However funny he might be, his material is sexually oriented and full of innuendo and double meanings. Tara is very uncomfortable listening to Fabian and does not find his routine funny at all.

1. Is Tara being harassed? Explain.

_____

_____

2. What should Tara do?

_____

_____

C. Anthony has been employed as a skilled laboratory technician at a scientific research facility for the past 10 years. Recently, he was injured in a motorcycle accident and now walks with a cane. His supervisor now speaks to Anthony very slowly and in a loud voice, assigning him the most menial tasks.

1. Discuss Anthony's problem.

_____

_____

2. How should he handle this situation?

_____

_____

Benefits

You might want additional things from your employer to be happy on the job. These are extras, added bonuses a company might offer to its employees. No rules and regulations govern these extras, and each company offers different ones. These should be discussed during the job interview and reviewed again during orientation. Benefits paid by your employer add to the value of your salary. For example, if you paid for them yourself, your medical insurance premiums might cost you $2,500 per year.

Smart TIP

Benefits add value to your earnings.

Basic Benefits

Benefits contribute to the welfare of the individual worker and, therefore, add to the productivity and morale of the organization. Some companies bear the cost of a complete benefits package. More commonly today, employees are required to share the cost through payroll deductions. Basic benefit packages can include:

1. **Health, Medical, and Dental Insurance** Many companies provide basic medical coverage for an employee and the employee's dependents. Various policies and types of coverage are available from a variety of available plans. Health insurance is limited to coverage provided for by the insurer through negotiation with the employer or, in some cases, a union. Medical insurance available through HMOs (health maintenance organizations) requires policy holders to pay a specific amount, called the *co-pay* amount, for each service, such as office and hospital visits, tests, x-rays, and physical therapy. Other types of health insurance require policy holders to pay a specific amount, called a yearly deductible, before they can receive reimbursement for medical expenses. Typically, reimbursements are calculated at 80 percent of the amount allowed by the insurance company for the medical service rendered. You will receive a copy of your insurance policy, an insurance identification card, and instructions for filing claims soon after your new-job orientation. Keep your policy and claim forms in a file at home for easy reference.

2. **Life Insurance** A policy paying a benefit to a designated person when the employee dies.

3. **Pension Plan** A form of investment and savings where funds are payable to the employee upon retirement, supplementing Social Security benefits. The 401(k) plan is the most popular pension plan available today. This plan allows investments with no taxes paid on the amount deducted from paychecks (nor the investment's earnings) if money is not withdrawn from the 401(k) fund before the employee reaches a certain age.

Other Benefits

Additional benefits can include:

1. **Discounts** A reduction in the selling price of products the company manufactures, sells, or represents to encourage employees to purchase and use what it makes. Sometimes the company's retail outlets are called company stores.

2. **Child Care** A place in the company building or nearby providing care for the children of employees while the parents are working.

3. **Group Travel** Discounts on air fares, package tours, and hotels and resorts might be made available to employees.

4. **Tuition Refund or Reimbursement** Plans providing benefits for courses or other training. Successful completion of a course is generally required before the employee is reimbursed.

Paid Vacations and Holidays

Many companies offer paid vacations and holidays, which is time you are away from your job but still receive your pay. Companies have different policies, which can also vary from employee to employee according to the length of time employed and the position held.

Vacations

Vacation policy should be discussed at orientation. Vacation time varies by company, position, and the length of time employed. Many firms allow employees to take their vacations whenever they wish if the workload permits. It is the employee's responsibility to find out how to schedule your vacation and to do so with consideration of your employer's needs.

Holidays

Holidays are days the company is closed or days when you do not have to report to work in observance of certain events. Some observed holidays are Thanksgiving, Christmas, New Year's Day, Martin Luther King Jr. Birthday, President's Day, Memorial Day, Independence Day, and Labor Day. At the discretion of the company, other holidays might be celebrated as well. If your company is open six or seven days a week and some employees must be there all the time, you might not actually get the holiday off, but could receive extra pay or time off at a later date. Find out the company policy regarding religious holidays.

Smart **T I P**

Avoid confusion; know your company's policies on holidays.

Leave Time

Leave is time away from the job that is neither vacation nor holiday. Again, companies vary in their policy and you should find out what the company policy is when you start working.

Sick leave

This is when you are absent from work due to an illness or injury. Usually a company allows its employees a certain number of paid days off during a year for illness or injury. For longer absences, perhaps a week or more, the company might require you to bring in a doctor's note or to see its doctor.

Personal leave

This is any day you take off for personal business. Most companies discourage use of personal days off except for special circumstances, such as a funeral, graduation of a close relative, or personal emergency. The number of days you can take depends on the situation. The company might even pay you for these days. Be sure to check the company policy before you rely on getting paid for personal-leave days.

Family matters

Companies can grant leave time for the following:

1. **Maternity leave**, offered to female employees, usually starts in the later months of pregnancy and can extend a few months after the baby is born. The employee does not get paid for the time off, but her job or an equivalent one is held for her until she returns.

2. **Paternity leave** is a rather new practice of some enlightened companies whereby fathers take a short paternity leave to help at home during and after the birth of a child.

ACTIVITY 3

Antonio was in a bad automobile accident. He felt lucky to have lived. The doctor told him he would be out of work for at least six months.

1. What kind of leave does Antonio need to take? Why?

_____

_____

2. Will Antonio be able to return to his job? How do you know this?

_____

_____

3. **Family leave** is now guaranteed under federal law to employees who work in large companies. Employees are permitted to take time off without pay to handle family emergencies and still retain their jobs.

4. **Bereavement leave** can be offered to an employee when a close relative dies. This time is to be used to come to terms with the loss and to settle the estate of a deceased. Each company handles this situation differently, and therefore, no general statement can be made as to the time allowed or whether the employee will be paid for the bereavement leave.

5. **Long-term leave of absence** is sometimes granted when an employee must take an extended time off from the job. Again, how this is handled depends on the company. Usually with a long-term leave of absence, the employee does not get paid and benefits, like medical insurance, can be suspended. In this case, no guarantee is made that the employee's position will not be given to someone else. If an employee is not going to be working for a long time because of a disabling illness or physical injury, this is called disability leave. Policies for disability leave and pay vary from company to company.

Additional Employee Expectations

Angela has worked in food service at a large hotel for five years. When she started, she joined the union. Her first job was cleaning and preparing vegetables. She remembers peeling and dicing mountains of potatoes and carrots. As she became more skilled, Angela was given more complicated tasks in the hotel kitchens. Because she exhibited a talent for baking and decorating pastry and cakes, the hotel sent her to a special school for pastry chefs. Today, Angela is the Pastry Director at the hotel and supervises the preparation of all pastry for the hotel's catering facilities and five restaurants.

Employees have expectations over and above those we have already discussed. Because companies want to retain employees, they often provide additional services or opportunities for their employees.

Training and Continuing Education

Your employer must provide training if you need to learn how to operate machinery or equipment used on your job. This is for equipment presently used, and for new equipment as it is acquired. Many companies offer training to employees who wish to improve their skills or take another job within the organization. Some considerations are:

Smart **TIP**

Never stop learning. Lifetime learning is an asset.

1. Training can take place in-house (within the company) or at an off-site training facility, depending on the type of training needed and the equipment to be used.

2. Training can take place during working hours, for which you still receive your salary, or after hours, which might be on your own time (with or without pay).

Training and staff development help employees produce quality service and products, thus enabling the company to remain competitive in the marketplace. To enhance their employees' ability to remain productive in the global marketplace, many companies encourage attendance at conferences, workshops, and continuing education classes.

Unions

By law, employees are guaranteed the right to join a union representing workers at a company. The conditions of employment are governed by the contract the union negotiates with management through the process of collective bargaining. Employee wages, benefits, vacations, advancement, and retirement are commonly specified by union contracts. These contracts usually also provide a grievance procedure for employees to follow when they have a complaint against management.

Feedback on Your Performance

You have the right to receive feedback about how you are doing on your job. You could find out, for the first time, during a job performance review (discussed in Unit 4), that your skills need improvement or you will be fired. This is too late to receive feedback from your supervisor. Many supervisors fail to coach employees, especially when unacceptable personal behavior is involved, or let them know where to improve before a formal review. Make a point of asking your supervisor for feedback. For example, ask: "How am I doing?", "What things can I do to improve my job performance?", or, "Have I been doing this correctly?"

Job Advancement

Employees should expect to learn and grow on a job. You can advance at work by earning a promotion. This is an "upgrade" of job and responsibilities within the company and is discussed in Unit 4. You can also move up in a company by following a career path. This means you climb the career "ladder" at your company by moving up to increasingly more senior jobs. Career paths are available in many fields. For example, a teacher's aide at your school might aspire to being a licensed classroom teacher. His or her career path involves completing college courses, earning a college degree, and passing a teacher's licensing examination. The career path continues upward to other positions such as vice principal, principal, and superintendent of schools.

Activity 2-1

Using Important Words and Information

A. **Important Words.** Your instructor will assign various projects to help you achieve the goal of adding these words to your business vocabulary.

1. Benefits	9. Harassment	17. Promotion
2. Bereavement leave	10. Leave	18. Salary
3. Commission	11. Maternity leave	19. Sexual harassment
4. Deductible	12. Net pay	20. Sick leave
5. Disability leave	13. Pay period	21. Straight salary
6. Discrimination	14. Pension plan	22. Take-home pay
7. Family leave	15. Personal leave	23. W-2 form
8. Gross pay	16. Piecework	

B. **Learning Log.** Summarize what you have learned from the material in this chapter and what it means to you. How could you apply this information and personal insight to yourself or your employment situation?

_____
_____
_____
_____
_____
_____
_____
_____
_____
_____
_____
_____
_____
_____
_____
_____
_____
_____
_____

Activity 2-2

Write answers to the questions in this section. Explain your answers completely using examples to illustrate. Be prepared to discuss your responses with the class.

1. Why should the employee expect the employer to provide certain things?

   _____

   _____

2. What would happen if these expectations were not met?

   _____

   _____

3. List eight deductions your employer can withhold when computing your pay.

   _____

   _____

4. Describe the items listed on a W-2 form and why you need this form.

   _____

   _____

5. How do employers provide a proper work environment?

   _____

   _____

6. Explain why following the safety rules posted in the workplace is important.

   _____

   _____

7. List and explain the various ways an employee can experience harassment.

   _____

   _____

8. List and discuss five benefits you would like in your personal benefits package.

   _____

   _____

9. Describe a workplace situation requiring your employer to provide training.

   _____

   _____

10. Describe the difference between a holiday, a personal day, a sick day, and a vacation day.

    _____

    _____

Activity 2-3

Salary Computations

An employer hires someone to do a job because the employer believes that person has the skill and knowledge to do the required tasks. The employee is selling skills and time and receives a salary. Complete the calculations required at the end of each of these cases and show your work. Be prepared to discuss and explain your responses with your classmates.

CASE 1: Alba works in an office as a data-entry clerk. She receives $295.00 every week. Each week the company deducts $46.95 in federal taxes, $15.29 in state taxes, and $25.21 for health insurance. What is Alba's net pay each week? Alba receives a paycheck every two weeks, so how much will her next paycheck be?

1. Alba's take-home pay each week is $ _____

2. Alba's next paycheck will be for $ _____

CASE 2: Grace manages a clothing store. She pays Mario $6.50 per hour and he works 20 hours a week while attending classes at the local college. She has to deduct $25.95 per week for taxes. Mario does not receive any benefits. How much money does Grace have to put into Mario's pay envelope?

The cash in Mario's pay envelope each week should be $ _____

CASE 3: Carol works as an electrician. She receives $15.50 an hour and works a 35-hour week. This past week, she worked 35 hours plus two hours overtime for which she receives time-and-a-half ($23.25 an hour). Her deductions will be: $89.56 in federal taxes, $35.98 in local taxes, $51.50 in union dues, and $15.00 for a pension plan. How much will Carol take home for last week? She worked 35 hours this week. What will be her gross salary for this week?

1. Carol's net pay for last week should be $ _____

2. Carol's gross salary for this week is $ _____

Activity 2-4

People on the Job

Interview two people who are working and ask them the following questions. Write the answers on a separate sheet of paper and be prepared to discuss your answers with your classmates. After the class discussion, prepare a summary of your findings using a word processing program.

1. What benefits do you receive from your employer?

   _____

   _____

   _____

2. Describe the safety conditions and regulations on your job.

   _____

   _____

   _____

3. Describe the physical environment of your job. Do you consider it healthy or unhealthy? Is it safe or unsafe? Explain.

   _____

   _____

   _____

4. Have you ever been harassed on the job? If yes, explain how.

   _____

   _____

   _____

5. Do you belong to a union? If yes, which one? What does the union provide to you?

   _____

   _____

   _____

6. How many vacation days do you get each year? What is your company's policy for personal leave?

   _____

   _____

   _____

7. What holidays does your company recognize?

   _____

   _____

   _____

8. What is your company's policy regarding sick days?

_____

_____

9. What benefits do you receive? What benefits would you like to receive that you do not have now?

_____

_____

_____

10. When you started your job, how did you learn to do all the things required of you?

_____

_____

_____

internet

Activity 2-5

Expectations and Benefits

1. Find and download articles discussing issues in the workplace, employee expectations, or employer expectations. Write your reactions to each of these articles.

2. Do an Internet search for information regarding employee benefits and the laws governing them.

Activity 2-6

The Team Approach

team

1. Develop and publish a compendium of government agencies that advocate employee rights.

2. Establish a resource file of interesting articles regarding employee benefits, harassment, and equality in the workplace.

Chapter 3

Skills
OBJECTIVES

After completing this chapter you will be able to:

1. List and describe 10 employer expectations.

2. Describe the role of the customer in business.

3. Explain what a company is and why it exists.

What Your Employer Expects from You

Dylan has finally landed a job as a sales trainee with Trendsetters, a men's clothing store chain. He is really excited about starting a career in retailing with a very exciting company. He has spent much time finding this job. He went on many interviews, spoke with a lot of people, and received all kinds of advice from everyone who knows him, and even some who didn't. Dylan is looking forward to learning all he can about the business. He has learned job hunting can be "the pits," and he wants to keep this job. He knows keeping this job depends on his performance and how he meets his employer's expectations.

Types of Employers

Before we go any further, you should understand the types of employers who might hire you. Throughout the first two chapters, we have been talking about an entity called the company, also known as the corporation, firm, organization, or business. A company can be a small, medium-sized, or large enterprise engaged in producing a product or providing a service to make a profit. Our economy is dependent on the health of profit-making businesses—the private sector—making up the largest percentage of the US workforce. Also employing large numbers of people is the public sector, which includes nonprofit organizations, businesses, and local, state, and federal governments.

"Companies, organizations, and agencies are like people. Each has its own "personality," reflecting the types of people who work there, the way they are managed, and the goals they are trying to achieve. This company personality is referred to as its corporate culture, and it contributes to the employer's expectations of its workers. Corporate culture consists of the behavior, actions, and values the people in a company or business are expected to follow. These traditions and conventions figure prominently in the way a company conducts its daily business.

These methods have proven successful in the past; therefore, everyone is expected to continue using them in the future. This corporate culture dictates the way things are done, how people work, behave, and make decisions. The new employee should be familiar with the company's history and its important figures to understand its present way of doing things.

Even though two companies are in the same industry, they probably have developed their own corporate cultures and ways of doing business. For example, Holland Corp. and Markham Company are in the same business, providing a similar product. At Holland Corp. the management likes to run a tight ship where everyone does his or her work with minimal waste or duplicated effort. The supervisors are busy making sure everyone works efficiently producing goods of the requisite quality the first time. Socializing among employees takes place only during lunch or after work. At Markham Company, however, employees socialize, the atmosphere is relaxed, and the paperwork seems to be overflowing. The end result is that although the office is a friendly and busy place, everyone has to stay until the job is completed, even if this means working after hours or on weekends, with no extra pay. Both businesses are operating in their own fashion within their own corporate cultures. The people who work in each company are part of the personality of the company.

Figure 3-1 Businesses have their own personalities.

ACTIVITY 1

Refer to the Holland Corp. and Markham Company examples above and answer the following questions.

1. How are these two companies similar?

_____

_____

2. How are they different?

_____

_____

3. Which company would you want to work for? Why?

_____

_____

The Need for Quality

"And do you promise to serve our customers faithfully, and to the best of your ability?"

Although companies are organized and managed in various ways, they have many similarities as well. Their primary goal is to make money—earn a profit—by meeting a marketplace need. By producing a product or service, companies expect to be successful in achieving their goal. The customer, consumer, or client is the ultimate boss who defines the need for a product or service and the acceptable levels of quality. Without customers, businesses cannot survive. Lost business, complaints, additional costs, and lawsuits result from poor quality. In a highly competitive marketplace, a company with these problems will be out of business. When products and services meet availability and performance standards, customers generally recognize the quality provided. No one wants to buy something that falls apart after a short time, does not meet real needs, or cannot be made available in a reasonable time.

How Quality Is Achieved

Smart **TIP**

Be a team player.

Each company or organization must be sensitive to the needs of its customers. It must be aware of what the customer wants and then set its own standards. Management must make decisions on how and when a product or service will be provided, and the procedures necessary to reach the company's goals. The company must rely on its employees, working together in a spirit of teamwork, contributing to the effort to make it a success, or else the company will fail and everyone will be out of a job. Employers, therefore, have certain expectations of their employees.

Basic Employer Expectations

Many expectations are fundamental to success on the job. In addition to your technical skill, you bring attitude and personality to the workplace. No matter how good you are with those skills or handling other job requirements, if you fail to meet your employer's expectations, you will not succeed. The following are the most important employer expectations.

Productivity

The employee is a member of a team whose efforts affect the future of the company. Each individual must be willing to learn and improve, accept new methods, cooperate with coworkers, and follow the leadership of management as it responds to customers' needs. At your job, you will be expected to assist in producing a quality product or service by making a commitment to quality and taking pride in your work.

Let's look at an example. Jimmy is a carpenter at a shop that makes kitchen cabinets. Every time he cuts wood, he must do so precisely, or the pieces will not fit together correctly. The customer wants cabinets with doors that stay closed, fit the space properly, and look nice. When the company purchased new computerized saws, Jimmy spent his lunch hours reading the saw's training manual. By learning how to operate the new equipment, and doing it on his own time, Jimmy is helping his company to produce a quality product and meeting his employer's expectation of him.

Smart **T I P**

Do your part: be productive.

Contribute to the Productivity of the Company

Employers expect their employees to do all they were hired to do conscientiously and in a timely manner. Each employee's output contributes to the ability of the department and company to reach their goals. Productivity affects the economic health of the company and employee wages, bonuses, commissions, and incentives. Other measurements of productivity are derived from the number of items produced, sales made, volume of work done, or projects accurately completed. When people are productive, they have a sense of accomplishment, of being part of a winning team, and they take pride in doing a job well.

Maintain Good Attendance and Punctuality

The employer expects a full day's work and pays for the employee's time by providing a salary for work performed. Attendance means being present and working at a specified time and place. Good attendance is required because every job in a company is important. If a worker is not present, someone else might have to do the work. When that worker is trained to do a specific job, the company might have to pay for a temporary replacement or leave the work undone. Also, work you produce could be used in another office or department of the company. When this occurs, you have personal customers within the company. If you are absent, your work cannot be done and passed on to the next department or person in the company chain. This is costly to the company, and that is why employers do not tolerate excessive absenteeism.

Smart **T I P**

Remember the importance of attendance and punctuality.

Punctuality means being *exactly* on time or a little ahead of time at the start of the workday or shift and returning to your workstation on time from breaks, meals, and errands. Punctuality is important; it is an important measure of your dependability. Continual lateness means you are not giving your employer all the time for which you are being paid. You can also be docked, which means money is deducted from your pay for time missed from work.

Figure 3-2 Leaving for work on time helps you have a good day at work. Starting work on time is part of the punctuality on which your employer depends and on which your company's success depends.

In cities where rush hour traffic is overwhelming, flex-time is being advocated by urban planners as a means of decreasing commuting delays and air pollution. Many firms, especially those competing in the global marketplace, adopt flex-time as a means of extending the hours the business is in open. Flex-time is a business practice encouraging employees to work their daily hours on a flexible schedule; therefore, some people might work 8:00-4:00, others 8:30-4:30, and some 10:00-6:00. Some people assume being late is okay if they stay late or work through lunch to make up the lost time. In other words, they bring their own idea of flex-time to the workplace without checking to see whether management approves.

✔ When You Are Going to be Late or Absent

Checklist 3-1

Do

- Let your supervisor know the day before or early on the morning of the day you will be absent so proper arrangements can be made to cover your position.

- Call if you will be late, giving an approximate time of arrival. Speak directly with your supervisor or a designee.

- Offer to make up missed time by working late, during lunch, during breaks, or by coming in early.

- Know the company policy regarding sick days and other days off.

- Whenever possible, schedule appointments on your own time during days off, weekends, holidays, or vacations.

- Make reliable child-care arrangements, including alternative plans in case your child-care provider is ill or the facility is closed.

- Have more than one way of getting to work. Investigate trains, buses, alternative driving routes, carpools, and people who can give you a lift if necessary.

Don't

- Be excessively absent.

- Be continually late.

- Rely on a relative to call when you will be absent or late.

- Forget to call or call late on the day you are absent.

- Use personal and/or sick days for child-care.

- Take care of personal business on company time.

- Abuse personal day privileges.

Honesty and Trustworthiness

Your employer expects you to be straightforward and fair in your dealings with customers, coworkers, and supervisors, and that you will not lie or steal. Doing an honest job means you always work to the best of your ability. Being honest means admitting your mistakes and not making excuses or blaming others. Honesty also means representing the company in a truthful manner to the public, customers, and clients.

Employers must be able to trust employees with money, equipment, and other valuables. Employees are often tempted to steal small items such as pencils, paper, pens, and supplies. Avoid the temptation; it is not worth the consequences. Stealing costs the company money and can lead to your immediate dismissal or arrest if the employer thinks the theft constitutes a felony. You can steal time by taking extended breaks, having poor punctuality, or being excessively absent.

The successful employee is expected to be supportive of the company and faithful to its efforts. Disagreements with company or departmental policies and procedures should be resolved through proper channels. Company secrets or confidential information should not be discussed with others. Sometimes you are faced with having to make a moral or ethical decision about your employer's policies and practices. If you find yourself opposed to the ethical positions of your company, you really should consider finding employment elsewhere.

For example, Helena is a traffic supervisor employed by an electric utility company. She is aware the company is polluting the local water supply. An avid environmentalist, Helena is angry with her employer. Only Helena can decide whether she will be able to remain loyal to the company. If she cannot reconcile these differences, she will have to consider terminating her employment at the electric company.

Smart TIP

Ethical behavior is a must.

ACTIVITY 2

Joe had many problems, things he had to do, and people he had to see, so he took time off from his job as a telephone customer service representative. It didn't seem like much time and he didn't think his supervisor would mind, but he was really out almost one day a week. When Mr. Brown asked him why he didn't come in yesterday, Joe responded, "My grandmother died and I had to go to her funeral." Joe did not realize his supervisor kept a record of his attendance until Mr. Brown asked him, "How come you have had six grandmothers die this past year?"

1. Which employer expectations did Joe fail to meet?

   _____

   _____

2. What impression is Joe giving?

   _____

   _____

Show Interest in the Company

Employers hire people to perform specific tasks in the course of producing quality goods and services. Workers are more than warm bodies
hired to fill up space at desks and machines, and employers expect them
to be enthusiastic and show genuine interest in the company. If you can
get excited about your job, you will be eager to be successful doing it.
Some important employer expectations showing employee interest in
the company are listed below.

 Showing Interest in the Company   **Checklist 3-2**

Show a positive attitude
1. Do not whine, complain, or express self-pity.
2. Smile and be pleasant, be considerate and respectful of others.
3. Show an interest in the job, department, and equipment used.
4. Do the work to the best of your ability.

Be enthusiastic
1. Accept all tasks involved in the job.
2. Do the work in a timely manner.
3. Help others when necessary.
4. Be cheerful and upbeat.

Show an eagerness to learn
1. Ask questions and write down the answers.
2. Accept correction and criticism gracefully.
3. Request extra training or take courses offered by the company or at local
   schools and/or training centers.

Cooperate with coworkers
1. Help coworkers when they are overburdened.
2. Do the jobs when asked even though you do not like to do them.
3. Assist others when they have a problem.
4. Be willing to work reasonable overtime and through lunch or breaks to make
   sure the job is done on time.
5. Accept coworkers who come from cultures other than your own.
6. Accept coworkers who have physical disabilities.

Be a team member
1. Work towards the team goal of completing a quality project, producing a quality
   product, or delivering a quality service. The company is your customer.
2. Respect the ideas, opinions, beliefs, and rights of others.
3. Do your share of the work; don't let others carry all the weight.

Figure 3-3 Working together maximizes chances of getting the job done.

Take Responsibility for Your Actions

As we mentioned before, when a business chooses you to fill a job, it has every reason to believe you will be able to do the job successfully. Otherwise, the company would have hired someone else. Even if you are unsure of yourself, the employer expects you will be successful. You must be accountable for your work and for your mistakes. Note and study the list of guidelines in Checklist 3-3 below. Everyone makes mistakes in the beginning. In the long run, *how* you correct your mistakes and *taking responsibility for your actions* are of great importance.

Be a responsible employee.

 Responsibility, Judgement, and Initiative   **Checklist 3-3**

You can show responsibility and dependability by:
* Carrying out instructions.
* Working without constant supervision.
* Checking work to make sure it is accurate, complete, and done on time.

You can demonstrate good judgment by:
* Making objective decisions on the basis of all the facts to further the productivity of the department and company.
* Asking questions when in doubt instead of guessing.
* Knowing when to ask for help.

You can show initiative by:
* Being a self-starter; do your work and help others without being told to do so.
* Taking a leadership role when necessary.
* Looking for better ways to get the job done.

Ashley duplicates and compiles documents into case records for a large law firm. She works with four others in a department overseen by an individual who supervises another corporate section. To do her job well Ashley must work as a team member. What expectations does Ashley's supervisor have of her?

_____

_____

_____

_____

Consequences of Not Meeting Expectations

Blair is a medical technician at a large university hospital. She makes the rounds to inpatients and draws blood samples for laboratory tests. At first, her attendance was terrific and she could always be depended on to help draw more samples when she finished her rounds. Lately, Blair has been calling in sick on Mondays, a very busy lab day. Although her technical skills are satisfactory, she is not meeting hospital expectations.

Blair will suffer consequences for failing to meet her employer's expectations. Let's listen in while Mr. Cruz, Blair's supervisor, is talking with her: "Blair, too often you are absent on Monday. It puts a burden on your coworkers, who must carry your workload in addition to their own. We need you to report to work every day. I expect to see improvement in your attendance before your next job evaluation in six weeks."

Mr. Cruz has begun the management process of dealing with an employee's unsatisfactory behavior or skill performance. Most companies follow a procedure similar to the one described here. Your company might be different. This procedure could have been described to you during orientation.

First, you are advised and warned by your supervisor. Your manager might meet with you informally to discuss any skill or behavior you need to improve. At this time, you can expect supervisors to make specific suggestions or offer training so you can perform better. Ask your supervisor, "Exactly what do I have to do to improve and meet your standards?" Both of you will set a goal to show specific improvement by a certain date.

Next, your supervisor will conduct a formal meeting with you. At this meeting you will discuss whether or not you have achieved the performance goals. If you have not improved, you will be notified, usually in writing, that you are required to make certain specific improvements within a given time frame. You should also be told what action the company will take if you do not make satisfactory improvement.

If you are unable to make the necessary improvements, these may be the consequences:

1. *You can receive a poor job performance evaluation.* This is formal notification of your continued unsatisfactory performance. It becomes a part of your employment record. A poor evaluation can delay raises, promotions, bonuses, or incentives you could have been awarded. You will now have to prove your worth to the company before it will grant you these rewards.

2. *You can be fired from your job.* This results from not meeting your employer's standards. Before resorting to this extreme action, most employers will give you counsel, guidance, and training. When you are fired, you are dismissed from your job (you are terminated), and you no longer work for the company.

3. *You can be given a poor reference.* A reference is a testimonial from someone who can verify your education, skill, and previous job performance. In the future, your employer might not want to report your job performance to others. Your reputation, the esteem and favorable impression others have of you, can suffer. Poor references are hard to live down; you have to work twice as hard to erase the bad impression you have made.

Keep in mind your employer believed in you when you were hired. Once you are trained, the company has an investment in your future success with them. Neither you nor your employer wants to fail with each other. Do take your supervisor's suggestions seriously, find out what you have to do improve, show improvement quickly, and eliminate reasons for firing you.

*S*mart **T I P**

Your most valuable asset is your reputation.

Figure 3-4 Businesses have their own personalities. How might this company's personality differ from the personality of the company shown in Figure 3-1 on page 45?

Activity 3-1

Using Important Words and Information

A. **Important Words.** Your instructor will assign various projects to help you achieve the goal of adding these words to your business vocabulary.

1. Attendance	5. Enthusiasm	9. Judgment
2. Company	6. Fired	10. Punctuality
3. Corporate culture	7. Flex-time	11. Reference
4. Docked	8. Initiative	12. Reputation

B. **Learning Log.** Summarize what you have learned from the material in this chapter and what it means to you. How could you apply this information and personal insight to yourself or your employment situation?

_____

_____

_____

_____

_____

_____

_____

_____

_____

_____

_____

_____

_____

_____

_____

_____

_____

_____

_____

_____

_____

Activity 3-2

Write complete answers to the questions in this section. Explain your answers completely using examples to illustrate your answers. Be prepared to discuss your responses with the class.

1. Why is the employer having expectations of their employees important?

   _____

   _____

2. The quality of the product manufactured or service offered is very important in today's business. Why?

   _____

   _____

   _____

3. Why is the customer the ultimate boss?

   _____

   _____

   _____

4. Discuss employer expectations. Which ones do you think are the most important? Why?

   _____

   _____

   _____

5. Why do employers expect a certain level of productivity from all employees?

   _____

   _____

   _____

6. Develop a list of guidelines on the subject of attendance and punctuality to give a new employee.

   _____

   _____

   _____

7. Develop a list of guidelines on the subject of taking responsibility for your work to give to a new employee.

   _____

   _____

   _____

8. As a employee, what are some of your expectations?

   _____

   _____

   _____

9. List the possible outcomes if an employee does not give the employer what is expected on the job.

_____

_____

_____

10. Why do employers expect employees to be honest?

_____

_____

_____

11. How does corporate culture affect you on the job? Why?

_____

_____

_____

Activity 3-3

A. **School to Work** Write complete paragraphs answering the questions below. Be prepared to discuss and explain your responses with your classmates.

1. What is the policy regarding attendance and punctuality at your school or job?

_____

_____

_____

_____

_____

2. Why should the student or employee understand and follow this policy?

_____

_____

_____

_____

_____

3. How will this relate to your working life?

_____

_____

_____

_____

_____

B. **Familiar Excuses** You are the boss and have to make decisions regarding your employees. These are some of the reasons your employees have given you for being absent or late. For each excuse given, state whether you would find it acceptable as an employer. Give reasons for your decision. If the excuse is unacceptable, write a statement explaining how the employee should correct his or her behavior.

1. I'm late because the police stopped all traffic because of a bad car accident.

   _____

   _____

2. I was absent because I had to wait for a package my sister mailed to me.

   _____

   _____

3. I was late because my cat knocked over my alarm clock and I overslept.

   _____

   _____

4. My mother wanted me to go to the Social Security office with her for a 10:00 A.M. appointment. I didn't come to work because it was too late when we got finished.

   _____

   _____

5. I didn't come in yesterday because I had to have my car battery replaced; it was getting old.

   _____

   _____

6. I'm late because I missed the bus.

   _____

   _____

7. I'm late because I had to iron my shirt.

   _____

   _____

8. I won't be in today because I have a doctor's appointment. I can't seem to get rid of this cold.

   _____

   _____

9. I will be absent tomorrow because my sister will be visiting us overnight and I haven't seen her in two years.

   _____

   _____

10. I'm late because my friend was late in picking me up again.

    _____

    _____

Activity 3-4

Employment Situations

Read each employment situation and each question fully. Discuss the questions listed and write complete answers to them. Be prepared to discuss your responses in class.

A. Joan always tells everyone about her boss's personal life and company business. She never seems to have a nice word to say about anyone in the company.

1. How do you feel about Joan? Why?

_____

_____

_____

2. What do you think you should do?

_____

_____

_____

3. What do you think the supervisor should do?

_____

_____

_____

4. Would you want to work with Joan?

_____

_____

_____

5. Would you want to be friends with Joan? Why or why not?

_____

_____

_____

B. John comes to work regularly but he is almost always late. He takes long coffee breaks and tries to extend his lunch hour as long as possible. Sometimes instead of working, he reads the newspaper at his desk. When he does do his work, he makes many mistakes and works very slowly. He gets angry when reminded that accuracy is important. Sometimes, you are asked to correct or redo John's work.

1. As a member of John's team, what do you think about this situation?

_____

_____

_____

2. List the employer expectations John is not meeting. How do you know these are difficult for him?

_____

_____

_____

3. What are the possible consequences of John's behavior?

_____

_____

_____

C. Mohan is a coat salesman in Nelson's, a fashionable downtown men's store. Management has just decided to carry a line of fur coats for men and asks Mohan to be in charge of buying and selling the fur coats for the store. Mohan does not believe people should wear fur. He is a member of an animal rights organization opposing the sale of fur coats. Philosophically, Mohan is not comfortable with the new responsibilities of his job.

1. What actions could Mohan take in this situation?

_____

_____

_____

2. Describe the employer expectations involved.

_____

_____

_____

D. Doris works for a major national magazine as a research librarian. She gathers information and assists writers in researching material for forthcoming articles. The magazine is printed under a deadline and Doris is responsible for getting the needed data in time for publication. Her work is so interesting that Doris finds she reads everything she comes across, even articles not pertinent to her current project. She is always behind in her work and sometimes has to say she checked facts when she really did not have time to do so.

1. Discuss Doris' productivity in her job. Cite examples to illustrate your answer.

_____

_____

_____

2. What can happen at the magazine because of Doris' behavior? Consider the owners, employees, advertisers, and customers of the magazine.

_____

_____

_____

Activity 3-5

Decision Making

Decide if each of the following statements is *true* or *false*, circle the appropriate word, and explain your reasoning for such an answer.

1. Asking questions when you don't understand something just shows you are not smart.　　TRUE　FALSE

   _____

2. Helping others with their work, even if doing so isn't your job, is a sign you are cooperative.　　TRUE　FALSE

   _____

3. People who whine, complain, and feel sorry for themselves show a positive attitude.　　TRUE　FALSE

   _____

4. Being a team member is important in getting the job done.　　TRUE　FALSE

   _____

5. Doing tasks you do not like or understand is a good policy.　　TRUE　FALSE

   _____

internet

Activity 3-6

Trends in the Workplace

Productivity, total quality management (TQM), customer relations, teamwork, and groupware (software programs that promote group decision making) are some of the terms heard in the workplace. Use the Internet to learn more about each of these terms. While you are exploring, note and define other terms you encounter.

Activity 3-7

The Team Approach

team

Learning about current practices in the workplace is important. To do so, group members are to develop an interview guide and interview people who are employed regarding their benefits, responsibilities, employer expectations, workplace rules, customers, and how their company operates. Group members should assemble their responses and write a report of their findings.

Chapter 4

Developing Good Work Habits

Skills

After completing this chapter you will be able to:

1. Discuss good work habits and how they affect relations with others.

2. Define and discus the concepts of privacy, loyalty, and confidentiality.

3. Explain the need for time management and prioritizing skills.

4. Evaluate grooming and hygiene with relation to the workplace.

*S*mart **T I P**

Develop good work habits.

Alicia has been working at the public library for the past two weeks. She is determined to do well on the job and make a good impression on her supervisor. Alicia has perfect attendance and punctuality, has offered to work late during emergencies, and has learned her new job easily. She has listened to and carried out the instructions given by her supervisor, and has accepted the positive criticism given about the quality of her work. Alicia has made new friends at work among her coworkers and often joins them for lunch. Sensitive to her surroundings and coworkers, Alicia stopped wearing her usual strong perfume when she became aware that others found it offensive. So far, Alicia has been pleased with her progress at the public library and practices good work habits every day.

What are Habits?

When you start your new job, you will take with you all the habits you have developed through your life. Many of your habits were learned at home; others, at school or with your friends.

Habits are defined as a usual manner of behaving, acting, or doing something. You may be loud and boisterous among your friends, but quiet, timid, and soft-spoken in the company of new people in a work environment. The way you behave at the dinner table at home might differ from your behavior in a restaurant. These are some examples of habits that can change from place to place.

Good habits are the ways of behaving that are acceptable and beneficial to an individual or society. Some good habits you might already practice include:

- Being respectful to others.
- Throwing trash in the appropriate containers instead of littering.
- Attending school regularly.
- Completing assigned tasks properly and on time.

- Being friendly to a newcomer in your neighborhood or class.
- Being honest in all your activities and responsibilities.
- Not smoking or chewing gum.

Bad habits are those behaviors or mannerisms that are annoying, detrimental, or unacceptable to individuals or society. Your parents and teachers have probably nagged you about your bad habits. Do these comments sound familiar?

- "Can't you ever hang up your clothes? They're all over the place."
- "You never get to class on time. Why are you always late? If you worked for me, I'd fire you!"
- "You're a mess! Look at yourself! You need a bath, a haircut, and some clean clothes."
- "You still haven't turned in your homework from last week. Why can't you hand your assignments in when they are due?"
- "Some of the words that come out of your mouth are disgusting. Do you always have to swear?"
- "The only person you ever think about is yourself. There are other people around here, too."

People can develop all kinds of bad habits over time. Oversleeping, being late, talking in an angry manner, showing disrespect for others, making excuses, and chewing gum are all examples of bad habits.

_H_abits on the Job

Work habits include all the ways people behave while on the job. Good work habits include punctuality, excellent attendance, the ability to accept criticism, friendliness, acceptance of responsibility, and the ability to get the job done properly and on time. Some bad work habits are keeping a messy work area, being unable to follow directions, talking back to supervisors, taking extra time at lunch and breaks, and leaving work undone.

Why Is Having Good Work Habits Important?

Simply put, everyone gains from good work habits. Workers gain satisfaction when they do their jobs well and get along with their coworkers. They earn praise, promotions, and raises. When workers produce quality products and services, the company earns a profit and can stay in business. When workers exhibit poor work habits, jobs are not done well, supervisors and coworkers are dissatisfied, company business suffers, and employees can be fired.

How Do Habits Influence Your Behavior on the Job?

Your work habits influence the way you actually accomplish the tasks called for by your job. If you are in the habit of completing tasks accurately, on time, and in an organized fashion, you will continue those habits on the job. Likewise, if you were late to school 20 times out of the last 30 days, you will probably repeat this habit at work unless you make a concentrated effort to change it.

How Can Habits Affect the Way Others Relate to You?

Your ability to get along with others and to work on a team are a reflection of the habits you bring with you to a job. Your friendliness, sense of responsibility, organization, and other good habits will make coworkers eager to work with you in a positive manner.

How Do Habits Affect the Quality of the Work You Do?

Producing quality goods and services is crucial to business success today. Companies rely on workers who have good habits and behaviors to produce quality. Your organizational skills, attention to details, ability to work on several projects at once, and desire to see a job through to completion are some of the habits affecting the quality of your work.

Gregory works the night shift in a distribution warehouse. He is a very fast worker and helps others when they fall behind. At the end of each shift, the workers must list all the shipping invoice ID numbers on a log sheet, total them, and leave the data in the file on the supervisor's desk. Gregory "forgets" to total his log sheets, clocks out of his shift quickly, and leaves before anyone else most of the time.

1. Discuss Gregory's good habits.
   _____
   _____
   _____

2. Discuss his bad habits
   _____
   _____
   _____

3. How do these habits affect his job?
   _____
   _____
   _____

Developing Good Work Habits

You have been developing good and bad work habits all your life. Some of these you learned at home; others you learned in school or in sports you have played or watched. As you plan to start a new job, concentrate on the good work habits that will help you to get ahead and be successful. Being aware of the bad work habits will enable you to recognize and change them.

Pride

The sense of accomplishment you feel when you have done something well, the respect you have for what you have accomplished is pride. To feel pride in your work, you have to pay attention to your:

- **Tools and equipment.** Keep the items you need to actually perform your work in good condition. Get in the habit of cleaning your equipment and putting it back in its proper storage space when you are finished using it. Arrange for routine maintenance and service promptly. Your work is only as good as the equipment you use to do it.

- **Workstation and work area.** Keep your desk or other work area clean, neat, and orderly. If you need files, pens, paperclip holders, desk blotter, toolbox, bookcase, or other items, request whatever you need from the Supply Department. Your work will be easier to do if you organize your workstation. Your work area is also a re-

Smart **TIP**
- - - - - - - - - - - - - - -

Take pride in all you do.

flection of your self image and the company's image. Customers choose businesses to deal with that make a good impression. Your work area should look as good as you do each day.

- **Output and production.** Output refers to the amount of work you produce within a given time. Production is the act or process of producing goods and services. Your employer expects you to produce a certain amount of work in a given time. Therefore, you need to put out enough quality work to justify your continued employment.

Be proud of yourself. In order to do so, you have to believe you are doing the best job you can. Your accomplishments can serve to reinforce your feeling of pride in yourself. Others sometimes recognize your accomplishments with compliments, which are expressions of praise. Do any of these sound familiar?

- "You always do the best you can."
- "We can rely on your giving 100 percent to your tasks."
- "You are really working up to your potential."
- "You should be proud of the good work you are doing."
- "I am very proud of you."

Self-Respect

You should show a specific image of yourself to the outside world. We refer to this as having self-respect, meaning you hold yourself in high esteem or regard. You can never show respect to others if you do not have it for yourself first. Self-respect shows through your grooming, hygiene, and work output.

Grooming refers to how you dress and present yourself to the outside world. Good grooming is an important habit to develop and maintain because it reflects you as an individual, on your performance on the job, and whether people will want to work with you. The following are some of the good grooming issues and suggestions for handling them.

Are you dressed appropriately for the job? If you are, others will be more likely to want to be seen with and work with you. If you come to work overdressed, your coworkers might think you have socializing on your mind instead of work. Likewise, dressing too casually sends out the message that work is easy, like playing a game, and shows a less dedicated attitude. Some companies have adopted a *casual dress policy*, but even that has limits, as discussed in Chapter 1.

Are you showing the appropriate image to others? How do you really look today? Image is how you choose to show yourself to the outside world. Before you exit your front door to go to work, try to see yourself as others will see you. Decide whether you are sending out inappropriate messages. For example, if your skirt is too short and tight, or, your trousers too low and tight, you could be sending out images and messages that have no place at work. Most businesses will tell you what forms of dress are expected or you can pick up clues by noticing how the most respected and successful employees dress.

Smart **T I P**

Respect yourself and what you do.

What kinds of accessories are appropriate? Just like with your clothing, your choice of accessories can be businesslike, dressy, or casual. For example, ladies who wear long sparkly earrings and extra eye makeup might look great on Saturday night, but they don't send out messages that mean business on Monday morning. And the fellows who wear lots of gold or silver chains outside their shirts, super baggy pants, and skinny leather neckties to work should save them for activities after work.

Some accessories can be dangerous on the job. Consider the horrible consequences if a long scarf or tie gets caught in equipment and pulls you into sets of gears and wheels. Other accessories can hinder your job performance. For example, big earrings get in the way of using the telephone. Shoes with run-down heels cause you to trip or fall. As mentioned in Chapter 1, use perfumes, colognes, after-shave, or other fragrances sparingly as others might be allergic to or offended by these odors.

Do you care for your clothes? You might have all the right choices in clothing, but still never look quite put together if you are lazy in caring for your clothes. Use this checklist as a guide. Your goal is to check off each item.

 ## Caring for Your Clothes

Checklist 4-1

- Do your clothes fit you properly? If not, take them to a dressmaker or tailor for alterations. Purchase new items that show you off to best advantage.

- Have you made all necessary repairs to hems, seams, and pockets? Check zippers, snaps, buttons, loops, and other decorations.

- Are your clothes and shoes cleaned, pressed, and shined? A few dollars budgeted for cleaning and repairing will pay off in the ways other people regard you at work.

- Do your clothing pieces match or coordinate? Colors, stripes, plaids, and designs should go with and compliment each other.

ACTIVITY 2

During orientation at your new job, the Human Resources Director explained the dress code policy for all employees. She remarked, "A sloppy person does sloppy work." Is this statement fact or fiction? Defend your response with examples.

_____

_____

_____

_____

_____

_____

_____

_____

Hygiene includes all the personal things you do to take care of your body. Proper hygiene is a must if you want other people to be comfortable working around you. Make a daily habit of following the simple rules shown in Checklist 4-2. Of course, some of them might have to be done more than once a day.

 The Do's of Proper Hygiene   **Checklist 4-2**

- Bathe or shower.
- Wash your hair. If you have dandruff, use a special shampoo to eliminate it. Use nonscented deodorant liberally.
- Brush and floss your teeth regularly, especially after eating.
- Trim hair, beards, and moustaches regularly.
- Manicure and clean fingernails. Women should refrain from wearing super-long nails.
- Take care of medical and dental problems as they arise. Poor health can affect your personal hygiene, grooming, energy level, and job performance.
- Get proper sleep or other rest.
- Maintain good nutrition and a regular exercise program. Both can boost your energy level and make you sharper in your activities.
- Be careful when choosing the scent of your perfume, as some scents might not blend well with your body chemistry and will not last or smell pleasant.

Respect for Others

When you show respect to others, you hold them in high regard or esteem by giving them special attention in a variety of matters. You can show your respect for others in a number of ways.

Respect the Cultures of Others

The global workplace is a meeting place for individuals who come from different cultures. **Culture** can be described as the values, beliefs, customs, and ways of doing things that influences a person's behavior and outlook. You should understand your own culture and respect the cultures of others with whom you work. We will discuss working with people of different cultures more fully in Chapter 9, but remember, learning about different cultures can be exciting.

Smart TIP

Show respect to others and their efforts.

Recognize the Work of Others with Compliments

A compliment is a flattering remark, an expression of regard or admiration. If you are not in the habit of giving compliments readily, practice some of these so it becomes easy for you to do.

"We're all out of praise. How about a little stinging criticism?"

- "Your explanation and suggestions helped me to complete this difficult report without problems."
- "Congratulations on your well-deserved promotion."
- "Welcome back from vacation. We really missed you and your sense of humor while you were gone."
- "I'm so glad you are recovered from your illness. You look like you are feeling well now."

Accepting compliments from others can be difficult if you are not used to hearing nice things about yourself. When someone compliments you, you can say: "Thank you very much," "That's very kind of you," or, "I appreciate your compliment."

Respect the Privacy of Others

Privacy is one's freedom from unauthorized intrusion by or interference from other people. Each of us has a need for certain things to remain private and be kept out of public view or discussion. Keep these tips concerning privacy issues in mind as you begin your new job.

- *Do not intrude on others' work space or belongings.* If you want to borrow something, ask the owner for permission. Remember, people can be very possessive about their *stuff.* Likewise, one's work space is a personal place. Do not barge into someone's office, for example. Rather, knock on the door before entering. If the office has no door, approach casually and wait to be recognized. Above all, do not interrupt if the person is talking with someone else in person or on the phone.

- *Do not butt into the private lives of others.* Avoid asking personal questions, such as, "How much did that new dress cost?" or "Are you dating anyone special?" Likewise, don't divulge personal information about yourself. You might develop a few close personal friends among your coworkers, but you are advised to let these relationships happen over time.

- *Keep your thoughts to yourself.* Your unsolicited comments to coworkers about their work or their private lives are generally unwelcome and will make them uneasy about your ability to mind your own business.

Keeping Things Confidential

An important habit to develop is the ability to keep matters private, secret, or confidential. You must recognize when things should be kept *confidential*. For example, your supervisor tells you his promotion will be announced in two weeks. Your ability to keep this information to yourself is a measure of keeping things confidential. Some tips about confidentiality follow:

- *Do not become a gossip or participate in a rumor mill.* A gossip is usually surrounded by many people who want to hear what he or she has to say, but is usually not well liked or trusted by others. Your best interests are served by distancing yourself from work-place gossips.

- *Do not repeat everything you hear.* Rumors can be harmful, hurtful, and detrimental to other people. Find out whether information is hearsay or from a reputable source.

- *Recognize information as Top Secret, For Your Eyes Only, or Public Knowledge.* Then keep it or pass it on accordingly.

Maintain Loyalty in the Workplace

Loyalty is the act of being faithful to a person, organization, or cause. In the workplace, this means you should always act in the best interests of your employer. (Discussed in Chapter 3.)

ACTIVITY 3

Akiba is a carpet installation mechanic for Horizons Carpet Co. The last time he accompanied you on a job, you overhead him tell the customer, "Horizons is a bad company to do business with. It never takes care of customer's complaints. I don't know how the company stays in business."

1. Do you think Akiba's comments were proper? Why or why not?

   _____

   _____

2. What do you think you should do?

   _____

   _____

3. List the consequences of Akiba's remarks if his supervisor finds out about them.

   _____

   _____

Using Time Efficiently

Smart TIP

Prioritize your time effectively.

By using your time wisely, you will be able to be more effective at your job. Time management includes attendance and punctuality, which have been covered at length in Chapters 1 and 3.

Time management also means arranging and planning the tasks to be done. Central to organization is the concept of prioritizing your work load. **Prioritize** means to assign a degree of importance to each task you have to accomplish. The four questions you should ask in prioritizing your work are:

1. *What is the most important thing I have to do?* This is the most urgent task you have. It could be, for example, a telephone call your supervisor wants you to complete right away.

2. *What things do I have to do first because of time pressures?* This could be a memo needing to be FAXed within the hour or a report to edit by lunch time.

3. *What jobs can I do later?* These are less urgent and can be done later in the day or week.

4. *What jobs should I give to others so all jobs can be done on time?* For example, you could have to deliver a report to your boss by tomorrow at 10:00 A.M. But the report has to be photocopied, and you know the photocopy team will need two hours to do it. Therefore, you have to get your edited report to the photocopy team this afternoon so you can have it for your boss by the deadline.

The following are some tips to help you organize your work:

- *Prioritize.* Arrange tasks in order of urgency and complete them in that order. Plan the steps for all special projects to meet the deadlines.

- *Become a list maker.* Create checklists of tasks to accomplish and check them off as they are completed. Write notes for yourself and leave them in strategic places to keep you on top of your work.

Smart TIP

Use a day book, calendar, or organizer and plan ahead.

- *Write down your daily schedule.* Write down your beginning of work-day routine and end-of-work-day routine. Then fill in the activities for the remaining time periods.

- *Keep a current calendar.* List appointments, names, phone numbers, and other important data. This will help you avoid double-booking time slots. You might also need to keep a calendar for your supervisor. This kind of planning ahead helps reduce stress, too.

- *Plan errands.* When you have to go to other departments or out of the building, plan your tasks and consider your route. This will eliminate extra work caused by inefficient routes or having to retrace your steps.

Proper planning helps reduce your stress level and the overwhelming feelings that you can't get everything done in the time you have.

Here are items from your to-do list for today. The time is now 10:00 A.M. Prioritize this list by writing the numbers 1 through 10 on the line to the left of each task indicating the order in which you intend to perform it.

_____ Call dentist to cancel 5:30 P.M. appointment tonight.

_____ Type letter to Mr. Parsons; send messenger out by 11:00 A.M.

_____ Reserve Conference Room for meeting next week.

_____ Appointment at 11:00 A.M. with Ms. Lavingood about vacation schedule.

_____ Secure temporary secretary in two days to help with advertising mailing. Call temporary agency to make arrangements.

_____ Lunch with Susan at 1:00 P.M.

_____ Annual departmental report due in three weeks. Send memo to all department managers requesting data by next Friday.

_____ Interview candidates for data entry position today at 2:30 P.M., 3:00 P.M., and 3:30 P.M.

_____ Call Delores to see Ms. Garner in 15 minutes about her excessive lateness.

_____ Call Mother to see whether I have to bring anything home for supper tonight.

Figure 4-1 Be sure you provide enough to balance what your employer brings to the bargain.

Activity 4-1

Using Important Words and Information

A. **Important Words.** Your instructor will assign various projects to help you achieve the goal of adding these words to your business vocabulary.

1. Compliment	6. Hygiene	11. Prioritize
2. Confidential	7. Image	12. Privacy
3. Culture	8. Organization of work	13. Production
4. Directions	9. Output	14. Self-respect
5. Habits	10. Pride	15. Work habits

B. **Learning Log.** Summarize what you have learned from the material in this chapter and what it means to you. How could you apply this information and personal insight to yourself or your employment situation?

Activity 4-2

Write complete answers to the questions in this section. Explain your answers thoroughly using examples to illustrate your answer. Be prepared to discuss your responses with the class.

1. Explain the difference between good and bad habits, including an example of each.

   _____

   _____

2. Why should you be known as a person who can keep things to yourself?

   _____

   _____

3. Discuss the following statement: "Gossip is usually looked on with disfavor in a company."

   _____

   _____

4. How do your habits influence your job performance?

   _____

   _____

5. Why is taking care of your personal hygiene needs important?

   _____

   _____

6. List three ways you can respect the privacy of others at work.

   _____

   _____

7. Analyze the ways you can practice confidentiality.

   _____

   _____

8. What does "prioritizing your work" mean?

   _____

   _____

9. Which questions should you ask when prioritizing your job tasks?

   _____

   _____

10. Understanding an individual's culture is an important aspect of understanding him or her. Explain what this means to you, the employee.

    _____

    _____

Activity 4-3

Employment Situations/Case Studies

Write complete answers to the questions posed in these case studies. Be prepared to discuss and explain your responses with your classmates.

CASE 1 Genevieve, a receptionist at a large company, takes messages for people when they are out of the office. Within an hour, everyone within earshot knows who called, left a message, and what the message was all about.

1. What do you think of this situation?

    _____

    _____

    _____

    _____

2. What is Genevieve's problem?

    _____

    _____

    _____

    _____

3. What do you think the coworkers should do?

    _____

    _____

    _____

    _____

4. What do you think Genevieve's supervisor should do?

    _____

    _____

    _____

    _____

5. Would you want Genevieve to take messages for you? Why or why not?

    _____

    _____

    _____

    _____

CASE 2 Martin is responsible for getting his children to school and day care each morning. He is excessively late to his job because he misses his train and his children are ill. He has to go to the telephone company and the electric company each month to pay his bills. These companies are only open from 10:00 A.M. to 4:00 P.M. What should he do?

_____

_____

_____

_____

_____

_____

_____

_____

_____

_____

_____

_____

_____

_____

Activity 4-4

Time Management Exercise

When you arrived at work this morning, you made a list of all the things you have to do. Prioritize your to-do list, with #1 being the first thing to do, #2 the second, and so on. The time is now 8:30 A.M.

_____ Set up conference room for 4:00 P.M. meeting.

_____ Mr. Lange wants me to see that coffee and pastries are ready for the 4:00 P.M. meeting.

_____ Mr. Lange wants to see Paul at 1:30 P.M. about late returns from lunch breaks.

_____ Type and photocopy Agenda for 4:00 P.M. meeting.

_____ Call Medical Department; make appointment for my annual physical.

_____ Confirm lunch date with Hazel from Accounting.

_____ Return phone call from Ms. Otis, a client, by 10:00 A.M.

_____ Put up posters in department announcing next week's Blood Drive.

Activity 4-5

Breaking Bad Habits

List a bad habit you believe you must break in order to be successful in a job. Then, describe the steps you would follow to break this habit.

Bad habit I want to break: _____

Steps I will follow to break this habit: _____

_____

_____

_____

_____

_____

_____

_____

_____

_____

_____

_____

_____

Activity 4-6

Reasons Why People Get Fired

A number of articles have been written discussing why people get fired. Research and download pertinent articles from the Internet, keep a log of the URLs you followed to find these articles, and write your reactions to them.

Activity 4-7

The Team Approach

team

Plan a handbook for new employees, decide on the salient points to be included, and develop a table of contents. Write the first chapter.

Develop Your Career Portfolio

The first question that you might ask is, "What is a career portfolio?" A portfolio is a collection of your work that represents what you know and can do. It is a quick way for a teacher or prospective employer to learn more about you because it is representative of who you are.

The second question you might ask is, "How can a career portfolio do that?" You are the one to develop and organize the information within the portfolio so that it contains representative samples of your work. It can be a quick picture of you, a means for initiating a conversation about your interests, aspirations, and abilities. You will be able to demonstrate your critical thinking, problem-solving, and decision-making skills, your ability to write, your use of resources, and your understanding of how to work with others. The portfolio should illustrate your self-esteem, sense of responsibility, and integrity. It can make you stand out from all the others as you interview for your dream job.

Now you might ask, "How can I develop a career portfolio?" Throughout *Working Smart* you will have an opportunity to develop materials to put into your portfolio, materials that will illustrate your understanding of the workplace and your ability to communicate and interact with others. This is only a beginning, however. Your portfolio should grow and develop as you do. It should reflect your thoughts, insights, and growth as you progress throughout your career.

Getting Started

Ideally, your portfolio should be in a loose-leaf book having plastic sleeves that will hold and protect the material you have selected. This binder and the way you present the information will be illustrative of you and, therefore, will give the viewer an opportunity to form a positive first impression of you.

Information to Include

1. A resume.
2. Three letters of reference from teachers and/or former employers.
3. A 300-word personal statement that states your professional goals and objectives. It should be clear, concise, and list your specific goals in a broad, general fashion. It must be printed on good-quality white paper.

Melbrook Sporting Goods, Inc. is a manufacturer of high quality sporting goods equipment. Melbrook specializes in outdoor sports equipment such as backpacks, sleeping bags, and camp stoves. It is located in a well-landscaped industrial park in a large building that contains a factory, corporate offices, storage facilities, and a loading platform for handling freight.

The time is 8:45 in the morning and employees are getting off the buses that run down the road in front of the building or driving into the parking lot. Many of the employees who arrived earlier bought coffee and rolls from the restaurant across the street, ate in the employee lounge, and are cleaning up the lounge area before they start their day's work.

Meet the New Employees

Three people are sitting in the corporate reception area smiling nervously at each other. Today is their first day on the job. Ms. Weber, the head of Personnel, asks Jean, the receptionist, to show them into her office.

Miguel Garcia, who will be a computer operator in the Accounting Department, is wearing a shirt, tie, and brown suit. He immediately takes the chair that Ms. Weber points to at a large table. His hand goes to his pocket and he takes out his cigarettes, but he does not light up when he realizes there are no ashtrays. He desperately wants that smoke; and, if not that, at least a cup of coffee.

Timothy Landers has been hired to operate some of the metalworking machinery in the plant. He is a recent graduate of the local technical institute, where he majored in metallurgy. He is dressed in dark blue slacks, white shirt and striped tie, and carries a small duffel bag with his tools and work clothes. When Ms. Weber shows him which seat to take, he does not respond. She repeats her request, he nods and takes a seat. He keeps his hands tightly clasped in his lap and sits very straight in his chair.

Kiesha Brown will be a new Customer Service Representative. After giving considerable thought to her clothes, she is wearing a green dress with a tight skirt and very high-heeled shoes. She is also wearing a number of bracelets and fairly large gold earrings that make a slight noise when she moves her head. She takes her seat at the table when invited to by Ms. Weber.

Ellen Post, who will be working in the Shipping Department as an order processor, comes running in 15 minutes late. As she walks into the room she immediately exclaims, "I got lost getting here, the traffic was as slow as molasses, and it was hard finding a parking space out there in the small lot. Anyway, it's so hard to get up and out of the house in the morning." Ellen is wearing a simple gray suit with white blouse, low-heeled shoes, and no makeup.

The Orientation Session

Ms. Weber welcomes everyone to Melbrook Sporting Goods and tells them the company manufactures equipment used in camping, hiking, and water sports. The production of reliable, quality merchandise is essential because the equipment must withstand hard, rugged outdoor use in all kinds of terrain and weather. Customers depend on this equipment for their personal safety. The equipment is in the mid- to upper-price range and is sold to the general public through stores specializing in camping and outdoor sporting goods.

Miguel, Timothy, Kiesha, and Ellen are given information packets, large folders containing information about the benefits the company offers and the products that are produced. The packets also have a number of forms to be completed. These include a W-4 for tax deductions, a personnel information card, forms for health and dental insurance, an application for bonding, a life insurance policy information form, and a drug testing information form. Ms. Weber reviews the information packets quickly and reminds the new employees to read them carefully when they get home that evening.

The forms are then reviewed slowly and everyone is given a chance to complete them. Miguel wonders why the personnel form requires information about his age, marital status, and religion, but answers all the questions anyway. Kiesha realizes she forgot her pen and social security card. Fortunately, Ms. Weber is prepared. She got Kiesha's social security number from her application and also lends her a pen. Timothy silently thanks his shop teacher for making him practice filling out the forms like these. Now he has a good idea of what to do and how to answer the questions.

A tour of the whole building is next. In the corporate offices the new hires get a quick glimpse of the Marketing, Accounting, Human Resources, Product Design and Product Research, and Purchasing Departments. In the plant, they see the various manufacturing areas, the shipping and freight handling offices, and the storage area. All four are amazed at the size of the place.

Back in Ms. Weber's office, company policy is reviewed: the workday is from 9:00 A.M. to 5:00 P.M., Monday through Friday, but frequently the plant runs overtime. Some of the office staff members elect to work from 8:00 A.M. to 4:00 P.M., and working flex-time is encouraged. Lunch is for one hour, the hour to be decided on by the immediate supervisor. Employees can take a 15-minute coffee break in the morning and in the afternoon. In case of absence or lateness, employees are to call their supervisors. If they are absent for an extended period of time, more than five working days, a doctor's note is required on returning to work. Supervisors must be notified of an absence as soon as possible so adequate coverage can be planned. All new employees receive two weeks vacation per year, and three weeks after three years of employment. A schedule of the holidays when the company is closed is included in the information packet. The safety rules to be followed in the shop are also included in this packet.

Introduction to Their Departments

The four new employees are then introduced to Mrs. Green, the Office Manager, and Mr. Berg, the Plant Manager. Mrs. Green will oversee the

rest of the orientation for Miguel and Kiesha; Mr. Berg will take Ellen and Timothy.

Let's follow Mrs. Green as she shows Miguel and Kiesha where they are to work and introduces them to their supervisors and coworkers. The newcomers are shown where they are to sign in every morning and told that a red line will be drawn in the sign-in book every morning at 9:00. Everyone who signs in under that line will be considered late, regardless of explanations. They are also shown the employees' lounge and told that each department has a place in the lounge where employees can hang their coats and lock up their personal possessions. Mrs. Green introduces Miguel to Mrs. Black, the head of the Accounts Receivable Department, and Kiesha to Mr. Sampson, the head of the Marketing Department, and goes back to her office.

Miguel Settles In

Mrs. Black welcomes Miguel to the department, walks him over to his desk, tells him to make himself comfortable, and to come into her office when he is ready. Miguel nods to those working around him and sits down. He turns on his computer and proceeds to investigate how it operates and what programs are installed. At noon, he gets up and leaves for lunch, returning at 1:00. Mrs. Black goes to Miguel's desk to give him his work during the afternoon and to explain how the department operates. Miguel does all he can until 5:00 P.M. and leaves for the day.

This sets the pattern for the rest of the week. Each day Mrs. Black has to call Miguel in to her office and give him his work for the day. He only asks questions if the material is unclear, yet his work is accurate and well done. He speaks with others when spoken to, but, other than nodding hello, does not communicate at all. He is very prompt, seems to work continually, and keeps his desk very neat.

Kiesha Learns About Her New Job

Mr. Sampson gives Kiesha a quick description of the Marketing Department and introduces her to

Mrs. Sadar-Wright, the Customer Relations Supervisor, who will be her immediate boss. Kiesha also meets the others in her department, staying to chat with each person. She tells each in detail how she hopes this job will be better than her last and explains all the problems she had at her old job. Mrs. Sadar-Wright tells Kiesha about her specific job responsibilities. She introduces her to Marilyn, a coworker. Marilyn will work with Kiesha for the next few days because she is an excellent teacher and knows the job very well.

Kiesha realizes that her big earrings will have to go because they get in the way when she is on the phone, which seems to be all the time. She likes talking with people. She finds the job interesting but the paperwork confusing. She leaves bits and pieces of paper all over, forgets where she put her pen, and thinks having to ask all those questions and filling in all those forms are silly. "So what if I make it all up," she thinks to herself. She knows that with so many products, she has a lot to learn, but is embarrassed always asking for help from Marilyn, who can be moody and seems to get annoyed when interrupted. So, she makes up answers to people's questions. "After all, who will know?" she thinks.

Ellen's First Impression

Meanwhile, in the plant, Mr. Berg shows Timothy and Ellen where the time clock, lounge, and employee locker room are located. Each is assigned a locker and told he or she will have to supply the lock. Ellen is getting more and more upset. "I'm a clerk hired to process orders, so why am I being shown the plant? I want to work in an office!" she thinks. As she walks around, she feels uncomfortable. Several men are looking and smiling at her and a few make "sweet" comments to her.

In her mind, she is finding all sorts of reasons why she should quit. "It is too hard to get here." "I don't like the people." "Mr. Berg looks mean because he does not smile." "I don't like where I have to work." "They don't seem to understand that I have a hard time getting started in the morning; and they expect me to sign in on time." "And these men, the way they look at me, and their comments—what creeps! I feel so un-

comfortable." When she meets Mr. Forman, head of the Shipping and Receiving Department, she definitely knows she made a mistake. Why, he's "old enough to be my grandfather."

Mr. Constantine is her immediate supervisor, and he seems all right. She thinks she might have some problems with the others in her department because they are too busy to chat and keep moving about the office area. She is upset to learn she has to wear work shoes, pants, and have work gloves and a hard hat handy to use when she will help pack items into crates. Mr. Constantine explains how the department operates and exactly what her chores will be. He then tells her to watch the others in the department and to explore the storage areas so that she will know where things are. Ellen is fascinated with all the products and decides to give this job a week, thinking "I do have my own desk and will be doing clerical work."

Timothy Is Welcomed

Timothy is introduced to Jack Jones, the metalworking supervisor, and the other people in the department. Mr. Jones shows him where to store his work gear, reviews the safety regulations, and points out the first aid box. He also describes the department's current work order and remarks, "Quality is the key to everything we do here because if we make a bad product, the company will be out of business." The other workers keep teasing Mr. Jones and Timothy. In a friendly way they tell Timothy about the job, how they need his help, and that they hope he is a good spot welder. One even predicts "This is the last time we'll see you in a tie."

Timothy returns to the employee locker room to change his clothes and then stores the rest of his equipment. He is given a welder's face mask and welding gun and shown what to do. Omar, a fellow employee, watches him work, slaps him on the back, reminds him to ask questions, and says they will all eat lunch together at noon. Timothy works slowly, trying to be as accurate as possible, and is glad to know that by the end of the week he will be working on something else.

FOOD FOR THOUGHT

Timothy, Ellen, Miguel, and Kiesha started work today at the Melbrook Sporting Goods, Inc. Let's see how well they did. Write detailed answers on a separate sheet of paper.

A. Preparation for the first day on the job is very important.

1. How well did the four prepare?

2. How could they have done better?

3. How did their preparation affect their first day?

4. How did their preparation influence their first impressions?

B. Employers have expectations of their employees. We have seen these four employees at work.

1. Why are these expectations important?

2. Each of the four met some, but not all, of these expectations. In the following chart, list the expectations the employees met and those they did not meet.

EMPLOYEE	EXPECTATION MET	EXPECTATION NOT MET
Timothy		
Ellen		
Miguel		
Kiesha		

3. What advice would you give them to improve?

EMPLOYEE	
Timothy	
Ellen	
Miguel	
Kiesha	

C. Employees have expectations of their employer. In short essay form, answer the following questions on a sheet of paper.

1. What employee expectations did Melbrook meet?

2. What were some of the difficulties the newcomers encountered that Melbrook will have to address?

D. Habits are very important when you are working. The things you do when you begin a new job frequently become habits that you will follow the whole time you are in that position. In the chart below, write the answers to the following questions.

1. What work habits did each person establish?

2. How could each one improve his or her habits? Make specific suggestions.

EMPLOYEE	
Timothy	
Ellen	
Miguel	
Kiesha	

E. Imagine you are the four new employees' supervisor and had to predict their future success on the job. On a scale of 1 to 10, with 10 being the highest score, how would you rate their future job success?

EMPLOYEE											
Timothy	0	1	2	3	4	5	6	7	8	9	10
Ellen	0	1	2	3	4	5	6	7	8	9	10
Miguel	0	1	2	3	4	5	6	7	8	9	10
Kiesha	0	1	2	3	4	5	6	7	8	9	10

Discuss your ratings with your classmates. How similar were your ratings?

F. To exist, Melbrook Sporting Goods depends on customers' satisfaction with their purchases, as well as the company's reputation as a manufacturer of quality merchandise. Each person employed by Melbrook contributes to this customer satisfaction and the production of a quality product. Write an essay covering the questions listed below using a word processor.

1. How do the jobs that these four employees do contribute to customer satisfaction?

2. What will happen if each employee does not make a contribution? What can the consequences be?

Unit 2

Smart Communications on the Job

Chapter 5

Importance of Communicating

Skills
O B J E C T I V E S

After reading this chapter, you will be able to:

1. Discuss the need for good communication skills in business.

2. Describe the communication process.

3. Enumerate the skills needed to be a good speaker.

4. Analyze the various aspects of nonverbal communication.

5. Indicate the role of culture in interpersonal communication

Smart TIP

Good communication is vital.

"**Y**es, Mrs. Jackson, I'll file the new report immediately," Claudia responded with a smile.

"I'll be happy to work on this project with you, Jason," Ronald snapped with a frown.

"Rosa, where did you put the new set of tools we received yesterday?" Hui asked with a quizzical look.

Claudia, Ronald, and Hui made themselves understood by communicating. Can you identify the aspect of communication reflected in each of their statements?

What is Communication?

Communication is the process by which information, thoughts, ideas, feelings, and questions are transmitted from one person to one or more other people. This process can happen in a number of ways:

- Person to person
- Person to group
- Telephone
- Computer message
- Video
- Written message
- Electronic message such as e-mail

Good communication is essential to the success of the employer, the employee, and the business. Without it, employees are not able to function effectively. All the people employed by the company, from the president on down, must understand clearly what is to be done and how the company goals and objectives are to be accomplished. Good communication with customers is also vital, as they are the reason for the business to be in operation. Therefore, employers look for and value employees who can communicate well.

Some Reasons People Communicate

- Develop social relationships
- Establish business associations
- Express thoughts and ideas
- Share emotions, ideas, and knowledge
- Help establish an understanding and meaning of observations
- Seek or impart information
- Ask for something *from* someone or *of* someone
- Entertain

The Communication Process

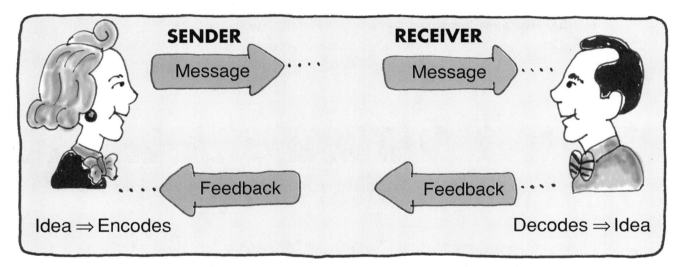

Figure 5-1 How a message is sent.

Communication is a very complex and, at times, delicate process. This process involves:

Smart **TIP**

Be a smart communicator.

- The Sender The person who conceives and conveys an idea to a receiver. The idea is converted into words, gestures, thoughts, diagrams, or pictures and is transmitted to the receiver. This process is called encoding the message.

- The Message The idea or thoughts that are transmitted. Usually in the form of words or pictures, they are understood if all parties involved in the communication process agree on their meaning.

- The Receiver The person or group who receives the message sent. The message needs to be *decoded* by the receiver to give it meaning. By decoding the message, the *receiver* understands what the *sender* is *expressing*. This message can be received through the ears (hearing words or sounds) and the eyes (seeing body language, pictures, written words).

- The Feedback The receiver responds to the message with comments, giving answers, asking questions, reacting or doing something. This sends a message called *FEEDBACK* to the *sender* showing how well the message was understood. The sender then furthers the conversation by reacting to this feedback by adding comments.
- Filters Filters include age, gender, cultural and ethnic background, language ability, education and experiences. Through these filters, we interpret what we hear and vocalize the messages we want to send.

Types of Messages

- **Written Messages** memos, notes, letters, advertisements, and electronic computer messages via e-mail, bulletin boards, and networks.
- **Verbal Messages** speaking face-to-face with an individual or a group or via the telephone and voice mail.
- **Nonverbal Messages** communicating through body language and posture.
- **Pictorial Messages** drawings, pictures, and charts expressing ideas or information.

ACTIVITY 1

Analyze the communication process in these situations. Who is the sender? Who is the receiver? What is the message? What feedback is given?

A. Kenya asks her coworker and friend, Taylor, to get her a box of file folders when he goes to the supply room. Taylor agrees to do so. He returns with a box of pencils and hands it to Kenya.

Sender: _____   Receiver: _____

Message: _____   Feedback: _____

Closing: _____

B. Jose tells his supervisor he is going out to buy lunch. She asks him to buy her a cup of coffee on his way back. Jose brings back a cup of tea.

Sender: _____   Receiver: _____

Message: _____   Feedback: _____

Closing: _____

Oral Communication

Oral communication occurs when words or sounds are used to transmit thoughts and ideas to others. Communicating thoughts and ideas is important so the receiver can understand the message and respond properly.

Musts for Good Communication

A good speaker does certain things to help the communication process:

Speak in an organized way. Organize your thoughts in a concise, logical manner and stick to the point.

Project a positive attitude. Express your ideas in a positive way. For example, compare these statements: "I can't talk with you now!" vs. "I'm on another line now. May I call you back in 10 minutes?"

Respond to feedback. Listen and respond directly to feedback. In this way you can find out whether your message was received as you intended. If the message was not understood, you can explain and clarify points as necessary.

Show respect and consideration for others. Etiquette is expected at every level of business and social communication. In American business culture, you can show respect and consideration in various ways:

1. Greet people in an open, friendly manner using their names when possible.

2. Make eye contact with the person to whom you are speaking. Looking down at the desk, over someone's head, or at your feet can be interpreted as disrespect, lack of confidence, or dishonesty.

3. Use good manners and social graces. This means shaking hands; removing your hat; holding doors open for others; and using phrases such as "please," "thank you," "you're welcome," "I'd be glad to," and, "I am pleased to have met you." It can also mean standing when someone older or senior to you enters the room, or it can mean waiting to be invited to take a seat before sitting down on your own.

4. Be aware of and accept differences in others. Physically challenged persons, people with special needs, and those who speak English as a second language appreciate help given in the true spirit of assistance. Treat them just the same as you would all the other people in the group, always being mindful they might need some discreet help from others.

5. Accept the cultural differences and language difficulties of others. Some people might not fully understand what you are trying to

Smart **TIP**

A positive attitude speaks up for you.

Smart **TIP**

Respond when spoken to.

Smart **TIP**

Giving respect gains respect.

say, but might not let you know. Therefore, be sensitive to others' verbal and nonverbal cues and encourage feedback. This could mean you need to repeat what you are saying in different words. Also, remember to speak in a normal voice—don't raise your voice as yelling does not help the listener understand better.

Things Good Speakers Do to Communicate Effectively

An effective speaker will do certain things to help the communication process:

Smart **T I P**

Speak clearly and distinctly to be understood.

Pronounce words properly. Be aware of how words should be pronounced; use a dictionary if you are unsure of the proper pronunciation. Because good diction minimizes confusion, the listener can understand what is being said. Chewing gum, or talking with your mouth full causes you to slur your words and makes understanding what you are trying to say more difficult.

Use standard business English. When you speak, use proper business English. Slang is not appropriate, nor should you bring street talk into a business environment.

Smart **T I P**

Tone of voice can say more than words.

Use a pleasant, friendly, sincere tone of voice. Emotions show through your speech by how fast you speak, the tone of voice used, and the volume of your voice. Try saying, "yes" in a *pleasant* voice, an *excited* voice, a *tired* voice, and then in an *angry* voice. Now try this phrase. "I got a $500 bonus today." Say it as if you are in shock, amazed, happy, disappointed. How did your rate of speech, the volume of your voice, or your tone change? The listener will respond more readily to a positive tone of voice.

The tone of your voice can also give your message a different meaning. Look at the following example. Brenda, a sale representative, is making a presentation to a prospective client. By saying each of the sentences and varying the word being emphasized, she changes the meaning of the message. Say each message with the emphasis on the italicized word.

Changing Emphasis Changes Meaning

Message	Implied Meaning
"*Our* new fax is fast."	"The other company's fax is slow."
"Our *new* fax is fast."	"Our old fax was slower."
"Our new *fax is* fast."	"Our computer isn't so fast."
"Our new fax *is* fast."	"It is, even if you think it is slow"
"Our new fax is *fast.*"	"This fax is really fast."

Avoid using offensive language. Be careful of using any words that might be offensive to the listener. **Auditing,** choosing your words and thinking of how you will say them before you speak, helps you to eliminate offensive language. These words can cause the listener to react emotionally, stop listening, and ignore the message. Being aware of the following could save you from an embarrassing situation:

S*mart* **T I P**

Speak as you wish to be spoken to.

- Be sensitive about certain subjects such as race, gender, age, disability, disease, religion, ethnicity, or economic status.

- Avoid stereotypes because they are based on biases built on generalizations about a "type," a "class," or a preconceived idea, not on a specific person, place, thing, or situation.

- Cursing and slang terms are frequently offensive to others. Although cursing might be commonplace in some work environments, be aware of new situations and business cultures where language of this kind is unacceptable and can be shocking. Avoid emotionally loaded words that make the listener react in a negative way.

Sample Words to Avoid

- lie (an untruth)
- fired
- stupid (when describing someone)
- retarded
- broad (meaning "woman")
- yeah (for "yes")
- Yo, man

- cheap (meaning "inexpensive")
- idiot
- goin'
- jock
- nope
- Akst (mispronounciation of ask)

ACTIVITY 2

List words or phrases you find offensive. Rewrite them so they are not offensive. Be prepared to discuss your list of offensive words and phrases with your classmates. Also, remember that what is considered offensive can vary greatly from place to place.

Offensive Words	How To Say Them Non-Offensively
1. _____	_____
2. _____	_____
3. _____	_____
4. _____	_____

Communicating Non-Verbally

Dion has been working as a food preparation assistant at Ristorante Baci for several months. Roberto, the owner and head chef, appreciates her work. The other day Roberto remarked, "You've done a terrific job preparing the salad and vegetables, Dion." Sometimes, he tells her that her work is good. Other times, Roberto nods his head, smiles broadly, applauds, or takes his chef's hat off in a salute. On the other hand, Roberto also makes his dissatisfaction clear. He shakes his head, pouts, stamps his feet, stands with his arms crossed in front of him, or closes his eyes. The food preparation assistants always know what the head chef thinks about their work. He communicates his positive and negative feelings both verbally and nonverbally.

What is Non-Verbal Communication?

Non-verbal communication is the act of sending messages without the use of words or sounds. Non-verbal communication includes facial expressions, the position of the head, the slope of the shoulders, gestures, and physical appearance. Some non-verbal expressions are universal, such as shrugging the shoulders to show lack of knowledge. Other non-verbal expressions are local or cultural. To be understood, everyone must know the meaning of the action.

In face-to-face communication, nonverbal communication is an important component of feedback. If you think carefully, you will probably remember someone who gave you the "raised eyebrow" look. That raised eyebrow could have said more than any words that were spoken.

Figure 5-2 Gestures can show a variety of attitudes.

Nonverbal communication gives additional meaning to what is said. It might also give the true meaning to the message being sent. Have you had someone tell you, "I'm happy," while looking at his or her feet? Or, "I absolutely agree," while shaking his or her head side-to-side? What were the real meanings behind these statements?

Use of Body Language in Communication

Body Language Body language is a way you express yourself using your body. It shows your true feelings and can either reinforce or contradict the verbal communication. When your words and body language disagree, the receiver will believe the body language first. This is because, unlike what we say, much of our body language is involuntary and difficult to control. Think about it—have you not ever smiled even though doing so was inappropriate?

Body Posture The way you hold your body when standing or sitting is called **body posture**, and it transmits nonverbal signals. You can show confidence, interest, an open attitude, and status through your posture.

Some posture messages common in the United States are:

- Body straight, shoulders up and slightly back, and head high, showing happiness, excitement, confidence.
- Body slouched, shoulders forward and down, head bent forward and looking down, showing sadness and unhappiness.
- Leaning forward in a conversation, showing interest in the communication process.
- Slouching in a chair or against a wall, showing disinterest.
- Standing or sitting stiff and tall, showing tension and lack of ease.
- Crossed arms and legs, showing skepticism and an unwillingness to accept the message.

Gestures Movements of the body, head, or hands in communication are referred to as **gestures**. Gestures have many uses in a conversation. Many people speak a great deal with their hands, sometimes using small movements of only the hands, and at other times making wide motions with the arms and hands.

Gestures can:

- Describe and underscore what is being said
- Be used as a means of letting other people know your general attitudes and mood
- Control the flow of conversation in a small group of people
- Be an unconscious display of one's inner thoughts

Smart **T I P**

Be aware of what your body is saying.

Smart **T I P**

Be considerate of cultures other than your own.

How we use and understand gestures are determined partially by our cultural or ethnic orientation. These influences help dictate how we use our hands, arms, fingers, head, facial features, and shoulders. Greeting someone is a perfect example. People in Europe and the United States will shake right hands when meeting; they will *salaam* in the Middle East and *namasta* in Southeast Asia.

Shaking Hands **Salaam** **Namasta**

Figure 5-3 Personal greetings may be based on cultural influences.

In the United States, the personal greeting is not a simple matter because gender plays such an important role. Men and women who are meeting professionally now commonly shake hands. Men greeting each other can shake hands, give each other a bear hug, slap one another on the back, or give a high-five sign. Professional women meeting each other can shake hands or "air kiss." When you meet someone whom you know, but cannot talk with at the time, you can catch that individual's eye, wink, or nod a greeting.

Figure 5-4 What are the nonverbal messages here?

American Facial Expressions

Facial Expression...	...Shows
• Raised eyebrows	• Surprise
• One raised eyebrow	• Doubt
• Narrowed eyes	• Thoughtfulness
• Wide-open eyes	• Innocence or wonder
• Winking	• Approval
• Smile	• Friendliness
• Frown	• Sadness
• Pursed lips	• Anger or deep thought
• Lack of facial strain: eyes open, slight smile	• Lack of concern
• Facial strain: eyebrows pulled together, eyes squinted, lips pursed	• Concern
• Forward-thrusting jaw	• Anger

Facial Expression All facial features—your eyebrows, eyes, lips, and facial tension—are parts of your **facial expression**. Some prevalent American facial expressions and their meanings are:

ACTIVITY 3

Look carefully at the following pictures of facial expressions. Describe the nonverbal message being sent.

①   ≠   ③   ④   ∞

Face 1 _____

Face 2 _____

Face 3 _____

Face 4 _____

Face 5 _____

Other Forms of Nonverbal Communication

You send nonverbal messages with your body using body language, gestures, and facial expressions. You can also communicate nonverbally by your behavior.

Use of Personal Space The way people use the space around them sends nonverbal signals to others. **Personal space** is the distance a person requires between himself or herself and those with whom he or she is communicating. This varies according to the relationship, the situation, and the cultural backgrounds of the people involved. Disagreements are common when people feel their personal territory has been invaded.

Some Ways We Use Personal Space

- Stepping toward someone with arm extended to give an order, or show anger or aggression.
- Standing over or sitting higher than someone else to show dominance, power, and authority.
- Leaning back or "giving someone space" by backing away to show disbelief or disagreement.
- Leaning forward, chest expanded, head tilted to look down on others.

Use of Silence Ursula always has a calm exterior. Nothing ever seems to bother her, and she is not given to outbursts of temper or emotion. However, her coworkers always know when she is angry because of her "silent treatment."

By remaining silent, even though responding verbally would be more appropriate, people demonstrate their feelings. Sometimes silence is used when a person is thinking about and formulating an appropriate verbal response. Then one has to look closely at the body language to interpret the message correctly.

Time Some people have no concept of time despite the watch they wear every day. They are never on time. When you are kept waiting, the message being sent to you can be interpreted as, "You are not really important. Whatever I am doing is more important than what we are going to do together."

Yu-Ming works in the Ambulatory Surgery Center of the Midland County Medical Center. She needs to speak with her supervisor, the Administrative Assistant to the department director, Ms. Coruzzi about a special project that is her responsibility. She made an appointment for a 10-minute interview with Ms. Coruzzi at 11:00 A.M. today. When she arrived at Ms. Coruzzi's office at 10:55 A.M., Yu-Ming was asked by the receptionist to "have a seat and wait." Now the time is 11:30 A.M.

1. How do you think Yu-Ming feels right now? Why?

_____

_____

_____

2. What nonverbal messages is Ms. Coruzzi sending to Yu-Ming?

_____

_____

_____

Barriers to Good Communication

Mr. Jackson, the manager of the Shipping Department of Loren's Ladies Dresses, is extremely angry. Dresses that were shipped three weeks ago are being returned from the stores. He does not know why they are being returned or what to do with them. Investigating, Mr. Jackson finds that Toni, a clerk in the Sales Department, was asked by the sales manager to call the stores to find out how well these dresses were selling. She called each store and told the store manager: "We need to know how these dresses are doing. Please send the unsold numbers back as soon as possible." The store managers believed Loren's wanted the unsold dresses returned.

Anything preventing or obstructing the communication process can cause a breakdown. Whatever causes this breakdown is known as a **communication barrier.** When you understand why and how communication is breaking down, you will have an idea of how to correct the situation.

"How can I listen to you if you don't say the things I want to hear?"

Barriers to Communication

Barriers Caused by Sender
- Misuse of language
- Sending more than one message
- Using generalizations
- Use of emotionally loaded words
- Poor speaking skills
- Disorganization of thoughts
- Preconceived ideas regarding the topic
- Negatively stereotyping the receiver
- Use of slang, "in-words," or an idiom

Barriers Caused by Receiver
- Interrupting the speaker
- Thinking ahead
- Pretending to listen
- Being intimidated by the speaker
- Preconceived ideas regarding topic
- Negatively stereotyping of sender

Barriers Caused by Poor Feedback
- Personal attack by the receiver
- Lack of feedback
- Feedback not related to the message sent

When Verbal and Nonverbal Messages Disagree

Whitney and Achmed, two lab technicians, are having a discussion at work. Whitney is standing with her head down, feet together, and her arms crossed when she says: "Tell me how you would do the job better, Achmed. I'm willing to listen to your suggestions." The stance of her body says something else. Achmed's response, "No, some other time, Whitney," is reasonable under the circumstances because he does not believe Whitney really wants to hear his message.

Nonverbal communication is difficult to control. You can betray your true feelings and beliefs even though you do not want to. This is because your actions, not the words you speak, are believed.

The listener becomes confused if he or she receives a mixed message. A **mixed message** is a discrepancy between the verbal and nonverbal messages, resulting in the meaning of the message being misunderstood. For example, when Roger returned from his vacation, everyone in the plant was anxious to hear about it. "I went fishing every morning, swam every afternoon, and partied every night. It was just great. I think you should all go there, too." Roger explained all this with a tense, sad look on his face and with his shoulders slumped forward. Do you think Roger was telling the truth about his vacation? What was the real message?

Noise As a Communication Barrier

Good communication is frequently beyond the control of all the parties involved. Let's look at the following situations to understand this:

1. Ana and Shawdell were deep in conversation regarding the programming of a new computer being installed at their work site. Suddenly, a loud banging noise coming from another office interrupted their conversation.

2. Ms. Garcia, an administrative assistant, was on the telephone confirming an appointment with a lawyer for her boss, Mr. Applewhite. There was a burst of static on the line and Ms. Garcia could not hear.

3. Mr. Jackson, a salesman at the Boston Shoe Store, was talking with a customer when a car drove by with its loud radio blaring. Both Mr. Jackson and the customer stopped talking and looked out the store window.

In these situations, the conversations were interrupted by noise. Noise is a kind of outside interference that results in a breakdown of communication. A barrier like this is usually beyond the participant's ability to control, and can interrupt or stop the communication process. Noise includes loud sounds, conversations, and music. Noise can also be physical interruptions, such as someone interrupting.

ACTIVITY 5

Which communication barrier is illustrated in each of the following examples?

Communication Barriers:
- Mixed message
- Personal attack
- Lack of feedback
- Misuse of language

- Pretending to listen
- Being intimidated
- Negative stereotyping
- Use of emotionally loaded words

Statement

1. "I'm very happy," Alex said in a sad, low voice.

2. "Everyone knows 'those' people don't do things the way we do them."

3. "Hey, Shortie, be careful."

4. "What's the matter with you? Don't you know anything?"

5. "Oh! I've been disconnected again by Mrs. Greene's assistant."

Communication Barrier

_____

_____

_____

_____

_____

A C T I V I T I E S

Activity 5-1

Using Important Words and Information

A. **Important Words** Your instructor will assign various projects to help you achieve the goal of adding these words to your business vocabulary.

1. Body language	6. Feedback	11. Personal space
2. Communication	7. Gesture	12. Posture
3. Communication barrier	8. Message	13. Receiver
4. Decode	9. Mixed message	14. Sender
5. Encode	10. Nonverbal communication	

B. **Learning Log** Using a word processing program, summarize what you have learned from the material in this chapter and what it means to you. How could you apply this information and personal insight to yourself or your employment situation?

_____
_____
_____
_____
_____
_____
_____
_____
_____
_____
_____
_____
_____
_____
_____
_____
_____
_____
_____
_____

Activity 5-2

Write complete answers to the questions in this section. Explain your answers using examples. Be prepared to discuss your responses with the class.

1. Describe the various ways communication occurs.

_____

_____

2. Why is good communication important?

_____

_____

3. Describe how the communication process works.

_____

_____

4. "Think before you speak." Why is this statement relevant in good communication?

_____

_____

5. Describe the characteristics of a good speaker.

_____

_____

6. How can you show respect and consideration for others when communicating?

_____

_____

7. Explain the statement: "Your body says more than your words."

_____

_____

_____

8. Why are facial expressions an important part of body language?

_____

_____

9. List 10 communication barriers that can interfere with communication.

_____

_____

_____

10. Describe noise and how it can interfere with communication.

_____

_____

Activity 5-3

Employment Situations

Write complete answers to the questions posed in the employment situations described in this section. Be prepared to discuss and explain your responses with your classmates.

A. Cassandra works at a prestigious law firm. Ms. Latham, her supervisor, approaches Cassandra's desk with a folder in her hand. When she leans over Cassandra's desk, saying, "You did a terrific job on this report. You really made me look good upstairs with management. Thanks a lot." Cassandra moves back in her chair, pushing away from her desk.

1. What nonverbal messages is Ms. Latham sending Cassandra?

_____

_____

_____

2. How do you think Cassandra feels after Ms. Latham's remarks?

_____

_____

_____

3. Do you think Cassandra minded Ms. Latham invading her personal space? Explain your answer.

_____

_____

B. Samantha is having a business lunch with Jordan and Ivan who, like her, are also executives. When she asks Jordan how a business meeting he attended went, he just continues to sip his soda. Later, while discussing an interesting point in a report Ivan wrote, Jordan says, "Well, what do you know, Ivan? You are so naive about business matters."

1. List the communication barriers in this exchange.

_____

_____

_____

2. Describe what you think happened to the communication process.

_____

_____

_____

3. How do you think the people at the luncheon felt about Jordan's comment?

_____

_____

_____

C. Sammy, Jason, Enrique, and Grace were discussing the new ad campaign their agency was developing. Grace said, "I really like the ad." Sammy and Enrique were not too sure whether they liked the ad, but they were glad to hear Grace's views about it. Jason kept talking about Alice, the new employee in their department. He kept interrupting, trying to draw Sammy and Enrique's attention into a discussion about Alice.

1. What barriers blocked good communication?

   _____

   _____

   _____

   _____

2. What could have been done to eliminate the communication barriers?

   _____

   _____

   _____

Activity 5-4

A. **Think Before You Speak** Each of the following comments can create communication barriers because it can offend others. Rewrite each to further good communication.

Poor Communication   Better Communication

1. "What a silly idea!" _____

   _____

   _____

2. "You never include me at meetings." _____

   _____

   _____

3. "You're never on time." _____

   _____

   _____

4. "Don't call me 'girl.'" _____

   _____

   _____

5. "Hey, what d'ya want me to do?" _____

_____

_____

6. "Are you dumb or something?" _____

_____

_____

7. "I can't do this job. You never teach me how to do anything." _____

_____

_____

8. "You're a lousy boss. I quit." _____

_____

_____

9. "Get outta my face." _____

_____

_____

10. "You people are all alike. You want to do everything your own way." _____

_____

_____

B. **Practice Makes Perfect** Developing good communication skills takes practice.

1. Listen in on two people speaking. Notice what are they doing to help the communication process? What are some of the barriers they are experiencing? _____

_____

_____

2. Listen to another conversation, and ask yourself the same questions. Note the common communication processes and barriers. _____

_____

_____

3. Observe people talking; note their nonverbal communication. What they are trying to say? How are their gestures similar or dissimilar to yours? _____

_____

_____

C. **Listen to Yourself** To learn to be a good communicator, you must learn how you communicate.

1. Make a list of the slang words and idiomatic expressions you use.

    _____   _____   _____

    _____   _____   _____

2. Do you erect other communication barriers when talking with others? And if so, with whom? What are these barriers?

    _____

    _____

    _____

    _____

    _____

internet

Activity 5-5

Communication Using the Internet

The Internet offers a number of ways to communicate. List, define, give illustrations, and provide instructions on how to use these different systems.

Activity 5-6

The Team Approach

team

Prepare a visual presentation showing common American body language mannerisms. Include postures, gestures, and facial expressions. Share your presentation with your class.

Chapter 6

Developing Listening Skills

Skills
OBJECTIVES

After reading Chapter 6, you will be able to:

1. Analyze the difference between hearing and listening.

2. Describe and discuss the skills needed to be a good listener.

3. Complete a self-evaluation of your listening habits.

4. Verbalize the importance of good listening in the workplace.

Susan works at the E-Z Breeze Ice Cream Store as a customer server. As customers come to the counter, she must take their orders and fill them. Mrs. Greene comes in with her three children and gives Susan her order. "Three cones, each with one scoop of vanilla and one scoop of cherry. One cone with one scoop of cherry. All cones are to have chocolate sprinkles, nuts and a cherry on top. And, oh, yes, lots of napkins." Susan must listen carefully to the order to make sure she gets it right, so Mrs. Greene will be satisfied and return again. Where can Susan easily make mistakes if she does not listen?

What Is Listening?

Most of us are aware of the mother who yells at her child, saying "Stop that! I told you before, and I'm going to tell you for the last time, don't eat anything from the floor. Don't you hear me?"

This child can easily answer, "Yes, I hear you, but I'm not listening." Hearing is the process by which sounds are registered on the brain. These sounds do not have any meaning when the person who hears them is not consciously aware of them. The child can hear the mother's voice as background noise and not pay attention to it. Listening is an active process requiring mental activity to give meaning to the sounds heard. The receiver must concentrate and contribute emotionally, intellectually, and even physically to the process to make the sounds understandable. The child, therefore, must hear the mother's voice, identify the sounds as words, and derive the meaning from the words, "Don't eat anything from the floor."

Why We Listen

We hear sounds all the time. We ignore some sounds while we concentrate on others. Take a moment. Close your eyes. Listen to all the sounds around you. Can you identify them? You hear many sounds all the time, but choose not to listen to most of them because you are listening to the sound you think is most important. These background sounds are called noise.

We tend to concentrate on and listen to things in which we are interested, which are of importance to us, and with which we agree. Some noises will catch your attention even if you are listening to something else—someone calling your name, for instance. A sudden noise like a sharp, loud bang or someone screaming for help will also get your attention.

Julio is having lunch with a group of friends. He is concentrating very carefully on what his friend Thomas is saying about his new car. He hears Fred mention his name in a conversation with three others. They are talking about the home run Julio hit in the company baseball game they all played on Saturday. As Julio's attention goes to Fred's conversation, he misses some of what Thomas is saying.

Listening Is Important

Listening is a very important part of the communication process. Studies have shown that we usually listen more than we speak. Listening to someone shows you care what that person has to say, that you are interested. You give that person respect because you are willing to spend the time and energy needed to listen.

Reasons We Listen

- To get information we need or want.
- To hear a joke, rumor, or gossip that interests us.
- To increase our understanding of a situation.
- To learn something new.

- To be friendly or likeable.
- To satisfy curiosity.
- To do a job properly.
- For leisure, as when listening to music, watching television, or attending a movie.

ACTIVITY I

Think back over your past 24 hours. You spent a good deal of your waking time listening. List all the times you listened and the reasons why you did so.

I Listened When	I Listened Because
_____	_____
_____	_____
_____	_____

Tamara, attending a company staff development seminar, is listening to Mr. Hart discuss some important events reported in the news. She realizes what is happening locally will have an impact on her position in the company. Tamara is listening for content. This means the listener is listening for all the facts or information within the message. The listener values what is being heard. This form of listening is usually used for information gathering, persuading, and learning.

Ms. Jones, Kevin's boss, tells him: "Adam is retiring and people should be notified." Kevin understands he has to write and distribute a memo to that effect. Kevin listened to Ms. Jones with *intent*; that is, he listened between the words for Ms. Jones' intention. He wants to understand the ideas and concepts in the message; the reason why the message was delivered to him. Intent is the meaning behind the message. When listening with intent, the listener must pay attention to the whole message, understand the meaning held within the words, and give feedback to clarify the thoughts and ideas being expressed.

ACTIVITY 2

While you are listening to the following comments, determine whether you are listening for *content* or *intent*. Circle your response.

1. "I think Alvin wants to plant a vegetable garden by those large rocks."

   CONTENT   INTENT

2. "Mercedes is the one who will be picking you up in her car at 3:35 this afternoon."

   CONTENT   INTENT

3. "I need a wedding gift for a couple who are each getting married for the first time; I don't want to spend too much money, but the gift must really be unique."

   CONTENT   INTENT

Skills Needed to Be a Good Listener

Being a good listener is not easy. A person who is a good listener is often considered a rare find.

Ryan is very popular with all the people at work. Everyone thinks he is smart, understanding, and a good friend. He is the person everyone goes to when they have a problem, are in trouble, or just want to talk. What is Ryan's secret? He is a good listener.

As noted earlier, listening involves intellectual, emotional, and sometimes physical input. Let's look at the skills needed.

Intellectual Listening

Intellectual concentration on the topic being discussed is the most vital part of listening. Without this effort, a person is not listening, but just hearing noise. Intellectual listening involves listening to the whole message and considering what is being said.

To listen intelligently you should:

1. Analyze the words and ideas being expressed to understand the message.

2. Understand the concepts expressed so you learn the full meaning of what you hear. Understanding the words spoken is often easy, but the meaning of the concepts can be confusing and the listener can fail to understand much of the message.

3. Evaluate the validity, that is, determine the truth of the ideas by examining the facts of what you hear.

4. Organize the ideas in a meaningful way. Sometimes the speaker throws concepts and ideas out in a slipshod fashion, and when this happens, listeners must reorganize the ideas to properly understand them.

5. Be able to give an accurate summary of the message.

6. Ask questions when you need to clarify, or make clear, what you have just heard. These questions have to be pertinent, relating directly to the matter at hand, and not be a *put-down* such as, "Don't you know what you are talking about?" Questions and comments like "Tell me more," "Do you mean ...," and "I don't understand" tell the speaker you are listening and want to understand what he or she is saying.

"You haven't been listening. I keep telling you that I don't want a product fit for a king."

Physically Active Listening

To be a good listener, you must be physically active in the process. This means your body is also involved in the listening process.

To be physically active while listening, you should:

1. Send a message with your body saying you are listening: sit straight or lean towards the speaker, nod your head, keep your hands and arms still.

2. Look at the person speaking. In the American business world, you should make eye contact with the speaker.

3. Send messages with facial expressions to tell the speaker you are listening. Smile or frown when appropriate.

4. Pay attention. Do not do anything else while listening, including reading, writing, or handling objects.

5. Do not interrupt the speaker. Wait until a break in the conversation so you can speak.

6. Do not talk at the same time others are talking. You should wait until your turn comes to speak.

*S*mart TIP

Being a good listener takes effort.

Controlling Your Emotions While Listening

Figure 6-1 Be a good listener.

Your emotions are involved in the communication process. Listeners should control their emotions to better understand the message and the speaker's point of view.

To control your emotions, you should:

1. Concentrate, putting feelings, ideas, and concerns unrelated to what is being said on hold for the time being.

2. React to the message, not the messenger. You might not want this individual for a friend, but do not allow yourself to become distracted because of the way the person talks, what that person stands for, or past bad experiences with similar individuals.

3. Listen to the whole message before deciding what you are going to say.

4. Try to understand the other person's point of view. Empathize, which means put yourself in the other person's place.

5. Avoid hasty judgments.

Poor Listening Habits

Kara and Jodi are talking. Let's listen in:

Kara: "My sister is angry with me because I forgot to call her on her birthday and now she won't let me borrow her car. Mine is in the repair shop and I need to go to Sandra's house to drop off work from the office."

Jodi: "Yeah, I know what you mean – everything is so complicated."

Kara: "Why do people have to be so sensitive? She should have understood we can't call from the office and I was working overtime on her birthday."

Jodi: "Boy, you have no time for yourself. I really like that silver-gray car Jim got."

Kara: "Yeah. Well, nice seeing you."

Poor listening habits are a problem for many people, leading to poor interpersonal relations because the listener is sending a message saying, "I don't care, I don't think that you, the speaker, are important. I'm more important in this discussion and so is what I have to say. I am not really interested in what you are saying." Let's look at what happened in this conversation to make Kara terminate it so abruptly. She was telling Jodi about a problem that was upsetting her, and really wanted some sympathy and a friendly ear. Jodi was not listening very well to what Kara had to say. Her mind was elsewhere—on Jim's new car.

Examples of Poor Listening

- Not paying attention when the other person speaks. This can happen when your mind wanders to other subjects.
- Criticizing the speaker.
- Letting your own emotions get in the way of the message so you stop listening.
- Receiving too much information at one time so you are overwhelmed and cannot follow what the speaker is saying.
- Thinking of what you will say next.
- Letting things such as noises, other people, or the surroundings distract you.
- *Tuning out* because the speaker has annoyed you by talking too fast or too slow, speaking in a monotonous voice, or gesturing too much. You might also tune out when you disagree with what is being said or find the speaker's appeal too emotional.
- Listening and reacting to only a part of what is being said; picking out only the part of the discussion that is of interest and ignoring the rest.

ACTIVITY 3

A. Is Dirk a good listener? Evaluate the following conversations overheard during the coffee break. Did he listen? Circle your responses and give the reasons for your answer.

Carole: "Are you going to the art show tonight after work?"

Dirk: "What time is it now?"

Dirk IS / IS NOT (circle one or the other) a good listener here because:

_____

_____

_____

_____

B. Carole: "I think Mr. Mori handled the situation very well when he wrote the press release."

Dirk: "I think you are right."

Dirk IS / IS NOT a good listener here because:

_____

_____

_____

_____

Activity 6-1

Using Important Words and Information

A. **Important Words.** Your instructor will assign various tasks to help you achieve the goal of adding these words to your business vocabulary.

1. Clarify	5. Intellectual listening	8. Noise
2. Content	6. Intent	9. Pertinent
3. Empathize	7. Listening	10. Validity
4. Hearing		

B. **Learning Log.** Using your word processing program, summarize what you have learned from the material in this chapter and what is means to you. Apply this information and personal insight to yourself and/or your employment situation.

_____
_____
_____
_____
_____
_____
_____
_____
_____
_____
_____
_____
_____
_____
_____
_____
_____
_____
_____
_____
_____
_____

Activity 6-2

Write complete answers to the questions in this section. Explain your answers completely, using examples to illustrate. Be prepared to discuss your responses with the class.

1. When listening, we sometimes say, "I hear you." What does this mean to the speaker?

   _____

   _____

2. Most people hear, but fewer people listen. Explain the difference between hearing and listening.

   _____

   _____

3. Explain what *noise* is and how it affects listening.

   _____

   _____

4. What makes a good listener?

   _____

   _____

5. Why do you think people like good listeners?

   _____

   _____

6. Poor listening habits can lead to poor interpersonal relationships. List four poor listening habits and explain why you think they can hinder communication and relationships.

   _____

   _____

   _____

7. List three things you can do when you listen intellectually.

   _____

   _____

8. Why is being physically active while listening important?

   _____

   _____

9. Describe how your emotions affect your listening.

   _____

   _____

10. List several things you can do to help people listen to you.

   _____

   _____

Activity 6-3

Employment Situations

Write complete answers to the following on-the-job situations. Discuss the listening skills used, good or poor, and how they would probably affect the person's job performance.

1. James has his eye on a pretty girl who just started to work in the office. She walks past and smiles while his supervisor is giving him instructions for a new task.

    Listening Skills   Effect on Job Performance

    _____   _____
    _____   _____
    _____   _____
    _____   _____

2. Alleya thinks her boss is simply not very smart. She tries to pay attention, however, when he talks to her about her job and project assignments for the day.

    Listening Skills   Effect on Job Performance

    _____   _____
    _____   _____
    _____   _____
    _____   _____

3. Mario likes to listen to rock music while working. He does not turn the volume down when his coworkers have something to say to him.

    Listening Skills   Effect on Job Performance

    _____   _____
    _____   _____
    _____   _____
    _____   _____

4. Because his supervisor, Mr. Kumaninsky, just moved to this country and still has a strong accent. John has to concentrate when speaking with him. He finds Mr. Kumaninsky hard to understand, especially when he speaks too fast, and John does not always pay attention to what is being said.

    Listening Skills   Effect on Job Performance

    _____   _____
    _____   _____
    _____   _____
    _____   _____

Activity 6-4

Listening Self-Test

A. **Rate Yourself.** One of the most important parts of the communication process is skill in listening. Poor listening habits lead to problems in communication. Rate your listening habits on the scale by circling a number from 1 to 5, using the following rating scale.

1	2	3	4	5
Usually	**Often**	**Sometimes**	**Rarely**	**Never**

1. My mind wanders if someone talks for more than a few minutes.   1 2 3 4 5

2. I don't listen if I don't like the person talking to me.   1 2 3 4 5

3. I interrupt others to respond to what they are saying.   1 2 3 4 5

4. I talk mainly about myself.   1 2 3 4 5

5. I make eye contact with the speaker.   1 2 3 4 5

6. I get so busy writing things down, I miss some of what is being said.   1 2 3 4 5

7. I ask speakers with foreign accents to speak slower so I can understand.   1 2 3 4 5

8. I never ask questions.   1 2 3 4 5

9. If I don't like the subject others are discussing, I tune out.   1 2 3 4 5

10. I find concentrating on only one thing at a time difficult.   1 2 3 4 5

11. I like to talk more than listen.   1 2 3 4 5

12. If I am not the topic of conversation, I change the subject and talk about myself.   1 2 3 4 5

13. If I don't understand, I stop listening.   1 2 3 4 5

14. If I don't like what other people are saying, I argue with them.   1 2 3 4 5

15. I look at the person with whom I am talking.   1 2 3 4 5

16. I fake paying attention.   1 2 3 4 5

17. I daydream when someone is talking.   1 2 3 4 5

18. I can listen to someone and read at the same time.   1 2 3 4 5

19. I have to move about when someone is talking with me.   1 2 3 4 5

20. I can't understand foreign accents so I don't speak to other people who do not speak good English.   1 2 3 4 5

Activity 6-4 *(continued)*

B. **Evaluate your responses.** On the basis of your answers to the Listening Self-Test, respond to the following questions.

a. List your good listening habits.

_____

_____

_____

b. List your bad listening habits.

_____

_____

_____

c. List things you can do to improve your listening skills.

_____

_____

_____

Activity 6-5

Role Play

In this section, you will act out the following situations with members of your class or group. The members who are observing will complete an evaluation form for each situation and rate the participants on their listening skills. The Role Play evaluation form will be provided by your instructor.

1. Carole is waiting on a customer at the Cornwall Dress Shop. She is very harried and impatient with the customer, who cannot seem to choose between two dresses. Other customers are waiting for help. Also, Carole is worried because her car is parked at a meter and the time is running out.

2. Darrell is an apprentice carpenter and is listening to his supervisor tell him how to use the new computerized lathe. Darrell knows how to use the machine because he used it in technology classes at school.

3. Randi is a hygienist in a dental practice with four dentists. Randi likes the patient she is working on and thinks he is a "hunk." Dr. Berg, one of the dentists, is giving her instructions on what he wants her to do. The patient keeps smiling and "making eyes" at Randi.

4. Jermal is a teller at a local branch of a large bank. He knows many of the customers who come in and likes to talk with them even when they are not at his window. Mrs. Gainer, a new customer, has a number of transactions needing attention. Jermal is in conversation with the person at the next window.

Activity 6-6

Evaluate Listening Skills in Random Conversations

Go someplace where people talk, such as a large store, and listen in on some conversations. Pick a conversation for this evaluation. Write your answers on a separate sheet of paper.

- Ask yourself, "Does the listener listen to what is being said." Discuss the facts behind your answer; what made you come to the conclusions you did?

- Repeat this exercise again. Now ask yourself, "How does the speaker respond to the listening ability of the listener?

- Review the conversations you have heard, list the communication barriers you noticed.

internet

Activity 6-7

Listening in the Workplace

Explore the Internet to find references to listening in the workplace. Download what you have found and summarize each point.

Activity 6-8

The Team Approach

team

As a group, write three scenarios regarding communication. Formulate answers to the questions developed for each scenario. Trade scenarios with another group and answer their questions. Share findings and decisions with other groups.

Chapter 7

Communicating in a Business Organization

Skills

OBJECTIVES

After working through this chapter, you will be able to:

1. Verbalize the role of communication in business.

2. Define and illustrate the corporate chain of command.

3. Differentiate between and cite examples of authority and responsibility within an organization.

4. Illustrate vertical and horizontal communication in a business situation.

5. Distinguish between formal and informal company communication.

Smart TIP

Communication processes are different in every company.

Joanna Lincoln, the owner of Lincoln Jewelry Supply, employs 10 people to do marketing and advertising, merchandise packaging, distribution, and clerical support. This is a friendly company and communication among staff members is easy and often informal. Karen is in charge of packaging outgoing orders and has to get several large orders out today. The day is busy at Lincoln Jewelry Supply and Karen has more work than she can handle. She knows, however, she does not have the authority to ask others to drop their work and help out; she must go through the proper communication channels. Karen approaches the owner and says, "Joanna, I need help in getting today's work out. Who can help me for an hour this afternoon?" By following established communication channels, Karen was able to get the help she needed without difficulty.

The Role of Communication in Business

Communication is the process by which information, ideas, and feelings are exchanged among people. When people are able to communicate effectively in business, they make possible the producing of quality products and services, meeting deadlines, making effective decisions, transferring information, and interacting with others. The role of communication in the smooth operation and success of a business is so important that most companies have established specific methods for all employees to get the information they need to do their jobs effectively. These channels of communication are referred to as the flow of information.

The **flow of information** is *how* information travels within a company. For example, management sets the policies and goals of a company after considering recommendations from departments and work teams. To be effective, management must pass this information along to others who are responsible for putting the policies into practice and achieving the stated goals.

A Recognized System of Communication

Every business must have a recognized system of communication, a formal method or procedure agreed upon and used by all employees. This is necessary to create a smooth flow of information. In small businesses, all the staff members know each other and communication is generally informal. Here you will find a great deal of face-to-face communication. Employees in small companies tend to be familiar with their coworkers' roles and responsibilities. Often, employees are expected to assist wherever they are needed. Although the smaller firms usually do not have elaborate communication networks, the savvy employee is aware of whatever system it does have, and is careful to follow it.

Large businesses have many divisions and departments. These can be located in one large headquarters, as well as across the United States and in other countries. In large companies, people have a greater need for a formal system of communication everyone can follow.

Figure 7-1 Your employer can help you understand the inner workings of the organization.

Chain of Command

The chain of command refers to the order in which information, orders, and responsibilities are passed along in an organization. The chain of command in a small business is shorter, as information flows directly from one person to another. As businesses increase in size and complexity, the chain of command is broadened to allow for specialization and different levels of responsibility.

To help all employees understand how this chain of command works, large organizations develop a chart for circulation throughout the company. The organization chart (or *org chart*) is a flowchart showing all departments and their relationships to each other. It illustrates the flow of authority, the power to command in an organization, and responsibility, being accountable for something.

The Line of Authority

Someone always has authority over you in a business organization, unless you own the company or are the president. The line of authority begins at the top of the organization with the president or owner and proceeds downward to include all the workers. It defines the flow of

Smart TIP

Following the chain of command is wise.

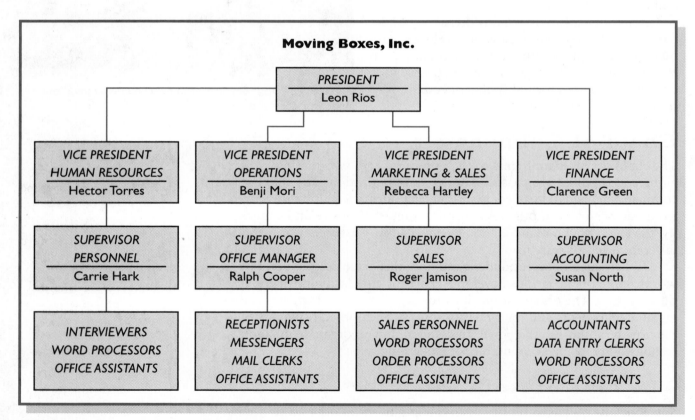

Smart T I P

Know how your company is organized.

information and responsibilities among individuals and departments.

The line of authority details the company hierarchy, a system of ranking people vertically in a business, according to their authority.

The company hierarchy answers the following questions:

1. Who is the boss?
2. Who answers to whom?
3. Who gives orders, directions, and work?
4. Who supervises you and other workers?
5. Who is in charge when your boss is not available?

The Line of Responsibility

The line of responsibility shows who is accountable in a business organization. It usually follows the lines of authority. It must answer these questions:

1. Who is accountable for what happens?
2. Who accepts blame for failure?
3. Who gets credit for successes?

Figure 7-2 shows a typical business organization chart.

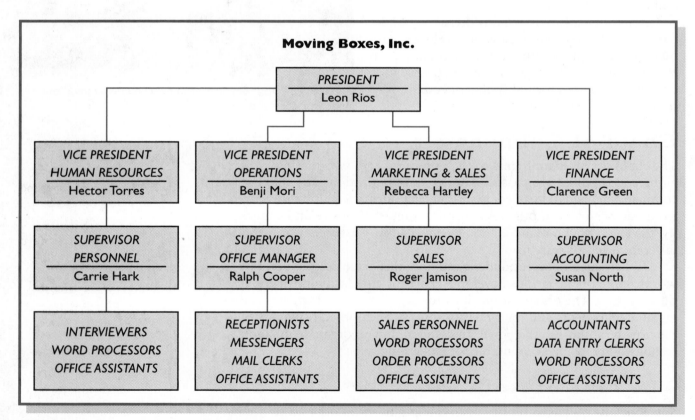

Figure 7-2 Typical Organization Chart: Moving Boxes, Inc.

Moving Boxes, Inc. is a wholesaler of corrugated boxes and containers used by moving and storage companies. This company is an example of a **line organization**. In this system, every person has one supervisor who is a manager in the organization. Employees at Moving Boxes, Inc. know their responsibilities, to whom they report, and whom they supervise.

Using Figure 7-2 as a guide, note the line of authority starts with the president, Leon Rios. The vice presidents, Hector Torres, Benji Mori, Rebecca Hartley, and Clarence Greene, are below the president, and they represent the next group of people in the line of authority. Moving downward from the vice presidents are the supervisors of specific departments: Hark, Cooper, Jamison, and North. The bottom row of squares shows who works in each department. For example, as a mail clerk, you report to Ralph Cooper, the Office Manager. Mr. Cooper is your supervisor and is responsible for giving you your work assignments.

In the line of responsibility, Roger Jamison, as Supervisor of Sales, is accountable to Rebecca Hartley, Vice President of Marketing and Sales. In turn, Ms. Hartley answers to the president. In this example, the sales staff reporting to Mr. Jamison will get the credit for increased sales or the blame for poor sales.

ACTIVITY I

Using the organization chart in Figure 7-2, fill in the blanks by supplying the name of the appropriate person for each of the following:

1. The line of authority starts with _____

2. Susan North's boss is _____

3. The order processors report to _____

4. The receptionists report to _____

5. Sales personnel take orders from _____

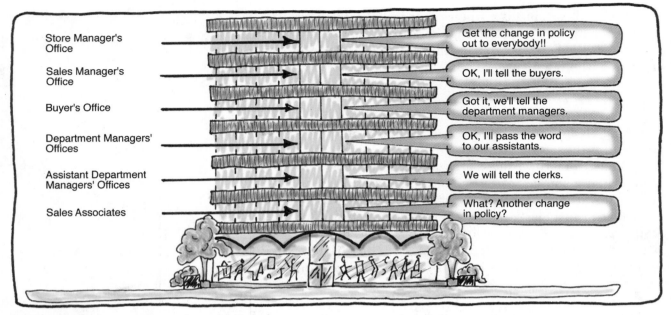

Figure 7-3 Downward lines of communication.

The Lines of Communication

The term lines of communication refers to the direct flow of information through the organization as detailed on the organization chart. The sum total of a company's lines of communication creates a kind of road map with many routes going to the same destinations. In business, planning is required for effective communication. This planning includes effective problem solving, decision making, production, and policy development at all levels of the organization.

✓ **Vertical Communication**   **Checklist 7-1**

- Flows downward from the top, where policy making takes place, to the lower levels, where policies are carried out.

- Completed work, finished products, and reports flow upward.

- A supervisor communicates with a person immediately under or above him or her; that person communicates with people immediately under or above himself or herself.

- Common forms of vertical communication are:

  1. Written memos and letters
  2. Formal reports
  3. Formal meetings
  4. Training sessions
  5. E-mail

- Flows between people or departments on the same level of the organization chart.
- A supervisor from Department A exchanges information with the supervisor from Department B but does not take or give orders in Department B.
- Common forms of horizontal communication are:
  1. Interoffice memos
  2. Telephone conversations
  3. Formal meetings
  4. Informal meetings and chat sessions
  5. E-mail

Let's look at Figure 7-4. The lines of communication are indicated by the dotted lines. In vertical communication, policy making flows downward from Mr. Rios through the vice presidents. For example, Moving Boxes, Inc. sets a goal to hire more female and minority employees. Hector Torres, the Human Resources VP, sends Carrie Hark a written memo directing her to achieve this goal. Mrs. Hark is responsible for communicating this information to her personnel interviewers. When the interviewers recruit more female and minority employees, they communicate this information back to Mrs. Hark.

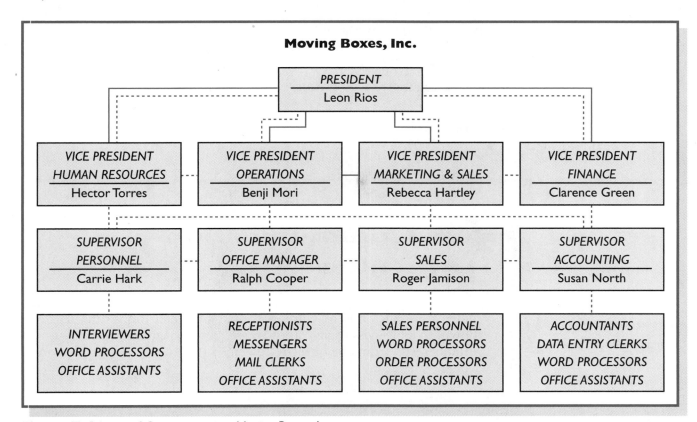

Figure 7-4 Lines of Communication, Moving Boxes, Inc.

Look at Figure 7-4 again. Mr. Torres sends a written memo to the other vice presidents explaining that Moving Boxes, Inc. wants to hire more female and minority workers. In the memo, he tells the vice presidents about the company goal and details his plans for working with them to place more minority workers in each vice president's department. This is an example of **horizontal communication**, where information flows between departments.

ACTIVITY 2

Circle the type of communication for each example, using the information in Figure 7-2.

1. Benji Mori sends a memo to Ralph Cooper.   Vertical   Horizontal

2. Susan North has a meeting with the data entry clerks.   Vertical   Horizontal

3. Mrs. Hark has a telephone conversation with Mr. Torres.   Vertical   Horizontal

4. Mr. Jamison sends the June sales report to the sales staff. Vertical   Horizontal

5. Mr. Jamison sends the June sales report to Ms. Hartley.   Vertical   Horizontal

6. Mr. Jamison sends the June sales report to the other   Vertical   Horizontal
   supervisors.

7. Ms. Hartley sends the June sales report to Leon Rios.   Vertical   Horizontal

8. Ms. Hartley sends the June sales report to the other   Vertical   Horizontal
   vice presidents.

How Communication Difficulties Arise

Smart TIP

Use the company communications systems effectively.

Every company strives to have an efficient and effective system of communication known to all employees. But communications can break down. In a business organization, these communication breakdowns usually result from one of the following:

Going Around Designated Levels of Communication

When you try to bypass, or *go around*, the lines of communication, you create problems for yourself and others in the organization. Suppose you have devised a new form for summarizing customer complaints. The line of authority indicates you should propose such a change to your immediate supervisor. If your supervisor has the authority, your new idea might be accepted immediately. Lacking such authority, your supervisor would have to suggest your new plan to his or her immediate supervisor.

Suppose, however, your supervisor says, "Thank you," and then does nothing with your idea. If you decide to bypass your immediate supervisor and go over his or her head, you can be sure your supervisor will be angry and probably will never willingly accept your new plan. In addition, your supervisor probably will distrust you in the future and could give you an unsatisfactory job performance rating. You might also get a bad reputation within the company for trying to go where you do not belong. Ultimately, you could lose your job if you continue this behavior.

Always try to solve problems first with your immediate supervisor before going up higher in the organization. When you go over your boss's head, you show disrespect for the lines of communication. People you have passed over will feel annoyed you did not come to them directly. You could be considered untrustworthy and pushy, even if your intentions were good.

*S**mart* **T I P**

Think before you act.

Communications Can Get Snagged

Messages sometimes get delivered to one part of the business organization, only to be stuck there without progressing to the next level. Look at this example: Theodore is an artist at JHR Advertising. Mr. Harville, the president, wrote a memo to Ted's boss, the supervisor of the Art Department, Ms. Archer. He asked her to prepare a newspaper advertisement for an anti-drug campaign. Ted has been designing all the agency's anti-drug ads for the past year. In the hallway today, Mr. Harville stopped Ted and said, "What's taking you so long, Ted? Where's that anti-drug newspaper ad I wanted?" Ted didn't know what Mr. Harville was talking about because Ms. Archer never told him about the memo. The line of communication got *snagged* with Ms. Archer because she did not act on the written instructions from the president.

What are the consequences of snagged communications?

1. The people who are supposed to do the work do not get the assignments to do so.

2. Time is wasted, increasing company expenses.

3. Employees can become demoralized when blamed for not acting on information they did not have.

4. The company loses money and goes out of business. People lose their jobs.

Employees See Only a Small Part of the Company Structure

Barbara Liu is a clerical assistant in an insurance company. She processes claims submitted by people who are insured by the company. She has no contact with other parts of the insurance company, such as marketing, advertising, and sales. As a clerk, Barbara is not in a position of authority or responsibility. She does the work assigned to her and is not part of the company's decision-making teams. In fact, her awareness of the company is limited to claim preparation. Last week the insurance company applied for an increase in its rates. Barbara doesn't understand why the company is getting negative publicity in the community.

In this case, management is responsible for informing all employees about matters affecting the company. Remember, the lines of communication are set up to make sure all workers know about the company so they feel they are a part of the business for which they work. Some of the communication techniques used to keep employees informed are:

1. Written memos and letters

2. Company newsletters and magazines

3. Formal meetings

4. E-mail

People in Authority Sometimes Exhibit Ineffective Communication Skills

$Smart$ **T I P**
- - - - - - - - - -

Beware! Not everyone is a smart communicator.

When your supervisor gives instructions to do something, your job is to carry them out. You follow the directions, secure in the knowledge your supervisor has given you the information you need to do your job. For example, you are asked to develop a price list of all the products your company manufactures by product name and product number. When you deliver it to your supervisor, he declares, "But you only included the product name, number, and price. I don't know how many of each item we have in stock right now." You reply, "You asked only for a price list. I didn't know you wanted inventory information." By not telling you he wanted inventory information, your supervisor displayed ineffective communication skills.

How Communication Difficulties Arise

- *Going around* designated levels of communication.
- Communications get *snagged* at one level.
- Employees see only a small part of the company structure.
- People in authority sometimes exhibit ineffective communication skills.

For each of the following situations, describe the communication difficulty involved and give suggestions as to how to remedy the situation.

1. Last week Ursula had a meeting with her boss, Ms. Positano, who requested a report due today. Ursula delivered the report this morning. Ms. Positano appeared at Ursula's desk, a look of anger on her face, and declared: "Why is this work late? You know I wanted this report yesterday."

   Communication difficulty: _____

   _____

   Remedy: _____

   _____

2. Porter, a construction worker, received a memo from the Human Resources Manager of the company for which he works, noting his excessive absences from his building site and the possible consequences if this continues. A dedicated worker, Porter has never missed a day's work since he started with the company. Angry about the poor record keeping at his job site, he marched into the president's office demanding to know how a foul-up like this could happen.

   Communication difficulty: _____

   _____

   Remedy: _____

   _____

*I*nformal Company Communication

During your coffee break this morning, you went outside to buy a cup of coffee and a bagel. In the elevator, you overheard people from another department talking about Nancy Carstairs, your supervisor: "Did you hear? I mean it's all over the place! Carstairs just brought the firm a $2 million client. They say she'll be a vice president before the week is out." This is news to you. How come you heard news about your boss from others? What you have just heard is the latest rumor through the company grapevine.

The Grapevine

Word-of-mouth communication spreading information quickly throughout a company is known as the grapevine. The grapevine does not follow any formal line of communication.

*S*mart **T I P**

Do not feed the grapevine.

Figure 7-5 Gossips at work

Several characteristics of the grapevine are listed below.

- Information is passed among friends, coworkers, and associates.
- Information might be incomplete.
- Information could be based on rumor or gossip. **Rumor** refers to reports or statements that are not confirmed. The conversation you overheard in the elevator about Nancy Carstairs is an example of a rumor. **Gossip** is more personal, being information of a personal nature about one or more individuals. Gossip can also be critical of an individual.
- Information can be distorted because of misunderstandings and assumptions by the participants in the grapevine.
- Information can become distorted through repeated telling. When people pass information along, facts, such as dates and names, can become confused and change the meaning of the message.
- Information might be exaggerated. By the end of the day, instead of Nancy Carstairs bringing the firm a $2 million client, the rumor could say a $20 million client.
- Information can include emotionally loaded statements caused by each person's personal feelings toward the people or events involved. These statements usually involve references to personal characteristics and behavior.

Office Gossip

In a work setting, a person who spreads rumor is usually known as the office gossip. Most gossips are recognizable, and you have probably known some in your life. Some characteristics of gossips are:

1. Gossips want to be *in the know*, so they tell everything to everybody as a way to gain status or importance.

2. Gossips are generally not trusted by coworkers, who are afraid the gossip will talk about them behind their backs. A frequently heard comment is, "I'm afraid to leave the room. The gossip will talk about me when I'm gone."

3. Gossips' friendships often form on the basis of getting and giving information. As soon as gossips are out of juicy news to pass along, people do not want to know them.

4. Gossips are used frequently by management to spread informal corporate information and news. Because these workers want to be liked by everyone, they willingly help managers pass along information. The news they pass along is usually unpleasant. For example, when a company plans to lay off 1,000 workers because business is bad, they "leak" information using gossips to spread the news.

 Simple Rules To Follow At Work **Checklist 7-3**

- Do not spread gossip.
- Keep what you know or hear to yourself.
- Do not feed new information into the grapevine or to the office gossip.
- Stand up for your coworkers when others speak ill of them.
- Don't engage in negative discussions about your supervisor.
- Remember, slurs against people are unacceptable and illegal.

ACTIVITY 4

A. We hear rumors every day, in school, at work, at home, and from friends. You should understand how people react to the rumors they hear. Keep a log with two columns; in the first write a rumor you have heard. In the second column note what you think about the rumor.

B. Many of us enjoy listening to good gossip. Describe some gossip you heard recently and how you felt when you heard it. Now consider the object of the gossip, take that individual's point of view.

Activity 7-1

Using Important Words and Information

A. **Important Words.** Your instructor will assign various projects to help you achieve the goal of adding these words to your business vocabulary.

1. Authority	7. Grapevine	13. Office gossip
2. Chain of command	8. Horizontal communication	14. Organization chart
3. Communication	9. Line of authority	15. Responsibility
4. Company hierarchy	10. Line of responsibility	16. Rumor
5. Flow of information	11. Lines of communication	17. System of communication
6. Gossip	12. Line organization	18. Vertical communication

B. **Learning Log.** Summarize what you have learned from the material in this chapter and what it means to you. How could you apply this information and personal insight to yourself or your employment situation?

_____
_____
_____
_____
_____
_____
_____
_____
_____
_____
_____
_____
_____
_____
_____
_____
_____
_____
_____
_____
_____

Activity 7-2

Write complete answers to the questions in this section. Explain your answers completely using examples to illustrate your answer. Be prepared to discuss your responses with the class.

1. Why is communication important to the smooth operation of businesses?

   _____

   _____

2. Describe the differences in the chain of command between a small and a large business.

   _____

   _____

3. How do the lines of authority and responsibility differ from each other?

   _____

   _____

4. What three questions of accountability must be answered in a business?

   _____

   _____

   _____

5. When reading an organization chart, how do you know who the supervisors are for each level in the business?

   _____

   _____

6. Describe the flow in vertical communication.

   _____

   _____

   _____

7. List four ways you can encounter communication difficulties.

   _____

   _____

   _____

8. What happens in a job situation if you go around the designated lines of communication?

   _____

   _____

   _____

9. List the rules about gossips and gossiping you should follow on the job.

   _____

   _____

Activity 7-3

The employment activities in this section are based on the organization chart below. Your responses should reflect the information in this chart.

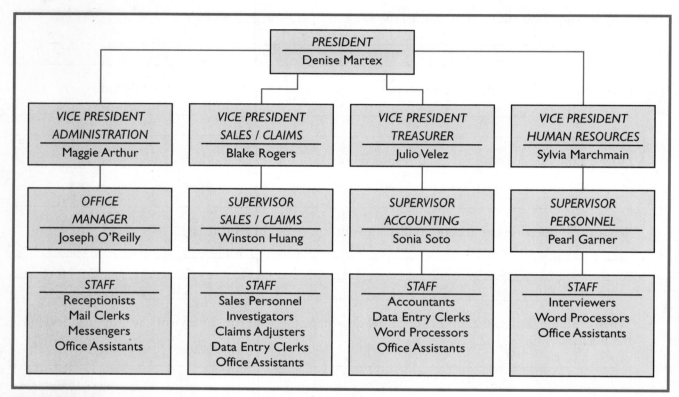

Figure 7-7 Organization Chart for the Martex Auto Insurance Co.

A. Fill in the blanks for questions 1-2. Give the name and title in questions 3-8. Draw the answers to questions 9 and 10 on the organization chart for Martex Auto Insurance Co. (Lines should be drawn where needed.)

1. The president's name is _____.

2. The treasurer's name is _____.

3. The VP of Administration reports to: _____   _____
   (Name)   (Title)

4. Winston Huang reports to: _____   _____
   (Name)   (Title)

5. The office manager reports to: _____   _____
   (Name)   (Title)

6. The claims adjusters report to: _____   _____
   (Name)   (Title)

Smart Communications on the Job • Unit 2

7. The mail clerks report to: _____ _____
                                           (Name)   (Title)

8. The personnel interviewers report to: _____ _____
                                                      (Name)   (Title)

9. Draw the horizontal line of communications among the VPs.

10. Draw the horizontal line of communications among the supervisors.

B. Jose, a data entry clerk, has a problem with an insurance claim form.

1. In the chain of command, whom should he ask for assistance?

_____

2. Discuss the appropriateness of him going to Joseph O'Reilly to find out how to handle this claim form.

_____

_____

internet

Activity 7-4

Business Communication Articles

On the Internet, locate and download articles on business communication appearing in the last year. Summarize each article, list the search words used to find it, and note its address.

Activity 7-5

The Team Approach

team

Ask each group member to interview two people regarding the communication processes at their workplaces. Concentrate on the lines of communication, authority, and responsibility. Develop a presentation on the findings to be given to the class.

Chapter 8

Applying Communication Skills

Skills

OBJECTIVES

After reading Chapter 8, you will be able to:

1. List and give examples of the methods of business communication.

2. Develop skills needed to be successful when using the telephone.

3. Understand the role the computer plays in business communication.

4. Verbalize the appropriate steps to take when receiving instructions.

"**G**ood afternoon, I'm Julia, customer service representative for Goodworks. How may I help you today?"

"Hi, Julia, I'm calling to find out whether my toaster has been fixed."

"Okay. If you will tell me your name and give me the red printed number on your repair stub, I'll look it up on our computer."

"I'm Marylou Kiley and the number is 5489-56.

"Please hold while I check the computer. Your toaster has been repaired and you may pick it up anytime Monday to Friday, 9:00 A.M. to 4:00 P.M. or until 12:00 noon on Saturday. Because the toaster was under warranty, you won't be charged for the repair."

"Thank you, Julia. I'll pick it up this week."

Julia is a customer service representative for Goodworks, Inc., manufacturer of small kitchen appliances and utensils. She talks with people all day as customers come to the service office in person. Julia's success is based on the fact that she is polite, courteous, and well spoken. She treats each individual as a worthwhile person and gives each her personal attention.

Julia knows customers will buy Goodworks' products because they like the design and quality of the products. Another important factor to customers is that they receive satisfaction from the company when a problem arises. A company representative who is polite, calm, understanding, and helpful is a very important public relations asset for the company. A satisfied public, willing to buy or use the company's services or products, is what keeps the company in business.

Communication in Business

Communication is the essence of business, for without it business could not exist. As we discussed in Chapter 5, companies use communication internally to let employees know what to do and what is expected of them. Supervisors communicate with those above them in management and with subordinates, those below them in the company's organization chart. Additional communication occurs among departments and individuals to coordinate the work being done.

To make its products or perform its services, a company must use suppliers, other firms that sell them the provisions they need. Therefore, one company might communicate with another about supplies, products, shipping, costs, services, or deadlines.

In today's *global marketplace*, companies exist and operate together—no company exists in a vacuum. Businesses need salespeople, special promotions, and advertising as this means to communicate to others what they have to offer and to attract customers. Customers are the ultimate *purchasers* of goods and services an organization wishes to sell. The term consumer is used to designate the person or business actually *using* the goods or services. The money received by a business for the sale of its products or services is called income. In many firms, each department might operate like a small firm whereby one department becomes the customer of the services offered by another.

*S*mart T I P

The customer is your business.

Communication Methods

Businesses, as well as individuals, communicate in many different ways:

*S*mart T I P

Use all methods to communicate with others.

- **Print** Written letters, memos, reports, and notes. Printed materials are called "hard copy."

- **Electronically** E-mail, Web sites, voice mail, television, video, movies.

- **Pictorially** Graphic images that are drawn, painted, or computer-generated. The pictorial method of communication also includes photographs, charts, and diagrams.

- **Verbally**
  - ◆ In-person conversation in meetings, informative discussions, chance encounters with people who walk in asking for assistance.
  - ◆ Telephone conversations between two or more people, voice mail.

Applying Verbal Communication Skills

Because verbal communication is such a vital part of business, workers like you need to understand and develop business communication skills. A valued employee will develop these skills to a fine art, especially when following and giving instructions, using the telephone, and dealing with customers. This chapter, therefore, will concentrate on these three aspects of communication.

Following and Giving Instructions

Figure 8-1 Your success at your work will depend in part on your ability to give instructions and on your ability to follow instructions.

Instructions are directions, information, or orders telling you what to do and how to do it. Without instructions, no one in the company would be able to produce a good product or service. Good instructions save time and materials because work does not have to be redone. Employees spend less time on a project and do not waste time trying to figure out what to do. Supervisors spend less time giving and repeating instructions, freeing them to help their subordinates when necessary.

Giving Instructions

Giving good instructions is not always easy. Supervisors frequently have more than one thing to think about or have not completely thought a project through. As a result, employees might not know exactly what the supervisors want done, how the job should be done, or the time needed to complete the job. When you have to give instructions, be sure to include the *who, what, where, when,* and any other specifics. If you receive poor instructions, be sure to ask questions so you know exactly what to do. For example, your supervisor could say, "Call the lawyer and say we have to meet to discuss tomorrow's court appearance." Your supervisor has omitted a crucial piece of information and you now have to ask, "Which lawyer do you want me to call?"

Following Instructions

By following instructions, you know what tasks to do in a specified order. Instructions help you avoid making mistakes and having misunderstandings and conflicts with other workers or supervisors. Your ability to follow instructions will probably be evaluated in your job performance review and will affect your continued success and employment with this company.

Smart **TIP**

Give directions as you would wish to receive them.

Smart **TIP**

Make sure you understand instructions.

✓ **Tips for Following Instructions** **Checklist 8-1**

1. Concentrate on what is being said or demonstrated.
2. Listen carefully.
3. Write down all important information, including facts, numbers, or even draw diagrams if you feel the need.
4. Refer to your notes when you are working on your own.
5. Think critically by considering what you are told, eliminating unnecessary information, and making sure you understand the whole process.
6. Organize how the job should be done, step-by-step in a logical order. Try to think of any needed steps that have not been mentioned.
7. Review all steps with the person giving you the instructions. Restate the instructions in your own words to make sure the person realizes that you understand him or her.
8. Request that the instructions be repeated if you are unsure about what you heard.
9. Ask questions if you are not clear about what is required.
10. Make sure you understand the order of importance when you are given several tasks at once.

ACTIVITY 1

Read the directions given by these supervisors. Put yourself in each employee's position and write in the space provided:

1. the steps you would take to make sure you understood the directions.

2. exactly what your supervisor is asking you to do.

A. Mr. Stroud: "Please complete the report I gave you to photocopy by 3:00 this afternoon. Staple the pages; I think we will need five copies. Use the ivory paper, I think that will be best. Maybe we will need seven copies. I'm not certain—better ask Mr. Green."

1. _____

_____

2. _____

_____

B. Ms. Anderson: "Go to the supply room and get a box of staples, five blue pens and one black one, six boxes of paperclips, two notepads, and a ream of computer paper. Oh, yes, remind me about the business meeting at 2:30 this afternoon."

1. _____

_____

2. _____

_____

Using the Telephone

Smart T I P
- - - - - - - - - - -

Speaking on the telephone is like a face-to-face conversation.

The telephone can be a friend or foe. Given the recent explosion of telephone technology, telephones are everywhere. Now you can see people talking on telephones while walking down the street, riding in cars or on public transportation, or just sitting at the beach. Businesses and their employees can be in instant contact with each other and their customers. The telephone today is an essential tool in the conducting of business.

In Chapter 5 we discussed the importance of body language in the communication process. On the telephone, you have conversations without seeing the other parties—you cannot see their body language and they cannot see yours. All you have to go by are your respective skills as speakers.

Skills You Need for the Telephone

1. **The voice must say it all.** Using your voice properly shows you are interested and knowledgeable. It should be well **modulated**—varied in tone, pitch, and volume; have **inflection** and emphasis. You need not yell, as a soft tone of voice will do. The preferred business style is to speak naturally, but slowly and distinctly.

2. **Smile.** Your facial expression comes through in your voice. If you are genuinely friendly, the person on the other end of the line will hear it.

3. **Gesture.** We are all in the habit of gesturing when talking. Continue to do so when speaking on the phone, even though no one can see you, because doing so makes you sound more natural to the listener. Gesturing helps put personality into your voice.

4. **Picture the person to whom you are talking.** Holding a conversation is easier if you can picture the person on the other end of the telephone. You are talking with an individual, not a black hole.

5. **Courtesy is essential.** Be friendly. Use the other party's name. If you experience a delay, tell the person. Do not interrupt; let the person finish talking before you speak. Respect the other person for what he or she has to say. If you have to say something negative, use tact and courtesy.

6. **Speak in complete sentences.** Your words must convey *exactly* what you want to say because your body language cannot be seen.

7. **Be polite.** This is your #1 priority. "Please," "Thank you," and "Just one moment" are a few important words and phrases you should use. Do not leave people hanging on the line or transfer calls without explanation. Apologize for company errors or delays, even if they were not your fault. You represent the company, and your behavior on the telephone reflects the company, as well as you personally.

8. **Speak clearly.** Avoid using company jargon or acronyms (a word formed by the first letters of a series of words) that outsiders might not understand. If you speak English with an accent, talk slowly to make sure you are understood. Do not eat or drink while on the phone; the sounds of your chewing can be heard over the line and will make your words sound garbled.

Making Telephone Calls

Making a telephone call for business is not like speaking to a friend. You are the representative of your firm when you speak with the other party. Planning the call is important; you must prepare for actually making the telephone call. The final step is making the call to your party.

 Preparing for a Business Call   Checklist 8-2

- Consider the business hours of the person or organization you are calling. Business hours vary from company to company and in different time zones. The person with whom you wish to speak could work an unusual schedule, or have unusual lunch and break times.

- For long-distance calls, calculate the time difference between your location and that of the person you wish to contact. Check on whether daylight savings time is observed in the state you are calling. Calls to European or Pacific Rim countries require special planning as they can be 12 or more hours ahead or behind you, putting them into a different day of the week. World time zone charts are available in the front of most telephone company directories and are easy to use.

- Decide on the important points you want to cover during the call and the outcome you expect. **Outcome** is what you would like to happen as a result of an action—the telephone call.

- Plan how you will say what you want. If necessary, choose words and phrases to say ahead of time.

- Before making the call, look up information you will need.

Jorge, an accountant in a large international firm, needs to clarify by telephone some figures he has received from the Singapore office. He has prepared for this call by determining the best time to call, he knows what he wants to find out, and has the information he needs in front of him. Jorge must now plan his call, for he knows that what he says and how he says it will reflect both him and his office.

 Making a Business Telephone Call   Checklist 8-3

1. Give your name and the name of your company to the person who answers the phone. For example, you might say, "Hello, I am Joyce Cohen calling from Fashion Designs." Or, "This is Bruce Amundsen, sales representative for Jordan Supply."

2. Know the name of the person to whom you want to speak, or the name of the department. Say, "I would like to talk with Mr. Thomas," "May I please speak to the supervisor of your complaint department?" or, "Who can help me with a billing error?"

3. Take responsibility for terminating the call. You might say, "Thank you for your help. I appreciate your kindness in speaking with me. Goodbye."

4. Cover all issues in one call so you do not have to call the person again that day.

5. When giving information, speak slowly and distinctly. Repeat numbers if necessary to make sure the listener has noted them correctly.

6. When leaving *voice mail* messages, speak slowly so the listener understands what you are saying. Give your name and that of your company, the date and time of your call, your telephone number—you can say it twice—and a message in as concise a manner as possible.

Smart **T I P**

A polite and pleasant telephone
manner projects a positive
company image.

Answering the Telephone

In addition to answering your own telephone, you might have to pick up the phone for others at your job. To do this, you need to know the company protocols for handling incoming calls.

Following Company Procedures Each company has its own policy as to how it wants the phone answered. In the following examples, Angelica is a receptionist at S&C Builders.

- How quickly is the phone answered? Angelica knows the phone should be answered within two rings if possible; otherwise the caller could feel ignored or think the company has a problem and is too short-staffed to handle its phones properly.

- How is the company name given? Angelica can say, "S&C," "S&C Builders," "Good morning, you have reached S&C Builders," "S&C Builders, quality construction for your building project," or, whatever the company directs her to say when she answers the telephone. Consistent handling of phone calls helps the company project a consistent, professional image.

- Is the person who answers the phone to give his or her name? First name or full name? For example, "S&C Builders, Angelica speaking," or, "S&C Builders, Angelica Johns speaking."

- Where are messages to be placed?

- Who handles specific types of calls? Who responds to customer questions about the product? Who takes the calls regarding billing, shipping, and sales? Who handles advertising matters?

Representing the Company When you answer the telephone on your job, you might be the first person in the company to whom your caller speaks. Remember, you represent the company and in so doing, you are helping to give callers an idea of what your company is like.

Transferring the Caller When you answer the telephone for a supervisor or coworker, you need to know how to place calls on hold and how to transfer calls. Several points should be remembered.

First, tell the caller if you have to put him or her on *hold*. Return to the call within a few minutes to keep in touch. You might say, "Thanks for holding, that line is still busy. I'll connect you as soon as possible." "Mr. Blackthorn is in conference and will return your call as soon as he is available." Or, "I'm sorry your call is being delayed, I will connect you to Mrs. Denby now."

If you must transfer the call, tell the caller you are doing so and give him or her the name of the person or department with whom he or she will be speaking. For example, "Your problem must be handled by Mr. Thatcher in Billing. I am transferring your call to him now on extension 35." Or, "I'm sorry, but I do not take customer orders. Let me transfer your call to our Order Department right away."

Computerized Telephone Answering Systems Firms are now using computerized systems to answer all incoming calls (those calls originating outside the firm). A voice gives the firm's greeting and then gives the caller a *menu* of options. The caller selects an option by pressing a button on his or her telephone keypad, and is transferred to the person or department requested.

Taking Messages

"If Mr. Dennis is not in, may I leave a message?" "Give Ms. Young a message when she returns to her office, please." You might be asked by the caller to take a message when the person wanted is unavailable. Take accurate, concise messages so the reader of the message knows exactly what the caller said and wants. Most firms have special forms for this purpose. (See Figure 8-2.)

(IMPORTANT MESSAGE)

FOR __Mrs. Loggins__   DATE __3/21__   TIME __1:30__   A.M. (P.M.)

M __r. Watson__

OF __Accounting Department__   ✓ PHONED

PHONE _____ __7210__ _____   RETURNED YOUR CALL
            AREA CODE   NUMBER   EXTENSION

MESSAGE __Wants to discuss budget for May.__   ✓ PLEASE CALL

_____   WILL CALL AGAIN

_____   CAME TO SEE YOU

__J.P.__   WANTS TO SEE YOU
SIGNED

Figure 8-2 Sample Message Form

 Taking Good Messages   **Checklist 8-4**

- Tell callers the person they are calling is "unavailable," "out of the office," "in a meeting," or "out of town." Do not give personal information, such as "Mr. Chu is at the dentist," or "Harriet doesn't want to be disturbed right now."

- Be businesslike in your manner.

- Get all the important information and record it on the message form. This includes:

  - ◆ Caller's name   ◆ Company the caller represents
  - ◆ Telephone number   ◆ Detailed message
  - ◆ City from which the call originates   ◆ Best time to call back
  - ◆ Caller's time zone

- Read the information back to the caller to verify its accuracy.

- Enter the date and time of the call.

- Place the message in the appropriate place to be picked up by the receiver.

Problem Calls and Callers

Answering the telephone can be a difficult chore when the caller is rude, angry, or otherwise impolite. Callers can threaten you or your job. Not infrequently, the person placing the phone call uses abusive language. You have to remain cool and tactful in this very stressful situation.

Let's examine the following situations:

	The Caller Says	You May Respond
1.	"You */*+#@! Can't you answer the phone faster? I'm in a hurry."	"I'm sorry you had to wait. How may I help you?"
2.	"How come you don't know where my package is? I'll have your job for this!"	"Sir, what is your name and order number? I will try to trace your package now."
3.	"You get me an appointment with Mr. Shiu and I'll take you out for dinner and dancing."	"That won't be necessary, but I will try to make an appointment for you."
4.	"+ !@#%&=*!@#+\! "	"I didn't quite catch what you said. How may I help you?"
5.	"You don't know anything. I'm going to report you to your supervisor."	"I'm sorry you're unhappy." (Report this conversation to your supervisor.)

ACTIVITY 2

Write your response to each of the following:

The Caller Says: **You May Respond:**

A. "Where is Mr. Browne? I've called three times. You're lying to me." _____

_____

B. "Make an exception for me." _____

_____

C. "I want an appointment for tomorrow. What do you mean I have to wait?" _____

_____

D. "I know the president of your company. I want that shipment now or I'll have you fired." _____

_____

E. "You sound real nice. Would you like to have dinner with me after work tonight?" _____

_____

The Computer in Business Communications

The computer is the standard business tool. Knowledge of how computers work, how they are used, and competency with various computer programs is called computer literacy. Because the field of computers is changing rapidly, you have the responsibility to keep learning about new developments, as well as changes to existing products. You become a more valuable employee when you are able to apply new computer skills to your job.

Computer hardware is the physical equipment that makes up a computer. Hardware includes the computer's internal circuitry and boards. The hardware cannot operate, however, without *software* or *programs,* which perform the work the users need to do.

One of the fastest-growing uses of computers is in the realm of communications, where the computer user is linked to other computers through cables, wires, and telephone lines. Networking is accomplished by connecting computers to each other through cables so they can share files, printers, and modems. This facilitates the communication process, with applications including:

- **E-mail** The user can send and receive messages with other computer users.

- **Computer conferencing** Two or more individuals can communicate directly by typing at their workstations. The text appears simultaneously on the other computer screen or screens, making forreal-time communication. This process enables individuals at different locations to work together, communicate, make decisions, and hold meetings. Computer conferencing participants can respond to what they read, add information, ask questions, and come to decisions just as if they were having a face-to-face conversation.

*S*mart **T I P**

The computer *is* a business tool.

Proper Etiquette in Electronic Communication

The increasing use of e-mail, newsgroups, chat rooms, and bulletin boards has led to the development of specific rules of behavior, manners, and etiquette when you communicate electronically. New technologies and ways of doing business mean new protocols, and users of the Information Highway are following new rules of etiquette.

*S*mart **T I P**

E-mail is a reflection of you.

- Type your text using regular upper- and lower-case letters. Using all capital letters is considered shouting and is not polite behavior.
- Be certain messages are short, clear, concise, and readily understandable.
- Use proper grammar and spelling, as bad grammar and spelling are considered bad manners.
- Read your message before you forward it.
- Answer your e-mail as soon as possible.
- An e-mail message should discuss only one topic, which is clearly stated in the "Subject" field of the message.
- Do not send confidential or sensitive information electronically, as e-mail is not private and can be read by others.
- Avoid "flaming." Sending terse, angry messages is considered flaming and is a breach of etiquette.
- Observe the chain of command within the organization and keep the concerned people apprised of new developments.

ACTIVITY 3

Write e-mail messages on a separate sheet of paper for the following situations:

1. Confirm the arrival of a shipment of books from the Jay Company.

2. Inform your supervisor of a change of time for a sales meeting from 10:00 A.M. to 1:00 P.M.

3. Your supervisor cannot attend the sales meeting at 1:00, so ask the Sales Manager for another time.

The Internet as a Business Tool

The Internet enables the user to gather information from various sources. These sources can include *newsgroups,* where you can ask for and receive information, and *chat rooms,* where you can communicate with others. Searches for information can be done using *search engines,* which are software programs that find requested Web sites and documents. You enter one or more descriptive words, called *keywords* or *descriptors,* and the search engine displays a list of all the sites and documents it can find that match your request. A word of caution here: Not all the information you receive will be useful to you or even accurate as, people with access to the Internet can post whatever information they wish.

Using Communication in Customer Relations

Roger owns and operates the Coffee Cup, a take-out shop in a busy office building. By 7:00 each morning, a long line of customers is waiting to buy breakfast. After 10 years in business at this location, Roger knows almost everyone by sight and remembers what he or she usually orders. Barbara walks in and Roger knows she wants a dark coffee and a lightly buttered bagel. As he writes the sales slip, Roger gives the order to Akiba and Carmen, the short-order cooks. Next in line is Lucy, who likes dry wheat toast, cottage cheese, and a diet soda. Barbara's order is ready and Roger bags it, hands her a slip for the cashier, and smiles as he remarks, "I hope your presentation is a success today, Barbara." This steady pace keeps up until 9:00, and is then repeated at lunchtime. Roger works hard to give his customers what they want, so they will remain loyal to his coffee shop.

Greta is a customer service representative for The Garden Supply Company, a catalog merchandiser specializing in garden supplies and outdoor accessories. She answers her next call, "How may I help you today?" A voice snaps back, "Is your shipping department illiterate? I ordered seven items, and I only received four of them in this package I've got here." What does Greta say next? She has to satisfy the irate customer on the other end of the telephone.

Both of these examples show the importance of customer relations, an important aspect of any business. The way customers are treated is crucial to having a successful business.

What Is Customer Relations?

The term customer relations refers to the way clients are spoken to, handled, and treated by the employees of a business. Businesses spend large sums of money to win customers and make sales, money that can be wasted if customers are not treated well. Customers especially do not like being ignored once they have made a purchase; they want to feel valued by the company. If problems arise, they expect the company to process their complaints quickly, cheerfully, and give them the satisfaction they want.

As mentioned earlier in this chapter, customers are the people who actually purchase goods and services, either for their own use or use by others. In professional firms in fields like law, accounting, and advertising, customers are called clients. The term is often used by social service agencies to refer to those who use their services as well. Medical customers are generally called patients. No matter what term is used in a particular business or industry, the user of the goods or services is a *customer* and should be treated as such.

Smart **T I P**

Keep in mind the value of the customer.

Most companies are divided into a number of different departments, each responsible for specific tasks. (See Chapter 7.) Therefore, each department is a *customer* of the other departments because it uses the services and goods generated by them. For example, Alexander Green works for an automobile manufacturer. He is in charge of the robotic equipment that puts doors on the cars coming through the assembly line. Alexander can do his job only if the proper doors are at his work station when the car being assembled arrives. If the department in charge of making doors slows down and fails to provide Alexander with the needed auto parts on time, the assembly line will have to stop. When production stops, companies cannot sell goods; and eventually employees are laid off.

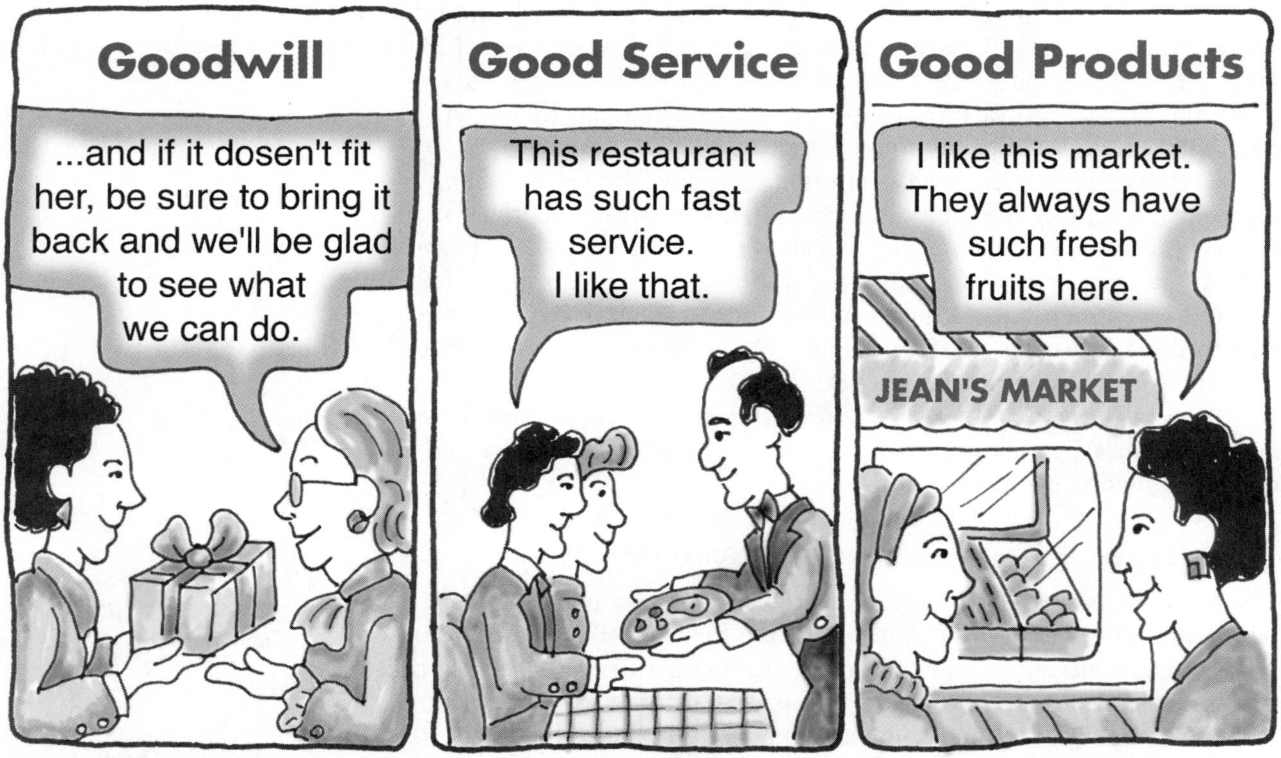

Figure 8-3 Customers come to a business expecting good products, good service, and goodwill.

How Customer Relations Work

Whenever you speak to a current or potential customer of your company, you are engaged in customer relations. If you make a good impression, customers are likely to remember you and your company when they have to purchase your product or service. Likewise, you could encourage someone who has never bought anything from your company to do so in the future. Your communication can be oral, written, or electronic, so everything you say or write is important. Most customer relations take place over the telephone, an example is when customers are told when they can expect delivery of an order. Sometimes, however, customer-relations activities involve face-to-face conversation. For example, this personal contact can occur when a customer returns an item to a store or a hospital patient goes to the billing office to discuss a bill.

The global marketplace is the result of easy, almost instantaneous communication, where buyers can find what they need anywhere. Shipping by air, land, or sea enables producers to get their products to market quickly. Therefore, to remain in business, many companies find developing customers in other countries necessary. Methods of doing business and customer needs might be different in these countries. If a customer is not satisfied with your product or service he or she can find another company that will meet those needs. Be very specific with respect to every detail of a transaction to prevent misunderstandings and difficulties. Remember, businesses in your country are responsible for learning how business is conducted abroad.

Figure 8-4 Customers are aware of more than just the purchase price. Good service is something customers look for.

✓ Tips for Good Customer Relations

Checklist 8-6

- Learn to recognize regular customers' voices over the phone and call the customers by name. Recognition means you value their business.

- Listen carefully.

- Use your telephone skills, even in person.

- Do not make customers repeat themselves. Take notes on the customer's problem or request. Include dates and times, order numbers, addresses, and other pertinent information as necessary. Repeat the information back to the customer to make sure it is accurate.

- Think critically. You should consider what the customer tells you, ignore unnecessary information, and pay attention to the heart of the problem or request.

- Do not interrupt. Customers often feel better when they are given free reign to talk. By interrupting, you can break their train of thought, miss crucial information, or increase the customer's anger and frustration.

- Ask questions to help clarify issues and information. Do not ask the same question repeatedly; customers will think you have not been listening to their responses.

- Solve problems and process requests according to company policy.

- Keep your word. If you say you will call back or take some other action, do it, and in a timely manner. Send the company brochure you talked about to that potential customer.

- Before terminating a telephone call or personal encounter, ask the person whether he or she wishes to discuss anything else or needs additional help.

- Follow up. Check with the client later to see whether everything was done satisfactorily; this shows you value his or her patronage.

HOW TO WIN AN ARGUMENT WITH A CUSTOMER:

YOU'RE RIGHT.

GOFF

If you can process the request immediately, do so because it's best to handle customer problems and requests promptly. You might say, "Mr. London, our people will be at your house at 4:00 this afternoon. Can I help you with anything else now?" Tell customers that, if you cannot handle the situation at hand, you will transfer them to someone who can.

Sometimes you need extra time to develop an appropriate solution. Say, "I have to look into that for you. I will call you back before the end of the day." Or, "The information you need is in our computer and it is off-line right now. May I call you back?" Then be sure to call back when you said you would. Should a delay or change occur, tell the other party.

Remember, without customers the business in which you are working could not exist and you might not have a job. Treat customers the same way you want to be treated when you are dealing with a company.

ACTIVITY 4

Warren is the customer representative for The Maple Tree, a boutique selling ready-to-wear clothing. He has just received a returned merchandise from a customer with a letter requesting a credit because the colors of the three sweaters were not satisfactory. The store policy states, "Half-price merchandise is not returnable." The sweaters were purchased at half price. Warren has to call the customer to discuss this matter.

1. What should Warren say to the customer?

_____

_____

_____

_____

_____

2. The customer says: "No one told me half-price purchases were non-refundable. Well, I guess you've lost a customer." What should Warren say now?

_____

_____

_____

_____

_____

Activity 8-1

Using Important Words and Information

A. **Important Words** Your instructor will assign various projects to help you add these words to your business vocabulary.

1. Client	6. Consumer	11. Instruction
2. Computer hardware	7. Customer	12. Modulated
3. Computer literacy	8. Income	13. Outcome
4. Computer networking	9. Incoming calls	14. Patient
5. Computer software	10. Inflection	15. Supplier

B. **Learning Log:** Summarize what you have learned from material in this chapter and what it means to you. How could you apply this information and personal insight to yourself or your employment situation?

_____

_____

_____

_____

_____

_____

_____

_____

_____

_____

_____

_____

_____

_____

_____

_____

_____

_____

_____

_____

_____

_____

_____

Activity 8-2

Apply what you have learned to answering the following questions. Explain your answers completely, using examples to illustrate your answers. Be prepared to discuss your responses with the class.

1. List several ways businesses communicate with customers.

_____

_____

2. Why should employees follow instructions properly?

_____

_____

3. You are showing a new employee how to use e-mail. What rules of etiquette would you give?

_____

_____

4. Why should you restate the instructions to the instruction giver?

_____

_____

5. List the eight skills needed for good telephone technique.

_____

_____

6. Respond to your caller, Mr. Emerson, who says, "That's not fair! Your company promised I would get that check in the mail today. Well, it isn't here. I counted on getting that check, I need it to meet my payroll. You're all the same, you never pay your bills."

_____

_____

7. What should you do if you have to transfer a telephone call?

_____

_____

8. Why is this statement true? "The customer is the most important person in your business."

_____

_____

9. List four ways you can make customers think they are valued by your business.

_____

_____

10. How is the global marketplace affecting American business practices?

_____

_____

Activity 8-3

Taking Messages

Using the following information, complete the message forms below. Use today's date and time, and sign your name as the message taker.

1. "I'm Claude Dufay from the Navajo Silversmith Workshop and I'd like to leave a message for Mona Rosenthal. Please tell her the silver jewelry order is completed and we are sending the package overnight express so she has it in time for the Indian Jewelry promotion this weekend. If she has any questions, I'll be available in my office in New Mexico at 505-432-8800 until 3:00 P.M. today."

(IMPORTANT MESSAGE)

FOR _____ DATE _____ TIME _____	A.M. P.M.
M _____	
OF _____	PHONED
PHONE _____	RETURNED YOUR CALL
AREA CODE NUMBER EXTENSION	PLEASE CALL
MESSAGE _____	
_____	WILL CALL AGAIN
_____	CAME TO SEE YOU
_____	WANTS TO SEE YOU
SIGNED	

2. "This is Mr. Gregory from Medical Billing at Lakewood Hospital. I need to talk with Omar Hakim in your office as soon as possible. The last check we received was returned by the bank with a notation that the account was closed. Are you still in business? What am I supposed to do with this now? I'm available until 4:00 P.M. today at 677-4686. After that, he can reach me at home, 789-1066."

(IMPORTANT MESSAGE)

FOR _____ DATE _____ TIME _____	A.M. P.M.
M _____	
OF _____	PHONED
PHONE _____	RETURNED YOUR CALL
AREA CODE NUMBER EXTENSION	PLEASE CALL
MESSAGE _____	
_____	WILL CALL AGAIN
_____	CAME TO SEE YOU
_____	WANTS TO SEE YOU
SIGNED	

Activity 8-4

Handling Customers

You are the expert and have been asked by several business managers to help solve some customer relations problems. What would you tell each of these employers about the situations below and how could the problems be corrected.

1. Megan is a sales representative at Linens for Rent. They supply sheets, pillowcases, towels, and bathmats to hotels and schools on a rental basis. Megan services accounts in her geographic area and usually handles problems and complaints from her accounts. Peter, the Accounts Receivable manager for Linens for Rent, notices the Graystone Hotel has an overdue bill. He telephones Graystone's Accounting Department and says, "Hello, I'm Peter from Linens for Rent. It seems your hotel has an overdue account balance. Therefore, we are suspending further deliveries to you." Peter then hangs up the phone.

_____

_____

_____

_____

_____

_____

2. Jonah has a cold and cough and calls Dr. Smith for an appointment. The receptionist tells him the first available appointment is for the following week at 11:30 in the morning. Jonah asks for an appointment at an earlier date and is told that none is available. He then asks the receptionist for a time later in the day so he does not have to take time off from work. The receptionist responds, "I guess then you don't want to see the doctor."

_____

_____

_____

_____

_____

3. LaTanya buys wool for a sweater she wishes to knit at a small store in her neighborhood that has been in business for three months. The sales clerk tells her she will need 15 balls of wool and cannot return whatever she does not need. LaTanya thinks she will only need 12 and does not want to buy more than that. The clerk grabs the three extra balls of wool and throws them on a shelf, telling LaTanya, "It's your decision, but we won't have these again if you need more."

_____

_____

_____

_____

_____

_____

Activity 8-5

Experience Pays

Using a situation from your own personal history and experience, write complete responses to the following:

1. Describe a situation where you were given instructions and did not follow them accurately.

   _____

   _____

   _____

2. Describe the reasons why you did not follow the instructions.

   _____

   _____

   _____

3. What were the consequences of your failure to follow directions?

   _____

   _____

   _____

Activity 8-6

Employment Situations

A. Both you and Patricia work at the reservations counter for an airline at a major airport. Following the airport rules and regulations, as well as the instructions given to you at the beginning of each shift by Mr. Johnson, your supervisor, is important. Today he told both of you, "Remind customers that special security procedures are in effect at the airport through the end of the month. No short-term parking will be available. Parking for passenger pick-ups at the arrivals terminal will be limited to three minutes." Annoyed at having to tell customers what she thinks is bad news, Patricia does not mention the security information to anyone.

1. Explain to Patricia the consequences of her inaction.

   _____

   _____

   _____

2. Help Patricia by telling her how to follow the instructions given.

   _____

   _____

   _____

Activity 8-6 *(continued)*

B. You are asked to schedule a conference call between New York, Paris, Singapore, and Dallas.

1. Using the telephone book in your area, find the time zones for each of the cities.

2. Using New York as your reference point, how many hours earlier is the time in each city?

	Time Zone #	Hours Earlier
New York	_____	_____
Paris	_____	_____
Singapore	_____	_____
Dallas	_____	_____

3. What time would be appropriate for you to schedule this call? Why?

4. How would you let all the parties know the time for the call? Explain the steps you would follow.

C. You are working in Chicago, IL and your boss is attending a conference in London, England. You have an important message and need to speak with him before the conference begins at 9:30 A.M. local time. What time should you place the telephone call to him. Why?

internet

Activity 8-7

E-mail Symbols and Abbreviations
Many symbols and abbreviations are used in e-mail, chat rooms, and on bulletin boards. Research and develop a glossary of such symbols and abbreviations along with their meanings.

Activity 8-8

The Team Approach

team

As a team, develop a multi-media presentation, report, or lesson using visual materials (charts, pictures, diagrams, or computer program), printed text, and verbal discussions on either of these themes:

1. The Customer is Vital for Business

2. The Global Marketplace and American Business

Developing Your Career Portfolio

You have now begun your portfolio. You have written a resume, collected letters of recommendation, and put them in an attractive binder you will be proud to show to prospective employers. Remember, the purpose of the portfolio is to present you in the best possible light. It is a representation of you—what you think of yourself, and how you showcase your abilities.

Now is the time to consider what else should go into your portfolio.

1. **Work Samples** The aim of including work samples is to show how you use or present information that you have learned in your field, and how well you organize these materials. Your career goals and ability to communicate should also be showcased.

   A. Go through all the work you have done for this course and related courses. Select reports, recommendations, projects, and tests of which you are proud and include them.

   B. Think of the type of impression you want to make and what you want your portfolio to say about yourself. Remember what you want to achieve with this portfolio.

   C. Look through the items you selected and choose those that best represent you and your objectives.

   D. Put them in your portfolio.

2. **Awards** Collect all awards and certificates you have received, and put them into your portfolio.

3. **Writing Sample** Write a 300-word essay in which you discuss the need for good communication skills in the workplace. This writing sample should show how proficient you are with the concepts of verbal communication, nonverbal communication, and listening skills. Your essay should be original, well organized, and clear in its point of view. Your style of writing – which includes sentence structure and vocabulary – is an important consideration when putting your thoughts down on paper. The essay should be keyed and saved on a disk, then printed for easy reading.

Ellen Post, Miguel Garcia, Timothy Landers, and Kiesha Brown have now had a chance to settle in at Melbrook Sporting Goods, Inc. They are learning about the company, the tasks required of them to be successful on the job, and the written and unwritten rules. They have also had a chance to meet their coworkers and develop a working relationship with their respective supervisors. Each has the need to communicate with others to do their job well. Let's see how they are doing.

Kiesha Brown

As a customer service representative, Kiesha has a position requiring direct contact with the public. A large part of her day is spent on the telephone talking with current and prospective customers. She must handle inquiries about the products the company manufactures, giving customers specific answers to questions. Frequently this type of call requires a great deal of time because the person is shopping for the best buy and has many questions and concerns to be clarified. Kiesha also handles complaints and problems customers might have.

Marilyn, the coworker who is training her, has given Kiesha a few scripts to study showing how to deal with each type of situation that arises. The company is very particular as to how telephone calls to the company are handled. These scripts are actually lists of responses and questions Kiesha should ask each person who calls. Directions are given about how to handle the problems. On the basis of the customer's responses, Kiesha could deal with the problem herself, give the call to Marilyn or Mrs. Sadar-Wright to handle, or transfer the call to another department for a solution. Sometimes Kiesha has to call a customer back with an answer to a question, give information about a product, or provide an update to a problem currently being addressed.

Kiesha loves speaking to customers on the telephone. She has always felt the telephone is her best friend. Just think, all these people to talk with! No one will complain that she is tying up the phone, as happens at home. Also, she does not have to pay the phone bills. What she doesn't like is talking with people who are hard to understand because they have accents or speak funny. Each morning she comes in, has a quick cup of coffee and a muffin with everyone else in the department, and settles into her chair in a relaxed position, ready to get to work.

Let's eavesdrop on a few calls Kiesha is handling this morning.

Call Number 1

Kiesha:	"Good morning, Melbrook Sporting Goods, Kiesha speaking. How can I help you?"
Caller:	"I have a problem with my bill. You people billed me twice for two items. Don't you ever know what you are doing? What kind of company is this?"
Kiesha:	(In a quiet tone of voice, smiling.) "I'm sorry about the problem with your bill. I'll transfer you to the Billing Department. I'm sure this will be corrected immediately."

Call Number 2

Kiesha:	"Good morning, Melbrook Sporting Goods, Kiesha speaking. How can I help you?"
Caller:	"I'm interested in finding out more about the frame in your backpack No. 238H. What can you tell me about it?"
Kiesha:	(To herself: "I never heard of that one before, who %^#@ knows or even cares? Marilyn is busy with May now; she'll just get angry if I interrupt to ask. Oh, well, I'll think of something. This caller sounds like a young kid anyway.) "What would you like to know? I'll see whether I can help you."

Caller:	"Is it welded?"
Kiesha:	(Guessing.) "Yes."
Caller:	"What is used to weld it?"
Kiesha:	"Good-quality materials are used on all our products."
Caller:	"How heavy is it?"
Kiesha:	"The welding is quite light."
Caller:	"That's not what I meant."

Five minutes later

Caller:	"Thanks, you are a nice lady, but I don't think you know much about backpacks."
Kiesha:	(Still smiling, voice pleasant.) "Thank you for calling Melbrook. I am sure you will enjoy Melbrook's products."

Call Number 3

Kiesha:	"Good morning, Melbrook Sporting Goods, Kiesha speaking. How may I help you?"
Caller:	"Young lady, I'm calling to see when my order will be shipped."
Kiesha:	(Recognizing the voice and picturing a man with white hair, smoking a pipe, and wearing slacks and shirt without a tie). "Why hello, Mr. Sims, how are you today."
Mr. Sims:	"Just fine, and you, Kiesha?"
Kiesha:	"Couldn't be better. Did you receive those replacement tent poles you had trouble with?"
Mr. Sims:	"Yes, the new ones are just fine. The weather is lovely, isn't it."
Kiesha:	"Yes, too bad we have to be indoors on a day like today. I hope the weather is like this on the weekend. Just our luck it will rain."
Mr. Sims:	"You got that right."
Kiesha:	"Let me connect you to the Shipping Department so you can ask about your order. Nice talking with you again, Mr. Sims."

Ellen Post

Ellen, an order processor in the Shipping Department, is not very happy. No one in the department wants to chat with her. Everyone is busy when she is around, but still find time to talk with each other. When she comes up to them, they turn away from her or find something else to do.

Ellen believes that if anything, she knows how to deal with people. She has decided everyone in the department will like her in spite of the fact that they ignore her. When she comes in each morning, she says hello to everyone in a friendly voice, but she is unaware of the frown on her face. Her shoulders are slumped forward and her head is down. As she walks, she shuffles her feet. As the day progresses and she goes about her duties, Ellen's mouth becomes pinched in a tight pout, her eyes narrow, and her brow creases. Her shoulders hunch up, her upper torso leans forward, and her arms hang away from her body. Ellen's coworkers tend to give her even more personal space when they do speak with her.

Karl, a fellow order processor, likes to discuss politics. He always has some opinion about what is written in the papers regarding a politician or the state of the nation. Let's follow a typical discussion that occurs during the coffee break each morning.

Karl:	"Did you read about the mayor's meeting yesterday? He is really going easy on all special-interest groups. He should show them who's boss."
Tim:	"Yeah, the streets are not safe any more, we need more police, and he talks about the city paying for a new statue in the park to make someone happy."
Karl:	"Right, and ..."

Ellen:	"You're a jerk—police aren't the answer anyway. People who live in that neighborhood aren't so hot. Which team do you think is going to win the ballgame tonight? I have money riding on it."
Karl:	"... and that statue could mean more taxes. Don't you think so?"
Sue:	"Our taxes are high enough as it is."
Ellen:	(Her mind on the clock.) "Yeah."
Karl:	"We need more creative government."
Tim:	"Yes, Karl, and we all know what you mean by that."

Recently, Ellen has been having a problem with Mr. Constantine, her supervisor. He is always trying to do at least five things at one time. As a result, his instructions are not always clear. He might tell you to fill one order and hand you a packing form for a different order. Ellen has, therefore, made a number of mistakes. She believes Mr. Constantine's job is to know what is being shipped, so who is she to question him? If the order is mixed up, it is not her problem. She was just following instructions–that's her job.

Miguel Garcia

Miguel, a computer operator in the Accounting Department, has maintained a pattern of behavior he established the first day he started working at Melbrook. He comes in each morning promptly at 9:00 and starts working. He nods a polite good morning to everyone, but does not have his morning coffee with his coworkers.

He does not participate in small talk, but sits quietly at his computer doing his assigned tasks. He does not look around, does not smile, his body squarely faces the machine. Should coworkers come to his workstation, Miguel does not like them to stand too close because he feels they are invading his private area. To show his dislike of being crowded, he will frown and pull back from the "intruder." He will answer any questions asked of him, respond to any statements made to him in a quiet, thoughtful manner. He listens thoughtfully and tries to understand what is being said. Miguel had a speech problem when he

was younger, and now he is aware of his diction and proud of how he pronounces and uses words. Should the need arise for Miguel to leave his computer, he walks with his head held high, eyes forward, and arms straight at his sides. When he holds papers or records, they are clasped close to his chest.

A large part of Miguel's job is handling the accounts receivable records and preparing bills. As a result, he will be called on to answer questions or handle problems regarding customer bills. He has found he receives more and more e-mail from customers and coworkers at Melbrook asking his opinion regarding handling billing problems. Miguel is surprised he does not mind this aspect of his job. Each call presents a problem, a puzzle to be solved, and he finds this a challenge.

Earlier, Kiesha answered a call from an irate customer who had a problem with a bill. She transferred that call to Miguel. Let's follow and see what Miguel did.

Miguel:	"Good morning, Accounting, Miguel speaking. How can I help you?"
Caller:	"Can't you people ever do anything right? I just get a run-around here. No one seems to be able answer a simple question."
Miguel:	"What is your problem?"
Caller:	"I was billed two times for two items. Who are you? What's your name?"
Miguel:	"My name is Miguel Garcia, I work in the Accounting Department. I'll try to help you. What is your order number?"
Caller:	"Which number is that in all this mess?"
Miguel:	"That is the number on the upper right-hand side, above your name."
Caller:	"Oh, 6794-9."
Miguel:	"One moment, I'm bringing it up on the computer. Okay, you are from Wood Lake Sporting Goods Outlet."
Caller:	"Yeah."

Miguel:	"And your name, sir?"
Caller:	"I'm Seth Worth, the owner of this outfit."
Miguel:	"Okay, Mr. Worth, let's see whether we can get to the bottom of this. You said you were billed two times for two items. Which particular items are you talking about?"
Worth:	"Those large tents and camping stoves. You blind? Can't you see that, dummy?"
Miguel:	(Working hard not to respond to Mr. Worth with anger.) "Okay, the problem is the large tents and camping stoves were billed to you twice."
Worth:	"Yeah, you finally got it."
Miguel:	"Mr. Worth, please hold while I trace your order and see what happened. It will take a few minutes."
Worth:	"I'm calling long-distance. This is costing me money."
Miguel:	"I'm sorry. I can call you back with an answer, Mr. Worth."
Worth:	"Nah, I'll hold."

Three minutes later.

Miguel:	"I'm sorry that took so long, Mr. Worth. I found the problem and you are correct. I will send you an amended bill today."
Worth:	"Fine. Nice doing business with you."

Timothy Landers

Timothy Landers works in the metalworking section of the plant. He has found he enjoys doing the creative jobs that come into the department. He likes the challenge of doing fine, difficult work to the customer's specifications. To do this type of work accurately and to the customer's satisfaction, he must follow directions exactly. This means he and Mr. Jones, his supervisor, have to discuss precisely what must be done. He listens and watches intently as Mr. Jones describes and demonstrates the required tasks. He breaks the job down into small steps and puts them in order. Then he restates the instructions and demonstrates to Mr. Jones how to do the task. Timothy is not afraid or embarrassed to ask questions and say he is confused.

Twice Timothy has found he must call a customer to check on the specifications of an order. This is something he hates to do. Mr. Jones tells him to relax, think of what he wants to say, introduce himself, and explain his problem. The customer will do the rest.

Timothy and his coworkers have a good relationship. They all like to tease each other and have many interests in common such as sports, music, and television shows. When they arrive in the morning, the men give each other bear hugs. They slap each other on the back when they tease or give compliments. This type of physical behavior makes Timothy uneasy, but he understands that this is the way things are done here.

Timothy usually has a smile that sparkles from his eyes, his shoulders are back, and his head held high. He likes to talk with his coworkers and participate in their discussions during their breaks and lunch. He finds these people have interesting opinions, are quite knowledgeable, and are willing to hear what he has to say. When anyone criticizes his work or says something Timothy believes is disrespectful, his demeanor changes. At such times his eyes narrow, his jaw juts out, his head comes forward, his torso bends forward, his stance widens so his feet are far apart, and his hands form fists. Nearby coworkers give him extra space and are careful what they say.

End of Unit 2

FOOD FOR THOUGHT

A. **Progress Report:** In many of the situations we find ourselves in daily, communicating with other people is necessary. This is especially true at work where you have to communicate with follow employees, supervisors, and customers. Let's see how Kiesha, Timothy, Ellen, and Miguel are doing.

1. Many of the messages we send are nonverbal. These messages are understood by those who see us. They can speak louder than words. What nonverbal messages are being sent by the four employees? What clues do you have to understand this message?

	Message(s)	Clues
Ellen:	_____	_____
	_____	_____
	_____	_____
Timothy:	_____	_____
	_____	_____
	_____	_____
Miguel:	_____	_____
	_____	_____
	_____	_____
Kiesha:	_____	_____
	_____	_____
	_____	_____

2. Using the telephone properly on the job is important for success. Answer the following questions about how our friends are doing.

a. The telephone plays an important role in Kiesha's job. List and evaluate her skills. What skills do you think she should improve?

_____

_____

_____

_____

b. What good advice did Mr. Jones give Timothy? What else would you tell him to do when he has to call customers?

_____

_____

_____

_____

c. Miguel has a chance to speak with customers on the phone when they have billing problems. What did he do to satisfy an angry customer?

_____

_____

_____

_____

d. Why do Kiesha and Miguel answer the telephone the way they do?

_____

_____

_____

_____

3. You should follow directions carefully. Respond to these statements by circling *Yes, No,* or *Not Sure* to indicate how well our friends followed instructions. State the reasons for your answers.

a. Miguel has problems following instructions.

Yes   Reasons _____
No   _____
Not sure   _____

b. Ellen knows how to follow instructions.

Yes   Reasons _____
No   _____
Not sure   _____

c. Timothy knows the value of following instructions.

Yes   Reasons _____
No   _____
Not sure   _____

d. Kiesha knows the value of following instructions.

Yes   Reasons _____
No   _____
Not sure   _____

4. Listening is a very important part of the communication process. Yet, not everyone knows how to listen. At Melbrook Sporting Goods, Inc. employees have to listen to each other, to their supervisors, and to customers in person and on the telephone. On a scale of 1 through 10, with 10 the highest score, how would you rate our friends' ability to listen? Discuss why you rated each person the way you did. Give examples to support your answers. Be prepared to share your answers with your classmates.

Employee

Kiesha   0   1   2   3   4   5   6   7   8   9   10
Reason: _____
_____
_____

Miguel   0   1   2   3   4   5   6   7   8   9   10
Reason: _____
_____
_____

Ellen   0   1   2   3   4   5   6   7   8   9   10
Reason: _____
_____
_____

Timothy   0   1   2   3   4   5   6   7   8   9   10
Reason: _____
_____
_____

Communicating in a Business Environment: Communicating effectively in business helps in producing quality products and services, meeting deadlines, making effective decisions, and interacting with others. The organization chart shows the structure of a company and how the departments relate to each other, as well as lines of authority and responsibility. Refer to the Melbrook Sporting Goods, Inc. organization chart, page 168, to answer the following questions:

1. The president's name is _____

2. John Holbrook wants to hold a meeting of all Production Department managers. Who would he ask to attend?

    _____

    _____

3. Which department managers would come to a meeting called by Tom Holbrook, Jr.?

    _____

4. Customer Relations is part of which department?

    _____

5. To whom does Jack Jones report?   _____   _____
                                              (Name)   (Title)

6. Mr. Constantine reports to whom?   _____   _____
                                              (Name)   (Title)

STUDENT: Answer questions 7-10 with a *yes* or *no* and state the reasons for your answer.

7. Does Miguel report to Andrea Bloom?

    _____

    _____

8. Does Ellen go to John Holbrook with her problems?

    _____

    _____

9. Can Kiesha go directly to Maud Mann with ideas?

    _____

    _____

10. Does Timothy have any reason to talk about business to Alice Green?

    _____

    _____

11. Draw the horizontal lines of communication among the heads of departments.

    _____

    _____

12. Draw the horizontal lines of communication among department supervisors within a department.

    _____

    _____

13. Tom Holbrook, Sr. has an idea about improving customer relations. What is the line of communication between Mr. Holbrook and Kiesha?

    _____

    _____

14. Maude Mann has a design idea and wants a prototype developed to field test. She will need Timothy's skill as a welder to help make it. What is the line of communication between Ms. Mann and Timothy?

    _____

    _____

15. Is the "grapevine" a part of this organizational chart? Answer yes or no. Explain your answer.

    _____

    _____

16. Does this chart show how rumors circulate? Answer yes or no. Explain your answer.

    _____

    _____

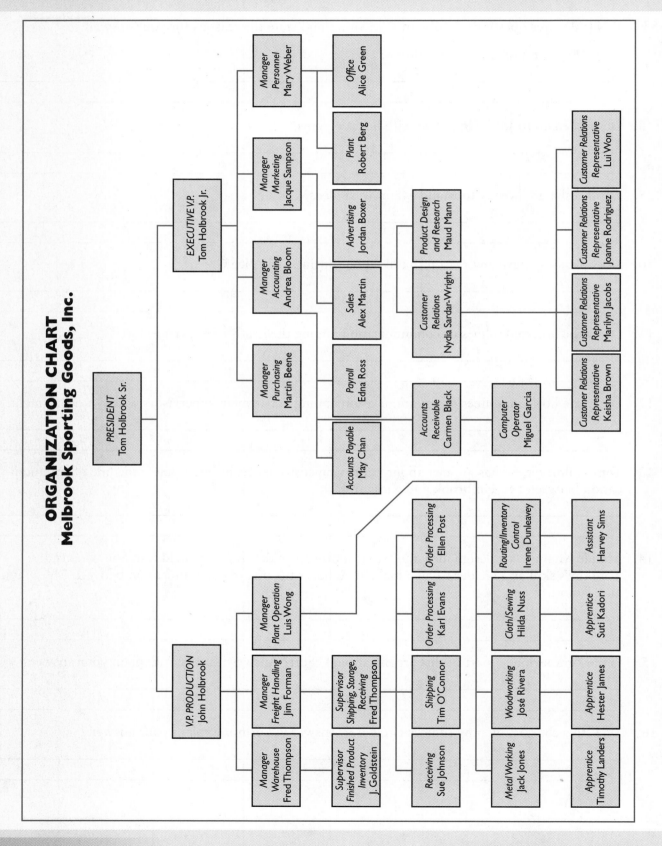

ORGANIZATION CHART
Melbrook Sporting Goods, Inc.

PRESIDENT
Tom Holbrook Sr.

EXECUTIVE V.P.
Tom Holbrook Jr.

V.P. PRODUCTION
John Holbrook

Manager Personnel
Mary Weber

Manager Marketing
Jacque Sampson

Manager Accounting
Andrea Bloom

Manager Purchasing
Martin Beene

Office
Alice Green

Plant
Robert Berg

Advertising
Jordan Boxer

Sales
Alex Martin

Payroll
Edna Ross

Accounts Payable
May Chan

Product Design and Research
Maud Mann

Customer Relations
Nydia Sardar-Wright

Accounts Receivable
Carmen Black

Computer Operator
Miguel Garcia

Customer Relations Representative
Lui Won

Customer Relations Representative
Joanne Rodriguez

Customer Relations Representative
Marilyn Jacobs

Customer Relations Representative
Keisha Brown

Manager Plant Operation
Luis Wong

Manager Freight Handling
Jim Forman

Manager Warehouse
Fred Thompson

Supervisor Shipping, Storage, Receiving
Fred Thompson

Supervisor Finished Product Inventory
J. Goldstein

Order Processing
Ellen Post

Order Processing
Karl Evans

Shipping
Tim O'Connor

Receiving
Sue Johnson

Routing/Inventory Control
Irene Dunleavey

Cloth/Sewing
Hilda Nuss

Woodworking
José Rivera

Metal Working
Jack Jones

Assistant
Harvey Sims

Apprentice
Suti Kadori

Apprentice
Hester James

Apprentice
Timothy Landers

Unit 3

Smart Relationships on the Job

Chapter 9

Attitudes and Relationships

Today is Marta's first day on the job as a quality control specialist for a food processing company. Her supervisor introduces her to Al, a co-worker, and asks him to show Marta around the work area. Marilyn notices that Al is greeted warmly by everyone. He is pleasant, seems to know his job well, and is willing to help others when asked. She is impressed because Al enjoys showing her around and he is comfortable handling the responsibility. Marta believes she will like working here; everyone seems so pleasant. She thinks she has already found a friend in Al. What Marta is witnessing is Al's good relationship with the company staff.

*T*he Importance of Good Interpersonal Relations

In earlier chapters we discussed what your first day on the job might be like, what your employer will expect from you, and what you can expect from your employer. Now we are going to look at interpersonal relationships. *Keep in mind you will spend more of your waking hours on the job than anywhere else.* You will interact more with people at work than with most other people in your life. Therefore, good interpersonal relationships are very important for your success on the job.

Interpersonal relationships involve interactions between and among people. Some interpersonal relationships are closer and more involved than others. Within your own family, you might have closer interpersonal relationships with some members than with others. The same is true of the relationships you have with people in your neighborhood, school, and workplace. When going shopping, you have a short, but interpersonal, relationship with the salesperson or cashier who helps you. On your job, you will have interpersonal relationships with many different people.

Having ongoing relationships with your supervisor and coworkers is important. In addition, be aware of how you relate to people with whom you interact briefly or infrequently. This can include executives, support personnel such as mailroom and duplicating employees, maintenance people, security officers, elevator operators, and business customers. You probably will not have involved relationships with these people, as your encounters with them usually will be brief. What might seem like a minor or passing encounter could, in fact, have important consequences for your personal or company success.

Attitudes Affect Your Relationships

One of the most important ingredients for good relationships is your ability to get along with other people. People relate to one another and are influenced by each other's attitudes and behaviors. Think about someone you like and admire. What do you admire about this person? Think of someone whose company you enjoy. Why? Consider how you react to other people—if they are polite and kind, you probably treat them with respect and kindness. On the other hand, if they are rude to you, you are likely to be rude to them.

Attitudes: What are they? An attitude is a state of mind, a feeling about a person, place, or thing. Your attitudes reflect the way you respond to and look at the world. An attitude can be expressed by your physical habits, such as the way you carry yourself, how your body is aligned, and how you talk. Attitudes also can reflect your emotions and values, such as the way you respond to different types of people, how you react to authority, and the manner in which you express your thoughts to others.

Positive Versus Negative Attitudes Is the glass half empty or half full? Is the weather partially sunny or partially cloudy? The answer depends on your attitude. A person with a positive attitude will tend to be optimistic and cheerful. He or she will see life as enjoyable, exciting, and good. On the job, supervisors tend to notice these types of people and value them. Having a positive attitude means seeing the glass as half full. Optimistic people feel good about themselves and their jobs and, therefore, they tend to be more productive and alert. Those individuals with a negative attitude are frequently angry, usually complain about everything, and never see the value or good in their work or life. Unhappy most of the time, they do not seem to like other people very much; their glass appears to them to be half empty.

Smart **T I P**

Your attitudes speak louder than words.

Smart **T I P**

Your attitudes say much about you.

Smart **T I P**

Positive attitudes draw people to you.

Characteristics of Positive Attitudes

People who have positive attitudes usually exhibit certain characteristics in their work and interpersonal relationships. These are characteristics you will want to cultivate.

Be willing to accept change. Positive people are generally willing to accept change. Learning new tasks, training on new equipment, or using new methods does not frighten them; they adapt to change easily. Often, people with positive attitudes are excited about change and accept it readily. In their excitement, they will help others and can be effective in creating positive changes in the workplace.

Be able to see other points of view. This means being able to accept new ideas and people's different cultural backgrounds, as well as being open to discussing someone else's opinions. This willingness to be open is a sign of flexibility. If you can accept differing points of view, you will be considered mature and accepting of others. Your ability to accept people from a wide variety of cultural backgrounds indicates tolerance, acceptance, and maturity.

Have a pleasant expression. A pleasant, friendly facial expression reflects a positive attitude, and shows you are calm, in control, and open to other people. When you appear pleasant and friendly, people you encounter will be relaxed and at ease. They will be comfortable with you and find you easy to talk with.

*S*mart **T I P**
- - - - - - - - - - - - - - - - - -
Accept responsibility for all you do.

Accept responsibility. A positive person is willing to accept responsibility. This includes being able to admit mistakes without blaming others or making excuses. Positive people are willing to correct their errors and learn from them to avoid repeating them in the future.

Accept Imperfections in Others. Understanding that others are not perfect, make mistakes, have personality quirks, and experience difficulties is a sign of a positive attitude. You should not become angry or impatient when others show they are not perfect. Remember, you are not perfect either.

Accept Constructive Criticism. When corrected, the person with a positive attitude will accept the correction graciously, often with a sense of humor. The ability to differentiate between constructive criticism and a personal attack is a sign of maturity. Even when being unfairly criticized, do not react in anger or create a confrontation. A straightforward, calm explanation of your side of the situation is a positive way of handling such a problem.

Be Willing to Follow Company Rules. Positive people realize regulations exist to guide the conduct of the people who make up the company. When rules are changed, these employees are able to readily accept the changes because they are flexible and not bound by rigid ways of thinking.

Show Respect for Others. Your positive attitude means being respectful of others and their beliefs or ways of doing things. Remind yourself that you need to show respect to everyone—including people of the opposite sex, from different cultures, followers of different religions, and from different regions of your own country. Most of the time, coworkers will characterize such a person as fair and open-minded, willing to listen to others, non-judgmental, and respectful of others without being critical. Accepting the attitudes of others is important, especially in today's multicultural, global business environment.

Smart **T I P**

To gain respect, you must give respect.

 Coworkers Like Someone Who: Checklist 9-1

- Smiles, is pleasant to be with, does not complain all the time, and shows a genuine interest in others.

- Makes them feel important by respecting their ideas and giving praise when it is due.

- Acknowledges other points of view and is willing to change ideas and behaviors when necessary.

- Is sympathetic, listens, and does not gossip.

- Gives credit to those who contribute worthy ideas and suggestions.

- Does not boast or act superior.

- Accepts responsibility for mistakes and tries to correct them.

- Avoids criticizing colleagues and gives them the opportunity to admit and correct errors without fanfare and publicity.

- Makes an extra effort on days when he or she does not feel up to par.

- Carries his or her own weight and does not impose on colleagues to get a job done.

For each of these examples, explain the positive work attitudes described:

1. Dirk has great patience while teaching Marion and Hugo how to operate a new piece of equipment the company just purchased. Additionally, Dirk is developing a safety manual for department personnel to follow when using this machine. _____

_____

2. April has a calm personality. When her supervisor corrects mistakes she has made, April accepts the criticism gracefully. _____

_____

3. Josh always seems to be very busy. His supervisor appears to give him more work than anyone else in the department, yet Josh has maintained his sense of humor and does not complain or whine about his workload. _____

_____

Smart **T I P**

People avoid others with negative attitudes.

Smart **T I P**

Do not take another individual's negative attitude personally.

Negative Attitudes

Negative attitudes can be contagious. One person with a negative attitude tends to produce a corresponding negative attitude in others. A person with a negative attitude is one who does not have good feelings about people, things, or situations. This person's world is not a happy one. This type of individual finds fault with everything and everyone, is not flexible or open to change, is inconsiderate of others, and intolerant of differences. Do not complain; complainers make other people uncomfortable. In fact, their grumbling makes difficult situations more strained as others try to deal with the very same problems. Being able to do your work without complaining shows a mature attitude and outlook toward the workplace.

People with negative attitudes generally have problems dealing with others. Coworkers are usually unwilling and unhappy about working with a negative person. For example, how would you like to work with someone who always criticizes what you are doing, the instructions your supervisor gave, the workload, and the state of the world? What would you think about someone who complains, gripes, and finds fault with everything? You might have to adapt to such people at times in order to complete your work. If you find you have no choice but to work with someone who has a negative attitude, just remember not to take his or her negativity personally. Avoid joining conversations in which others are complaining about their jobs or other coworkers. By setting a good example, you can help your coworkers change their own negative behaviors.

The following case studies describe on-the-job situations dealing with coworkers. Your answers should be based on the preceding material.

A. Hector, a carpet layer, was upset when he was told he had to work with Jim on a job in a private home. Jim has a reputation for complaining about everything. He criticizes the customer's furnishings, the choice of carpet, the company that made the carpet, his employer, and the way his coworkers worked. When Hector and Jim returned to the office, Hector told the supervisor he did not want to work with Jim anymore.

1. Describe Jim's attitude. _____
_____

2. Describe Hector's attitude. _____
_____

3. What would you have advised Hector to do?
_____
_____

B. Larry was asked to attend a training program to learn how to operate a new computer system. When his supervisor approached him about the training program, Larry excitedly replied, "What a great idea! We need that kind of computer system in this department. Thanks for letting me get additional training." He thought, "I hope I get a chance to take on new job responsibilities." Nora also was asked to attend the training program. She told her supervisor, "I can't leave work to attend a training program. Work will pile up, and I will end up having to work overtime to catch up. Besides, I am satisfied with the way I've always done my work. This is just another scheme someone in the executive offices dreamed up so they'll look good. Count me out."

1. Describe Larry's attitude. _____
_____

2. Describe Nora's attitude. _____
_____

3. Given the choice, who would you like to work with on your first week at this company? Give reasons for your response.
_____
_____

4. Who has the better prospect for success on the job, Larry or Nora? Explain your response.
_____
_____

The Importance of Tact in Relationships

Smart **T I P**

Tactful people consider the feelings of others.

How often do you find yourself avoiding some people because they always seem to say the wrong thing? They express themselves in such a way that it hurts or offends you. These people lack tact. **Tact** is skill and grace in dealing with others. It means *how you say something* is as important as *what you say.* Tact enables you to maintain good interpersonal relations by not offending others.

Courtesy and Respect

When you are working, you might be in contact with many of the same people for hours on end. With other coworkers, you might work periodically or meet infrequently. In each instance, your tact, along with your **courtesy** (behaving politely), show respect for others. **Respect** means you treat others with a high degree of consideration and esteem. Simple words such as "please," "thank you," and "you're welcome" are courteous and respectful. Remember, you should treat other people the same way you would like to be treated.

Smart **T I P**

"Please" is a magic word.

Using tact in your dealings with others fosters goodwill; they will like to be with you, help you, and interact with you. Being tactful is not difficult. Think first before you speak. Try to say what you mean without offending the listener. Consider how other people will react when they hear your words; do not be demeaning or disrespectful to others.

Using tact is especially important when you have something negative to say. For example, Sue made an error in adding a column of figures. When Jake found it, he turned to her and said, "Boy, you're dumb. Anyone could've added that column of figures, even a five-year-old." Put yourself in Sue's shoes. How do you think she felt? Jake was not considerate or respectful of Sue's feelings. In a word, Jake was tactless.

The *I Statement*

Positive or negative attitudes are evident in your manner of speaking. Why do some people seem to have "natural tact," while others suffer from "foot-in-mouth disease?" You can learn to express yourself more effectively by watching how you use language.

When using an *I statement*, you tell someone what you feel or need. This is different from a *You statement*, where you tell a person what he or she should think, feel, or do. Don't blame the other person because he or she will not listen to you. Blame is a way of attacking or condemning another person, and that person will probably react emotionally and, turn you off or tune you out. Rather, you want the other person to listen to you, note what you have to say, and do something you want. Tact is needed. Use an **I statement** to tell others how you *feel* and *what you want*.

The Two-Part *I Statement* This consists of 1 how you feel and 2 what you would like to happen, all stated in a positive, tactful manner.

When you have to correct someone, try to describe the person's behavior; do not personalize your words or assess blame. Express your feelings and concerns in a brief and simple statement. Saying "I'm sorry, but I had to make some corrections. The report will need some rewriting." is better than "You didn't write this report very well. You made many errors."

Smart **TIP**

Be assertive—not aggressive.

Smart **TIP**

Blame is a communication barrier.

Feeling	What You Want

Figure 9-1 The Two-Part *I Statement*.

Look at the following example:

The *I statement*:
"Mr. Brownley, I'm confused about how you want me to mail these letters; please repeat your instructions."

The *You statement*:
"Mr. Brownley, you didn't give me good instructions; what should I do?"

ACTIVITY 3

If you were Mr. Brownley, which statement would you prefer to hear directed toward you? Why?

_____

_____

The Three-Part *I Statement* This consists of 1 your feeling or concern, 2 what is causing it, and 3 what you want to happen, as shown in Illustration 9-2. An example is, 1 "I am upset, John," 2 "that you forgot our appointment," and 3 "Let's set up another one now."

Figure 9-2 The Three-Part *I Statement*.

In an *I statement* consisting of either two or three parts, the section describing what you want to happen can be preceded by the connecting words: *but, so,* or *therefore.* Look at Figure 9-3. Thus, in the previous example, you might say, "I am upset, John, that you forgot our appointment, *but* let's set up another one now."

Figure 9-3 Connecting words used in the *I Statement*.

ACTIVITY 4

In the following *I statements*, indicate the part that describes your feeling by underscoring it with one line; what you want to occur, with two lines; and the cause of your feeling, if stated, by circling it.

1. "Buddy, that's great, you have just given us three excellent ideas; but let's hear what Mario has to say."

2. "I am pleased, Alexia, you stayed late to finish your work, but could you complete your work assignments on time from now on?"

3. "Evelyn, I am very happy you came to the meeting today, so could you listen to what the others have to say?"

4. "I cannot see the chart, so please move your chair a little to the left."

5. "Johnson, you have a 100 percent 'on-time' record for the past six months; therefore, you will be responsible for drawing the red line, to indicate latecomers, in the Attendance Book each day."

Try practicing the *I statement* when you find yourself in a variety of situations. You can use it in social and family gatherings, or other interactions. The *I statement* can help diffuse situations that can lead to conflict. Here is an example: Ted is angry at Bruce for not returning his basketball. Ted remarks to Bruce: "I'm angry you haven't returned my basketball, so please return it in time for tonight's game."

*S*mart **T I P**

Use *I statements* every day.

ACTIVITY 5

Write *I statements* for each of the following situations using the examples in the previous section as guidelines.

1. Your car is not ready at the repair shop at the specified time.
   I Statement: _____
   _____
   _____

2. You ordered a rare steak and, when served, it was well done and you think the waitress did not listen to your order.
   I Statement: _____
   _____
   _____

3. Your brother has his radio on full blast when you are studying for an important exam.
   I Statement: _____
   _____
   _____

4. One of your best friends has a broken ankle, cannot drive, and needs to get to a medical appointment at the hospital all the way across town. You have to tell your boss you intend to drive him there.
   I Statement: _____
   _____
   _____

Activity 9-1

Using Important Words and Information

A. **Important Words** Your instructor will assign various projects to help you achieve the goal of adding these words to your business vocabulary.

1. Attitude	5. **"I" statement**	8. Respect
2. Blame	6. Negative attitude	9. Tact
3. Courtesy	7. Positive attitude	10. **"You" statement**
4. Interpersonal relationship		

B. **Learning Log** Summarize what you have learned from the material in this chapter and what it means to you. How could you apply this information and personal insight to yourself or your employment situation?

_____

_____

_____

_____

_____

_____

_____

_____

_____

_____

_____

_____

_____

_____

_____

_____

_____

_____

_____

_____

_____

Activity 9-2

Write complete answers to the questions in this section. Explain your answers completely, using examples to illustrate them. Be prepared to discuss your responses with the class.

1. Think of someone you like very much and with whom you like spending time. Describe the things you like about this person and the reasons you like to be with him or her. Describe this person's attitude.

_____

_____

_____

2. Why are attitudes important in interpersonal relationships?

_____

_____

_____

3. How does a person express positive attitudes?

_____

_____

_____

4. What positive attitudes do you find appealing? Why?

_____

_____

_____

5. What negative attitudes bother you the most? Why?

_____

_____

_____

6. Describe a situation where a person's attitude made you angry.

_____

_____

_____

7. Describe a situation where a person's attitude made a difficult situation easier for you.

_____

_____

_____

8. Why is being tactful important when dealing with others?

_____

_____

_____

Activity 9-3

Write complete answers to these case studies. Be ready to explain and discuss responses with your classmates.

CASE 1 Maria is the youngest of four children and the only girl. She thinks life is unfair because she cannot do the same things as her three older brothers. When she goes out socially, Maria is pleasant in her manner and she smiles frequently. She is very interested in the people around her, especially those from different cultures. She likes to discuss the foods they eat, the music they like, and is eager to learn about their customs and traditions. At work, however, Maria finds new ways of doing things difficult and does not really want to learn new tasks. When Maria does make an error, she will probably blame someone else for it and then pout or sulk when asked to make corrections.

1. Would you want to work with Maria? Why/Why not?

   _____

   _____

2. Would you want to know Maria socially? Why/Why not?

   _____

   _____

3. You are Maria's coworker, and you have a positive attitude. How would you handle working with Maria?

   _____

   _____

CASE 2 A member of a nearby tribe of Native American Indians, Dancing Wolf is always willing to help coworkers. He enjoys the challenge of learning and operating new equipment. He is always smiling and has a pleasant word for everyone. When faced with a problem or the need to make a decision, Dancing Wolf asks other people for their opinions before deciding. He does, however, feel constrained by rules. Most of the time he looks for a way around them and then makes up all sorts of excuses when he is found out. He also blames others for almost all the mistakes he makes. He corrects his errors grudgingly.

1. List Dancing Wolf's positive attitudes.

   _____

   _____

2. What attitudes should Dancing Wolf try to improve? Why?

   _____

   _____

3. How would Dancing Wolf's attitudes affect your working relationship with him?

   _____

   _____

Activity 9-4

Attitude Evaluation

A. For each of the *statements* given, rate your own attitude by placing an **X** in the appropriate column: *Always, Sometimes,* or *Never*.

	Always	Sometimes	Never
1. I control my temper.			
2. I get to work every day.			
3. I do what I am told.			
4. I avoid horseplay when working.			
5. I cooperate with others.			
6. I follow orders promptly.			
7. I do not complain about tasks.			
8. I get along with my boss.			
9. I dress appropriately for my job.			
10. I do the best job I can.			
11. I like working with foreigners.			
12. I am responsible for my work.			
13. I am responsible for my mistakes.			
14. I take care of equipment.			
15. I do neat, accurate work.			
16. I accept criticism easily.			
17. I am learning new skills.			
18. I get along with others.			
19. I am honest.			
20. I treat everyone equally.			

B. For the statements that you answered *sometimes* or *never*, identify them by circling the letter. On a separate sheet of paper, write each letter and its statement. Now, consider how you could change your attitude. Explain the steps you can follow to do so. Be prepared to discuss your findings with other team members in class. This sample, which illustrates how to set up your responses, can serve as a guide.

Number Circled: _____ Statement: _____

Steps I can follow to change this attitude.

1. _____   5. _____

2. _____   6. _____

3. _____   7. _____

4. _____   8. _____

Activity 9-5

Practicing the *I Statement*

Write a three-part *I statement* for each of the following situations. Share your *statements* with others and compile a sampling of interesting answers others have given.

1. You are talking with a bank teller when another depositor walks up and interrupts you.
   Statement: _____
   _____
   _____

2. Someone cuts in front of you in a line.
   Statement: _____
   _____

3. The restaurant waitperson incorrectly totals your bill.
   Statement: _____
   _____

4. Fran, your sister, always takes your favorite hat without asking.
   Statement: _____
   _____

5. Your friend nibbles at your serving of fries when you are out to lunch together.
   Statement: _____
   _____
   _____

6. You go out of your way to an office supply superstore advertising a special on items you need for your computer, only to find out the items are sold out when you get there.
   Statement: _____
   _____
   _____

7. For the third time in two weeks, your friend Mia cancels a date to go see a popular new movie.
   Statement: _____
   _____
   _____

8. Rory, a coworker, still owes you the $5.00 you lent him when he left his wallet at home two weeks ago.
   Statement: _____
   _____
   _____

9. You brought your watch to the repair shop three times in the past month, but it still does not keep proper time.

Statement: _____

_____

_____

10. A stranger is blocking the exit to the building you want to enter.

Statement: _____

_____

internet

Activity 9-6

Attitudes in the Workplace

Surf the Internet for statistics regarding how often people lose their jobs because of negative attitudes such as lateness, refusing to accept criticism, whining, and rudeness. Also find out how often people are recognized and promoted for their positive attitudes.

Activity 9-7

The Team Approach

team

Develop three scenarios using the two- and three-part *I statements*. Have another team role-play these scenarios and critique their *I statements*. Compile a list of the different, acceptable responses offered by the other team's members.

Chapter 10

Your Relationships with Your Coworkers

Skills

OBJECTIVES

After reading this chapter you will be able to:

1. Develop a list of basic rules fostering good interpersonal relationships with coworkers.

2. Discuss the importance of accepting differences in people.

3. Establish a set of guidelines for good teamwork.

4. Differentiate assertive, passive, and aggressive behavior

Yvonne is a computer repair person in the technical support department of a large firm. She is polite, tactful, and willing to help and listen to others. When faced with a difficult repair problem, the other people in her department will stop and help her, as she does when they have difficulties. Others within the firm ask for Yvonne when they need someone to repair a computer problem. One vice president told her, "Your smile is a welcome sight."

Harlan is one of seven case counselors in a government unemployment center. The counselors' offices are separated by thin partitions and workers have to leave their doors open for proper air circulation. Coworkers sometimes overhear Harlan's discussions when he is interviewing clients. He frequently tells people, "Nobody else around here knows his job. I'm the only decent counselor. You're lucky you got me and not one of them." Harlan wonders why he is never asked to join the other counselors for lunch or to go out with them after work. Could his remarks to clients have anything to do with it? Of course, his remarks are overheard. You probably would not like working with someone who had unkind things to say about you. You too, would avoid socializing with that person. You might even say Harlan has an attitude problem.

Yvonne and Harlan are interacting with others at their workplace. They have developed relationships with their coworkers that are both positive and negative. Working with others is a major activity when you are on the job.

Good Relationships With Coworkers

Good coworker relationships provide the social contact you need to make the workday as pleasant as possible. Coworkers can also provide needed support in accomplishing job duties and helping you solve problems on the job. Much of your success on the job depends on your getting along with coworkers. To do your job, you will have to rely on others, both individually and in groups.

Gain Coworker Support

People have to want to work with you for you to get your work done with ease. Others have to care about what happens to you and help if you get stuck with a problem or extra work. You want people to watch out for you, to help you when you ask for assistance, or to support you during difficult times. When people are willing to work with you, you have earned a measure of success that will be reflected by your increased productivity.

For example, Amelita is well-liked by other employees in her company. She has a big project in production and a completion deadline of 5:00 P.M. today. Pat, Jose, Sung Ho, and Safed offer to help her over the lunch hour so she can meet her deadline. When offering their help, Safed said, "After all, Amelita, you always help us when we need it. We can all take turns grabbing our lunch and help you at the same time."

Build a Good Reputation

Although you may not be aware of it, your reputation, the image other people have about you, begins the moment you walk into the company's building. You make a first impression and that is the cornerstone of your reputation, which grows and follows you throughout the company. People form opinions about you on the basis of your work habits, your attitudes, and your relationships with your coworkers. Before you move to another department or office, your reputation precedes you. When you meet someone new, what is that person thinking? "I've heard Mr. DuBraque is a really nice guy. Do you know he stayed late last Friday just to help Mr. Graham rearrange his office furniture?" Or, "I don't want anything to do with Mr. DuBraque after the way he yelled at that nice Mr. Graham."

Smart **TIP**

Your good name is invaluable.

Basic Rules of Good Coworker Relationships

Every relationship takes effort to develop and maintain. Your coworkers expect the same things from you that you expect from them. You must work to uphold your part of the relationship. To avoid problems, you need to develop the ability to critique your own behavior. Make sure you are following these basic rules of good relationships.

Have a sense of humor. Learn to strike a balance between taking your job seriously and maintaining a sense of humor. No matter how overworked or tired you might be, being able to smile and laugh, especially on those days when everything seems to go wrong, is a big help.

Smart **TIP**

A smile is always welcome.

Smart **TIP**

Be polite when you interrupt someone.

Learn from your coworkers. Just by watching your coworkers, you can learn how things are done in the company. Do not be afraid you will embarrass yourself by asking questions about how to do your job. Remember to be polite if you have to interrupt someone to ask a question. Avoid butting in on others' conversations. If you show courtesy and consideration, others will be glad to help you.

Smart **TIP**

Learn from others.

Keep your eyes and ears open. Observe how the people at work dress, talk, and do their work. You might dress conservatively for your first day and then discover that more casual dress is acceptable on the job. The type of language you use at work can also be crucial to your success. For example, if you are used to swearing, do not bring this bad habit into the workplace. Watch how others perform their tasks; follow their lead unless your supervisor gives you different instructions. Observe the **tempo**—the speed, or pace of the work. Does everyone work furiously, at a breakneck speed, or is the tempo more relaxed? Match your tempo to the prevailing work tempo.

Be friendly and respectful. Work is the same as any other social situation. To receive friendship and respect from others, you first must give it. Those on your level or below you on the career ladder deserve the same respect as supervisors, executives, and customers. Remember, everyone likes to feel important, to be treated with respect, and to believe they are accomplishing something. Your respect for others can go a long way toward helping them feel positive about both themselves and you.

Bob is the supervisor of the public relations office of a small textile firm. He always smiles and has a pleasant comment for the company's custodial staff. He tells the staff members how great the office looks and how much he appreciates each little effort they make on behalf of the company. When Bob needed help to set up an exhibit for visiting textile buyers, the custodial staff was more than willing to do so by moving furniture and shampooing the carpets.

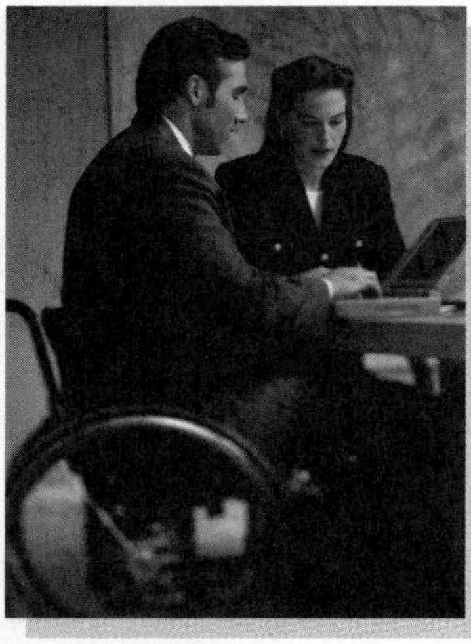

Figure 10-1 Learning new techniques means being flexible and accepting change.

Work with everyone equally. You might find you like working with some people and dislike working with others. You naturally want to be with the people you like, to seek out their company, and to share information with them. You want these people to *be on your team.* But you cannot ignore someone you dislike, nor can you be obvious about your feelings. When you have to interact with people you dislike, treat the situation as you would any other job task and try to do your best.

Raj, an agricultural technician at the Fortune Nursery, helps grow plants for sale to gardeners. He thinks Toby, another technician, talks too much, is too serious about her work, and is a snob. He also knows Toby is the most knowledgeable about landscaping difficult terrain and the placing of plants in the best places for optimum growth. Raj treats Toby with respect and asks her opinion about work, even though he knows they will not be friends.

Accept the differences in people. You are an individual, a unique person different from others. In the workplace, you will meet people who are *like you* as well as people whom you consider to be *different*. People do not look alike, they do not act alike, and they do not have the same experiences, feelings, and thoughts. These differences influence their actions and behaviors.

$\mathcal{S}$mart **T I P**

Work with everyone on your team.

✓ **People Differ By Their:**   Checklist 10-1

- Experience
- Lifestyles
- Ethnic backgrounds
- Beliefs and values
- Education
- Socioeconomic status

- Family situations
- Geography
- Advantages and disadvantages
- Likes and dislikes
- Dress
- Housing

The biases and prejudices you might have about different types of people should not be allowed to influence your working relationships with them. Accept each person for who he or she is, recognizing that someone is as different from you as you are from him or her. Accept differences in others by:

1. Trying to understand them without resorting to preconceived or stereotyped ideas, such as blondes have more fun or are dumb.

2. Respect the right of people to be who they are. Do not try to change them, as you would not like them to try to change you.

3. Practice **tolerance**, accepting the opinions and practices of others differing from your own.

4. Talk with people to learn about them—how they think, what they like to do, and how they are similar to you.

5. Avoid making judgments about individuals based their appearance, dress, way of speaking, or where they live.

You can learn about your job and your company by socializing with coworkers during breaks and lunch hours.

Figure 10-2 When you are willing to accept others, they will tend to accept you.

A. Jared and Estelle are trainees in the art department of an advertising agency. Jared is friendly to everyone and eager to help wherever he is needed. Coworkers enjoy working with him and are eager to teach him new things. Estelle, on the other hand, seems to have a chip on her shoulder. She says very little and makes sure she doesn't do more than her share of the work. Frequently, she snarls at coworkers when they ask for her help.

1. How would you like working with Jared? Explain your response.

   _____

   _____

   _____

2. How would you feel about working with Estelle? Explain your response.

   _____

   _____

   _____

3. What would you say to Estelle about her future on the job?

   _____

   _____

   _____

B. Jamie works as a counter person in a bakery; Helga and Stefan started working there today. You just overheard Jamie remark, "I'm not going to work with those foreigners. They live in the wrong part of town, they talk funny, and they probably don't even have visas to work in the USA." You know Helga and Stefan because they live in your neighborhood. Also, they just received their United States citizenship papers and are very proud to be able to work at the bakery.

1. What do you think about Jamie's remarks? Explain your answer.

   _____

   _____

   _____

2. What does Jamie have to learn about Helga and Stefan?

   _____

   _____

   _____

3. List three things Jamie needs to learn about accepting people with differences.

   _____

   _____

   _____

Social Skills at Your Job

Proper social skills include being nice to your coworkers. You should say "Good morning," "How are you?" and "Goodbye." You also have to show consideration for coworkers by asking about their health if they have been out ill or inquiring about a parent or child who might be ill. You might be expected to celebrate happy occasions with coworkers and acknowledge their successes. This might mean signing a greeting card, chipping in for a donation or gift, or remembering a birthday. These are all parts of being a member of a team at work.

"There are some egos in here gumming it up."

Working on a Team at Work

A team is a group of people working together to achieve a common goal. We are all aware of teams in sports, where all members work together to win the game. What happens when one member of the team does not do his or her job? Well, the same thing happens in business—the company does not produce a product or service that customers want. If this happens often enough, the company can go out of business.

To be a member of a team, you must play by the rules:

1. *Do your job to the best of your ability, and do not expect others to cover for you.* Other members of the team do not like having to pick up the slack for those who do not do their jobs or who constantly have to be shown what to do.

2. *Offer to assist others when they need help.* Be happy to help when asked. When one member of the team falls behind, chip in to help. You will be considered a good team member if you do.

3. *Accept teasing and bantering when they are done in a friendly, good-natured way.* Many times, team members will joke and tease each other to show comradeship, to see how another person reacts, to get a desired reaction, or to pass the time as they work. Remember to laugh with them, and take friendly teasing with a smile.

4. *Respect the rules.* Every company has written rules by which all employees must abide. These have been discussed in Chapter 3. Every person on the team is expected to follow some *unwritten rules* as well. Two important unwritten rules are (1) **territorial rights**, where an employee has "ownership" of a work area, desk, drawers, or tools; and, (2) **unofficial hierarchy**, where the newest members of the team are expected to do certain chores for others who have been on the team longer, like making the coffee, cleaning up, or running errands.

5. *Don't do other people's work.* Some members of a team will take advantage of newer members, those who are more efficient, or those who are always willing to help everyone. Learn to draw the line between being cooperative and letting others take advantage of you.

Smart **T I P**

"The Team" is significant in your working life.

Smart **T I P**

Follow the team rules.

Handling Problems Tactfully

As we have just discussed, you want to be a team member in *good standing*. This means you have to work well with other team members, be accepted by them, and maintain good relationships with them. The dynamics of the team change when you join it. You are a new person who contributes ideas, handles tasks, and has an outlook different from any other team member, past or present. The other members of the team might tease or test you to see whether you will be an asset to the team and work well with its members. This is frequently called **hazing**. It can take many forms, from teasing, to playing tricks, to interfering with your productivity.

When problems occur with another person, you must take immediate action. You need to be able to stand up for yourself, but at the same time you must remember to be gracious when you are teased. Laughing at yourself along with the others will be the quickest way to stop the hazing and become an accepted member of the group. Becoming angry could cause others to continue the hazing. If you are too defensive, co-workers might not want to work with you, thinking you are not a good sport or will not fit into their group.

You are the newcomer to these work situations. Tom, the teller at the window next to you, is always asking you to show him how to do a transaction. You are falling behind and seem to be making mistakes in your own work. What can you do? Janet, a photocopy-machine operator in your section, always asks you to help her with her work, giving you more work than you can handle. How can you say "No?" Seth, the computer operator in your department, is always teasing and embarrassing you. How can you make him stop?

When you confront problems like these, you need to be able to handle them gracefully. In Chapter 9 you learned tact is skill and grace in dealing with others. Knowing how to say things tactfully will give you confidence in standing up for yourself.

In social terms, people can express assertive, passive, and aggressive behavior. Being **assertive** means you stand up for your rights, express what you want, or state what you believe without hurting other people's feelings. In contrast, being **passive** means you let others dictate to you and do what they want without consideration for your feelings. While you should be assertive, you need to avoid being **aggressive**, which is dominating, attacking, or forcing your desires on others.

To illustrate this concept, let's examine how Lily Rodriquez handles her situation.

Lily Rodriquez is one of three Patient Records Clerks at a local hospital. Arnold, her supervisor, gives her many of the difficult cases in addition to her usual work. He is always telling her, "You really know how to handle this. You know what you are doing and I can rely on you." Lily thinks he is taking advantage of her by giving her more work than the other clerks in the department. Additionally, she thinks this situation is not fair because the work is not being distributed evenly among all the clerks. By being passive, Lily probably will remain angry and might complain to others about how *unfair* the workload is. Even so, she will continue to do the extra work without discussing how she

Smart **T I P**

Take hazing and teasing with good humor.

Smart **T I P**

Be tactful when standing up for yourself.

feels with Arnold. Lily would be considered *aggressive* if she yelled at Arnold about how unfair he is, refused to do the work, or simply told him, "No, I won't do it. Give it to someone else for a change." Being *assertive* means Lily has to express how she feels, why, and tactfully ask Arnold to distribute the work more evenly among all the clerks.

ACTIVITY 3

In the following situations, describe each person's behavior as *assertive*, *passive*, or *aggressive*, Write your answers in the spaces provided.

1. Alice went to the movies because her friend Ana said, "I won't be able to go if you don't come with me." Alice had already seen the movie. Alice is being _____
Ana is being _____

2. Traci had trouble finding a parking space in the company lot this morning. She went to the personnel office to discuss her solution to this problem. Traci was being _____

3. Larry did not want to help Juan carry some heavy equipment. Even though Juan yelled, called Larry names, and made threats, Larry quietly explained he could not lift anything heavy because of his recent back injury. Larry is being _____
Juan is being _____

Using the *I Statement*

Being assertive means you are sensitive to the feelings of others, while you are expressing yourself. You use tact to let others know how you feel about their actions and how you would like to have them change their behaviors. The best way to do this is by using the *I statements* discussed in Chapter 9.

*S*mart **T I P**

The *I statement* tactfully asks others to act.

Part 1	Part 2	Part 3
Your Feelings or Concerns	What is Causing it	What You Want to Happen

Figure 10-3 The *I Statement*.

Remember, the *I statement* is composed of either two or three parts. The first part is always a statement of how you feel, what you think, or how you are being affected by a situation. The last part is what you want the other person to do. When the statement has three parts, the middle part is the cause of your feeling. These statements are directed toward the person's behavior and do not constitute a personal attack, as they are honest and respectfully worded.

To see how this works, let's take another look at Tom, Janet, and Seth, whom we met earlier in this chapter on page 186.

ACTION DESIRED: You want Tom to let you do your job.	
Inefficient Statement: "Tom, just do your work and quit asking me how."	*I Statement:* "Tom, I'm getting frustrated; please take notes so you can do it yourself the next time."
ACTION DESIRED: You want Janet to do her own work.	
Inefficient Statement: "No!"	*I Statement:* "I'm sorry, I have more than I can handle now, too. Please ask someone else."
ACTION DESIRED: You want Seth to stop teasing you.	
Inefficient Statement: "Stop it, Seth! I hate when you do that."	*I Statement:* "I feel embarrassed when you tease me, Seth. I would appreciate your not doing it anymore."

ACTIVITY 4

Develop *I statements* for the following situations. Write the exact words you would say on the lines provided.

1. Heather always leaves work 10 minutes early, leaving you to clean up and close the office.

_____

_____

2. Jacques always borrows your tools and does not return them.

_____

_____

3. Ingrid takes credit for all the work you do.

_____

_____

4. Barry repeats everything you and other crew members say on the job to Sal, the construction supervisor.

_____

_____

Activity 10-1

Using Important Words and Information

A. **Important Words.** Your instructor will assign various projects to help you achieve the goal of adding these words to your business vocabulary.

1.	Aggressive	5.	Reputation	9.	Territorial rights
2.	Assertive	6.	Team	10.	Tolerance
3.	Hazing	7.	Teasing	11.	Unofficial hierarchy
4.	Passive	8.	Tempo		

B. **Learning Log.** Summarize what you have learned from material in this chapter and what it means to you. How could you apply this information to gaining personal insights about yourself?

_____

_____

_____

_____

_____

_____

_____

_____

_____

_____

_____

_____

_____

_____

_____

_____

_____

_____

_____

_____

_____

_____

_____

_____

_____

Activity 10-2

Write complete answers to the questions in this section. Explain and give examples to illustrate your answers. Be prepared to discuss your responses with the class.

1. Why would you want to have good interpersonal relationships with your coworkers?

     _____

     _____

2. What is a sense of humor, and why is it important on the job?

     _____

     _____

3. List all the basic rules of good coworker relationships.

     _____

     _____

4. Why is being a good team member important?

     _____

     _____

5. List four ways you can show your acceptance of coworkers who are different from you.

     _____

     _____

6. Explain the two unwritten rules of the workplace.

     _____

     _____

7. Being assertive is important. What does that mean?

     _____

     _____

8. Compare and contrast assertive and aggressive behavior.

     _____

     _____

9. Describe a coworker who exhibits passive behavior.

     _____

     _____

10. Name the three parts of the *I Statement*.

     _____

     _____

Activity 10-3

Employment Situations

Write complete answers to the questions posed in the employment situations in this section. Be prepared to discuss and explain your responses with your classmates.

A. Lucy is a very hard worker who always gives a helping hand when asked. Her supervisor, Mr. Calendar, has just given her a project to complete in a very short time. She asks Angela, a coworker in the same office who doesn't seem to have a big workload, to help her. Angela replies, "No, Mr. Calendar gave the work to you to do. That's not my job."

1. How do you think Lucy will react in this situation?

   _____

   _____

2. What exact words should Lucy say in response to Angela?

   _____

   _____

B. Ignacio works for a construction company at a building site in the business section of town. Rosa is the crew chief, while Glenn, Steve, Harriet, and Mark make up the rest of the team. Lunch is informal; most crew members grab a piece of sidewalk to sit on, eat their lunches together, and watch the passing parade of pedestrians. Ignacio shouts comments to the pedestrians. Some typical ones are, "Hey, Gorgeous, you're looking good!"; "Where did you get the muscles, Macho Man?"; and "Yo! Fatso, why don't you join a circus?"

1. How do you think Ignacio talks to his crew?

   _____

   _____

2. How do you think Rosa and Harriet feel about Ignacio's remarks? Why?

   _____

   _____

3. Write a response to Ignacio's comments for Rosa, the crew chief.

   _____

   _____

4. Why are Ignacio's comments so offensive?

   _____

   _____

5. Why did Ignacio's comments go beyond respectful civil discourse?

   _____

   _____

Activity 10-4

Terrence has been on the job for a week and feels it has been the best week of his working life. His co-workers are polite, the work interesting, and his supervisor pleasant to be around. At the beginning of the second week, one of his fellow workers tells Terrence he needs to report to the Personnel Office. Terrence, afraid he is about to be fired, leaves his work station and goes to the Personnel Office. When he gets there he finds that no one had requested him. Returning to his work station, he sees all the other workers are suddenly very busy and smiling.

1. What just happened to Terrence?

   _____

   _____

   _____

   _____

   _____

2. How should Terrence handle this situation?

   _____

   _____

   _____

   _____

   _____

3. Write a personal note to Terrence. It should specifically mention any discomfort you are experiencing, on your own or as part of the group.

   _____

   _____

   _____

   _____

   _____

   _____

   _____

   _____

   _____

   _____

   _____

   _____

Activity 10-5

How Assertive Are You? A Self-Inventory

A. For each of the statements given, rate your own attitude by placing an **X** in the appropriate column, *Always, Sometimes,* or *Never.*

	Always	Sometimes	Never
1. I can express my feelings easily.			
2. I can tell someone how I honestly feel.			
3. I find not attacking a person difficult when I don't like what he or she says or does.			
4. I complain about situations, but don't offer any solutions.			
5. I tell people what to do directly.			
6. I am not embarrassed to tell people what I think of them.			
7. I get angry and yell when someone upsets me.			
8. I let people make me angry and don't say a word.			
9. I let people take advantage of me.			
10. I am afraid to tell others the truth about how I feel.			
11. I do not see the necessity of expressing my feelings to someone else.			
12. If people do something I do not like, I tell them off.			

B. For the statements that you answered *sometimes* or *never,* identify them by circling the letter. On a separate sheet of paper, write each letter and its statement. Now, consider how you could change your attitude. Explain the steps you can follow to do so. Be prepared to discuss your findings with other team members in class. This sample, which illustrates how to set up your responses, can serve as a guide.

Number Circled: _____ Statement: _____

Steps I can follow to change this attitude.

1. _____   5. _____

2. _____   6. _____

3. _____   7. _____

4. _____   8. _____

Activity 10-6

Practicing *I Statements*

Write *I statements* for each of the following situations.

1. Your coworker continually criticizes your way of dressing, which makes you uncomfortable. You want him to stop.
    Statement: _____
    _____
    _____

2. Ms. Alton, a coworker, is always complaining about having too much to do. Your supervisor dumps a pile of her work on your desk and walks away.
    Statement: _____
    _____
    _____

3. Jane is always late and wants you to cover for her by telling everyone she just stepped out for a moment. You don't want to lie to protect Jane.
    Statement: _____
    _____
    _____

4. Frank, a member of your work team, is always going outside to smoke.
    Statement: _____
    _____

5. Joel likes to use a strongly scented after shave, which causes you to sneeze whenever you are near him.
    Statement: _____
    _____

6. Sadie is always talking about how wonderful her children are.
    Statement: _____
    _____

7. Andre interrupts conversations with a story of his own.
    Statement: _____
    _____

8. Rasheed is an excellent team member, and you know he will get the job done. He never cleans up after himself, however, leaving you to do all the work.
    Statement: _____
    _____
    _____

9. Laurie never contributes to celebrations such as promotions, retirements, and coworkers' milestones such as marriages.

   Statement: _____

   _____

   _____

10. Tony tells all his coworkers how to do their jobs.

    Statement: _____

    _____

internet

Activity 10-7

Getting Along with Coworkers

Search the Internet using the terms "coworkers," "interpersonal relationships," "team members," and "personal interactions," then describe the results of your searches. Compile a list of useful URLs. Write a brief description of the information given at each address.

Activity 10-8

The Team Approach

team

Have each team member write a skit to be role-played by the team regarding interpersonal interactions with coworkers. Critique and analyze the way each situation unfolds. Try the skit again incorporating the team discussion.

Chapter 11

Skills

After you have read this chapter, you will be able to:

1. Discuss the importance of good interpersonal relations with your supervisor.

2. Identify and discuss the three types of supervisors according to their management style.

3. List the responsibilities of the supervisor.

4. Discuss criticism in the workplace; what it is, why it is necessary, and how it should be handled.

Your Relationships with Your Supervisor

Andre, Sara, and Jason work as sales assistants in various shops at a nearby mall. They always eat lunch together in the mall's food court. Leslie comes running up to her friends in tears. "Ms. Manning is horrible, she's a lousy manager. She's always making us redo things and complains if we don't get them right," she sobbed. "I had to move all the clothes to new racks, even though everything looked fine where it was. Ms. Manning always worries about every little thing. She's not friendly, and I don't like her at all!"

Mr. Lowell stomped into his office, barked for his mail, and slammed his door. Kate, his secretary, sighed, thinking "It's going to be a long day." She decided to hold Mr. Lowell's calls until he had a chance to drink his coffee and read his mail.

Like virtually all employees, Leslie and Kate have a professional relationship with their supervisors. How successful they will be on the job and how satisfying their work experiences will be depends on this relationship. As with any interpersonal relationship, this is a two-way street. The supervisor has expectations and has to understand the employee. At the same time, the employee has to understand the supervisor, that person's role, and style of management.

Leslie and Kate react to their respective situations quite differently. Leslie is finding relating to her supervisor difficult. She does not understand the demands the supervisor is making of her. Kate, on the other hand, has learned to understand her supervisor. She knows where he's coming from, she manages her response to him, and behaves in an efficient and positive manner. Leslie has yet to learn good interpersonal relations with her supervisor.

What Is a Supervisor?

A **supervisor** is an employee who manages the work of one or more employees. These employees are called the supervisor's **subordinates**. Supervisors have varying titles, according to the type of business they are in. Similarly, companies choose to use different titles for the same position. You are probably aware of the term *boss,* which many people use when referring to their supervisor. Some other common titles include manager, department head, foreperson, and crew chief. Those whom the supervisor oversees can be called employees; staff, crew, or team members; or division, department, or project personnel. Many employees have a more specific job title like mechanic, computer operator, or accountant.

Supervisors are responsible for assigning work to their subordinates and for making sure the work is done according to company policies, standards, and goals. Most supervisors are responsible for hiring and firing employees, and so monitoring the day-to-day activities of each subordinate is a major task for the supervisor.

Smart **T I P**

Your supervisor sets the workplace tone.

✔ **Supervisors**   **Checklist 11-1**

- Give out work assignments
- Plan work schedules
- Ensure accuracy of work
- Make sure deadlines are met
- Monitor employees' performance

- Train employees
- Keep records
- Maintain subordinates' morale
- Report to his or her own supervisor

Supervisor Styles

Developing a good relationship with your supervisor is vital. To do this, you need to be aware of your supervisor's attitudes toward work and supervision. Every supervisor is different, an individual who brings his or her own unique style to the job. Management experts have analyzed different ways of relating to and supervising others. These different ways are called **management styles**. A supervisor might fit one style exactly, be a combination of styles, or use different styles as needed for different situations. Understanding these styles will help you relate to your supervisor.

Smart **T I P**

Each supervisor supervises differently.

The Authoritarian Supervisor.
This type of manager likes to be in charge of the whole operation. He or she wants to be a leader with a group of followers who are kept under tight control. Subordinates are given little opportunity to plan, make suggestions, or have a say in making decisions. Because this kind of manager operates in a totalitarian manner—always needing to get his or her own way—this style is sometimes referred to as being *dictatorial* or *despotic.*

Smart TIP

Understand your supervisor's management style.

Authoritarian supervisors rely heavily on the *power* and *status* of their positions to make others do what they want them to do. They believe in very close supervision of their subordinates, telling employees exactly how to do their jobs and constantly checking to see what is being done. These types of leaders place a high value on the accurate completion of each job, to their exact specifications. They do not welcome the opinions of others or have long discussions with staff members. As a result, they do not always consider their employees' needs or another, better way to do a job.

Tips on Handling the Authoritarian Supervisor

- Do not argue—this is rule #1.
- Listen, nod, and do the work as assigned even if you think you have a better way of doing it.
- Keep your feelings and ideas to yourself.
- Stay in close communication with your supervisor.
  - Explain what you are doing.
  - Ask for direction.

Mr. Rodney is an authoritarian supervisor. He has organized his supply storage room in a very particular way, and no one can change it. Every item in the room is kept in a specific order on the shelves. Theo, an employee of Mr. Rodney, realizes that many of the frequently requested items are stored on the high shelves. To get these items, workers have to use a ladder. Theo believed these items should be moved to a lower shelf. Mr. Rodney would not even consider such a suggestion. This would mean moving some items "out of order," which was something he could not tolerate.

The Participative Supervisor.

Also known as a *democratic* manager, the participative supervisor uses the team approach to getting a job done. The entire staff is encouraged to take part in running the project, department, or company. Here the channels of communication between the supervisor and the department members are wide open.

The participative supervisor believes leadership and supervision mean overseeing staff members, giving general direction, involving everyone in planning, and then letting people do their jobs. The entire staff is involved in planning and decision making, and reaches what is called a consensus, which is a general agreement by those concerned. The supervisor discusses the work to be done, encourages analysis and discussion, and then delegates the authority and work.

Smart TIP

You cannot change your supervisor's management style—*you* have to adapt.

Working with a participative manager will give you the opportunity to develop your decision-making skills and overcome fears you might have about handling responsibility. With a participative supervisor, be prepared to attend many meetings. You should be prepared to take part in these meetings and express your ideas and opinions. Also, take the time to fairly assess the ideas and opinions put forth by your coworkers. Confidentiality of matters discussed during meetings should be maintained.

Tips on Handling the Participative Supervisor

- Always remember, you are a member of a team.
- Work is to be done in the manner specified by the consensus.
- Accept the fact that not all your ideas will be accepted.
- You will probably not agree with the all the decisions.
- Be patient when things seems to take longer than necessary.
  - ◆ You might think the supervisor is not leading, but is letting others do his job.
  - ◆ You might believe the endeavor lacks direction, but the process takes time.

Mrs. Jackson calls a staff meeting every morning at 9:15 A.M., and each person in her department is expected to attend. The atmosphere is informal and some people bring their coffee and rolls. During these meetings, Mrs. Jackson outlines what has to be done during the day and notes upcoming tasks. She encourages discussion of current issues, anticipated problems, and anything else staff members consider important. Lively discussion of the topics takes place and tasks are assigned.

The Laissez-faire Supervisor. This type of manager shows employees how to do their jobs and then lets them do the work as they see fit. Laissez-faire (pronounced *lay-say-fair)* translates as "free reign" and carries with it the connotation of freedom. A laissez-faire supervisor keeps a distance from the day-to-day work activities, and so most of the pertinent communication occurs among the employees, with occasional direction given by the manager. Because of the lack of direct leadership and supervision, some people find working for this type of supervisor difficult.

Laissez-faire supervisors give employees a great deal of freedom, little supervision and direction, and trust their employees' judgment and abilities. Some supervisory tasks, such as handing out assignments and monitoring schedules, can be taken on by other staff members. Laissez-faire supervisors are nondirective, meaning they tend to not give direct instructions. They can be very supportive of their staff, however, and can be effective managers if they have a group of experienced, mature employees.

*S*mart **T I P**

Observe how successful colleagues work with your supervisor.

*S*mart **T I P**

Remember! Work with your supervisor's management style.

Tips on Handling the Laissez-Faire Supervisor

- Be self-directed and willing to work on your own.
- Do not become angry or frustrated by your supervisor's lack of direct participation.
- If your supervisor has relied on you in the past, he or she will probably do so again. If problems occur, you could be the first employee to be blamed because you were in charge.
  - ◆ Maintain the quality of your work as an example for others.
  - ◆ Keep your productivity high during times of minimal supervision.
  - ◆ Ask coworkers to share information, direction, and instructions.
  - ◆ Approach your supervisor when more guidance is needed, instead of waiting for your supervisor to come to you.

Mr. Alvarez is a laissez-faire supervisor. As the chief accountant for a large company, he has hired five people who have training and experience as bookkeepers. Because of their backgrounds, he is satisfied they are competent to do their jobs. Mr. Alvarez outlined the responsibilities to the members of his staff, showed them how the company likes the work done, and then left them to do their specific jobs.

ACTIVITY I

Identify the management styles of the following supervisors. Then, describe how Mrs. Brown should handle this kind of supervision.

SUPERVISOR A: "Mrs. Brown, did you mail those letters to the lawyer? Did you call to confirm my lunch appointment? Remember, I must have that report by 5:00 P.M. today."

1. Management style _____

2. How Mrs. Brown should handle Supervisor A? _____

   _____

   _____

SUPERVISOR B: "Good morning, Mrs. Brown, everything going okay? Any problems? I'll be in my office if you need anything."

1. Management style _____

2. How Mrs. Brown should handle Supervisor B? _____

   _____

   _____

SUPERVISOR C: "Good morning, Mrs. Brown. Can you have everyone in my office for a brief meeting in 15 minutes?"

1. Management style _____

2. How Mrs. Brown should handle Supervisor C? _____

_____

_____

SUPERVISOR D: "Mrs. Brown, I thought I told you I wanted the heading on this report to be three inches down from the top, not two-and-a-half. It's 2:00 already and I told you I must have five copies of the report by 2:30 this afternoon."

1. Management style _____

2. How Mrs. Brown should handle Supervisor D? _____

_____

_____

Successful Working Relationships

Once you have an understanding of your supervisor, you are on your way to developing a good interpersonal relationship with him or her. Attitudes and behavior are also important ingredients. Remember, when you have a positive attitude, a pleasant demeanor, and understand what makes a good employee, you make the supervisor's task easier because you are easier to supervise. In Chapter 3, you learned what an employer expected of an employee. Someone who meets these expectations usually develops a good working relationship with a supervisor. Some additional factors determining good relations with a supervisor are your:

Be dependable! Be reliable!

1. Willingness to learn the job thoroughly, perform it carefully, and ask questions when necessary.

2. Eagerness to explore new ways to solve problems or improve work methods.

3. Willingness to work and do the tasks required in a cheerful manner, without excuses. Ask for assistance if a task cannot be completed in time, give assistance to others, and work overtime when needed.

4. Ability to learn from mistakes to avoid making the same mistakes in the future, not making excuses for your mistakes or blaming others for them.

Figure 11-1 Supervisors and subordinates depend on each other in the workplace.

Smart **T I P**

You are never too old to learn.

5. Ability to follow directions accurately and ask questions when in doubt.

6. Willingness to accept criticism gracefully.

7. Honesty and a candid manner in keeping your superior informed about the progress of your work.

8. Concentration on doing a good job, but not being a supervisor's doormat. Supervisors want and need employees who can think for themselves and who will tell them honestly, yet kindly, when a problem exists or they have a better way of accomplishing a task.

ACTIVITY 2

Are the following employees acting in a way that will develop good interpersonal relations with their supervisors? On the lines provided, explain your answers.

Employee 1: "Fred always does it this way—why should my supervisor always complain when I do it like he does? My supervisor's always on my case."

_____

_____

_____

Employee 2: "Mr. Rivera doesn't look at the clock when I come back from lunch, so he won't know whether I take a few more minutes each day and come back late from lunch."

_____

_____

_____

Employee 3: "Charlotte, I see Mary is having trouble getting everything done today. Can you give her a hand?"

_____

_____

_____

Employee 4: "Ms. Chu, I have finished all the work you have given me. Is there anything else you need me to do?"

_____

_____

_____

The Importance of Good Morale

Your supervisor is responsible for maintaining good employee morale. *Morale* is the attitude and feeling employees have about their work and their workplace. Employees with good morale have confidence in themselves and others, usually like being together, and have discipline, enthusiasm, and loyalty.

Smart **TIP**

A team player makes an extra effort.

 Good Morale Means...   **Checklist 11-2**

- Employees like to come to work, willingly work extra hours, and give extra effort when needed to make the project, department, or company a success.
- Employees believe the supervisor is interested in them, cares about them, and is willing to support them.
- Employees have a good feeling about doing a job well, of belonging to a winning team, and enjoy the satisfaction of doing something worthwhile.
- The supervisor of these employees has the satisfaction of knowing his or her staff members are doing the best they can and will make that extra effort when necessary.

Good morale is something that develops over a period of time. Some days morale will be low: The supervisor will be in a bad mood, have a number of problems, or be distracted. Employees, too, can have problems interfering with their work. But if morale is good, then all parties understand one another and do not let passing problems ruin good working relationships.

Smart **TIP**

Feel good about yourself and the job you are doing.

Criticism on the Job

Your supervisor's job is to give you direction, make suggestions, and critique the work you do. So you, the employee, need to handle constructive criticism well. *Criticism* is a judgment made by others expressing disapproval of how you handled a task or a situation and points out specific mistakes you made.

 Criticism Can Be Helpful   **Checklist 11-3**

- It can help you learn how the job is to be done.
- It can provide ideas for doing the job better.
- It can motivate you to do the job more accurately.

Constructive Versus Destructive Criticism.

Remember not to take criticism as a personal attack. *Constructive criticism* is criticism directed toward a behavior, something you did or did not do, a mistake you made, a further step you should have taken. Criticism should be given in a calm manner. If the person giving the criticism is angry, frustrated, or under stress, though, those emotions and others can be heard in the voice. When you receive constructive criticism, accept it gracefully. Try to smile and promise to make the changes requested. This can be hard, but it is something you can learn to do over time.

Destructive Criticism.

The criticism that comes across as a personal attack is known as *destructive criticism.* Demeaning statements can be made without any effort to suggest how the problem should be corrected. Many reasons exist why a person would give destructive criticism. When this happens to you, you need to be able to separate the words from the personal attack. Ask yourself, "Is the criticism justified?" If the answer is *yes,* then you should react as you would to constructive criticism. If the answer is *no,* you will need to put into practice what you have learned about using tact and being assertive.

Handling Criticism.

Criticism is commentary critical of you that points out you made a mistake or acted improperly. Your first reaction might be to defend yourself and deny any problem exists. Or you could become defensive and give excuses or reasons for the problem. Another common reaction is to just silently accept the criticism without considering its validity or source.

None of these methods helps your working relationship with the person making the criticism. When you become defensive, the critic thinks you are not understanding what he or she is saying and will continue to criticize, which will make the situation worse, resulting in bad feelings and damaged relationships. Being passive shows you have little confidence in your abilities and will accept things said about you without defending yourself. This can result in you losing self-respect as well as the respect of others, who might see you as weak and unsure.

✓ When Criticized,

Checklist 11-4

You Should Not:

- Get angry
- Make excuses
- Complain
- Blame others
- Whine or cry
- Criticize your supervisor in turn
- Walk away
- Throw a temper tantrum

It Is Best To:

- Be aware of your reaction to criticism.
- Understand the source and the reason behind the criticism, and consider its validity.
- Formulate a response. Accept the criticism with grace, make the needed changes, and state your point of view assertively.

Homer works in the Order Department of Technical Supply, Inc. As part of his job, he must work with Mr. James, one of the purchasing agents. When Mr. James is under pressure, he will yell and scream, tell you how inefficient you are, how many mistakes you have made, and how late you are in handing in your work. Homer realizes Mr. James acts this way with everyone and does not take an attack from Mr. James personally. He listens to the comments and, where criticism is justified, he tries to make corrections. If he thinks the criticism is unjustified, he tries to ignore it.

*S*mart **T I P**

Ponder *why* you are being criticized.

ACTIVITY 3

Assume you are the employee in this activity and your supervisor, Renee, criticizes you. How do you react to these words? Write a tactful and assertive response to your supervisor. (Be prepared to role-play these situations with class members.)

1. "This is not what I wanted you to do. I said you should follow the example I gave you."

   _____

   _____

   _____

2. "You are 10 minutes late for the third time this week."

   _____

   _____

   _____

3. "If you have finished all your assigned tasks, you should help Shawn instead of sitting there and reading the newspaper."

   _____

   _____

   _____

*S*mart **T I P**

Be adult!

Handling Problems with Your Supervisor. We have discussed the importance of using tact in maintaining good interpersonal relationships on the job. The importance of tact does not diminish when you communicate with your supervisor—in fact, it becomes even greater. Being tactful with your friends and coworkers is even easier because you see them more as your equals.

Your supervisor, however, is not your equal, but someone who has authority over you. He or she has the power to fire you, or give you a promotion or a bonus. Some supervisors do not consider the feelings of the subordinates, giving orders and criticism without thought. Others when under a great deal of pressure from their own supervisors, unthinkingly pass the pressure on to their workers. The management style used definitely influences how workers do their jobs. No matter how well you get along with your supervisor, sometimes you will have problems or disagreements.

Mr. Rabson is under a great deal of pressure from the top executives of the firm to improve his department's productivity. He reacts by yelling, giving many orders, and making many demands. Soon, his entire department is stressed-out, its members yelling and sniping at each other.

Ms. Chanis is also under a great deal of pressure from her supervisor. She reacts by working long hours, carefully reviewing all projects from her staff, and holding long department meetings. Soon, many in her department are working long overtime hours, putting extra effort into their projects, and preparing for meetings.

How well you deal with Mr. Rabson when he yells at you or Ms. Chan when she wants you to work more overtime is important. You will need tact to deal effectively with supervisors under conditions like these.

We have discussed using tact in Chapters 5 and 6. To briefly review, you want to make a statement, let your feelings be known, or have your supervisor respond in a certain way. You do not want to be defensive, pass blame, or offend another person. To do this, use the *I* message.

- The **first part** of the message is where you describe your feelings or opinions: "I am having difficulty…," "I don't agree…," "I don't like…"

- The **second part** is where you tell the other person what you want: "Please repeat your instructions," "I would like to hear more of what you have to say," "… but could you please tell me first…"

When resolving problems with your supervisor, try to include the **middle part** of the *I statement*, with which you describe why you think what you do:

- "I am having difficulty following these instructions *because they are unclear to me*. Could you please repeat them?"

- "I am having trouble getting this important report done on time *because of all the telephone calls that are interrupting my concentration*. Please have LaToya answer the phone for the next few hours."

- "I am not able to work late without any notice *because I have to hire a babysitter*, so I would appreciate your letting me know ahead of time when this will be necessary."

Notice how the middle part of the statement softens the impact of what you are saying. By including this statement, you are less likely to be seen as angry or someone who is blaming others.

"Are those impersonal form letters ready yet, Ms. What's-Your-Name?"

The following situations could happen to you. How can you respond to your supervisor in a tactful manner?

SITUATION A: Ms. Harran, your supervisor, always comes to your workstation about 20 minutes before you leave work and asks you to complete a new task or make some corrections to earlier work before you leave.

1. What do you dislike about this situation?

_____

_____

2. What do you want to happen?

_____

_____

3. What should you say? Write the exact words.

_____

_____

SITUATION B: You have allowed your tasks, which are your sole responsibility, to pile up. At the same time, you need time off to register for classes at night school.

1. What do you dislike about this situation?

_____

_____

2. What do you want to happen?

_____

_____

3. What should you say? Write the exact words.

_____

_____

SITUATION C: You are the next in line in your department to get an office with a door. When an office becomes vacant, you write a memo to your supervisor, Madge O'Leary, requesting you be allowed to move in to that office. You do not receive a reply. The following Monday you see Richie, a staff member who has less seniority than you, moving his belongings into the office.

1. What do you dislike about this situation?

_____

_____

2. What do you want to happen?

_____

_____

3. What should you say? Write the exact words.

_____

_____

Activity 11-1

Using Important Words and Information

A. **Important Words.** Your instructor will assign various projects to help you add these words to your business vocabulary.

1. Authoritarian supervisor	5. Destructive criticism	9. Non-directive
2. Consensus	6. Laissez-faire supervisor	10. Participative supervisor
3. Constructive criticism	7. Management style	11. Subordinate
4. Criticism	8. Morale	12. Supervisor

B. **Learning Log.** Using a word processing program, summarize what you have learned from the material in this chapter and what it means to you. How could you apply this information and personal insight to yourself?

_____
_____
_____
_____
_____
_____
_____
_____
_____
_____
_____
_____
_____
_____
_____
_____
_____
_____
_____
_____
_____
_____
_____

Activity 11-2

Dealing with Your Boss in Employment Situations

Complete answers to these questions. Explain your answers thoroughly, using examples to illustrate. Be prepared to discuss your responses with the class. Collect and discuss the most interesting responses.

1. Explain what a supervisor means to subordinates.

   _____

   _____

2. Of the management styles described in this chapter, which type do you prefer? Explain why.

   _____

   _____

3. Of the management styles described in this chapter, which type would you least like to work with? Explain why.

   _____

   _____

4. Why should you have a good working relationship with your supervisor?

   _____

   _____

5. Describe three ways to handle an authoritarian supervisor.

   _____

   _____

   _____

6. How does the participatory supervisor reach a consensus in the department?

   _____

   _____

7. Describe the characteristics of a laissez-faire supervisor.

   _____

   _____

8. No one likes to be criticized, yet it is an important part of your relationship with your supervisor. Why is this true?

   _____

   _____

9. List five factors determining the quality of your relationship with your supervisor.

   _____

   _____

   _____

   _____

   _____

10. Explain the statement, "Morale is essential to the health of a business."

_____

_____

Activity 11-3

How can an employee re-word the following statements so they are tactful and assertive?

1. "It's 4:30. I have a date. I can't do this job. I don't care if it is an emergency."

_____

_____

_____

2. "So I made a mistake, it still looks okay. It's the way I always do it."

_____

_____

3. "I'm doing the best I can. If you don't like it, do it yourself."

_____

_____

_____

4. "Boy, are you grouchy today. What's eating you?"

_____

_____

5. "Why should I care? This product stinks."

_____

_____

6. "Why should I do her job, too?"

_____

_____

7. "I can't help it. Either the train is late or there's too much traffic. So I'm a few minutes late each day. What's the big deal?"

_____

_____

_____

8. "It's not my fault if the machine's messed up."

_____

_____

_____

9. "I do what I'm paid to do, no more, no less."

_____

_____

10. "Not overtime again! Ask someone else today."

_____

_____

Activity 11-4

Reacting to Criticism

Listed below are some of the ways you can react to criticism. How does the speaker react? Match the statement given with a reaction. Write the number of the reaction on the line to the left of the statement. You can use an answer more than once.

Reactions to Criticism:

1. Throw a temper tantrum.

2. Agree that you made a mistake.

3. Argue.

4. Pass the blame.

5. Agree to do better.

Statements:

_____ A. "Max told me this is always done this way."

_____ B. "Okay, I'll know that next time."

_____ C. "Why should I have to redo this? I worked hard on it and it looks fine to me."

_____ D. "No, do it yourself."

_____ E. "It's not my fault the computer messed up."

_____ F. "I'll mess these papers up if I want to. I worked hard on them."

_____ G. "So what if I made a mistake? I'm human too."

_____ H. "I'm sorry it didn't turn out the way you wanted it. I'll redo it."

_____ I. "Who are you yelling at?"

_____ J. "You can never make up your mind. First it's one way, then I'm wrong. Then it's another way, and I'm wrong. Decide what you want to do before telling me how to do it."

_____ K. "I'm sorry, I must not have understood all the instructions; could you please repeat them."

_____ L. Kick the wall and yell, "Why are you so critical?"

Activity 11-5

Practicing *I* Statements

Write *I statements* for the following situations.

1. Your boss has assumed you will stay late for the third time this week to complete a project. You want to get home for your son's ball game.

    _____

    _____

    _____

2. Louise, your employee, wants to leave early to take her cat to the vet.

    _____

    _____

    _____

3. Mr. Frey, an executive in your company, asked you to work on a project without speaking to your supervisor first.

    _____

    _____

    _____

4. Your supervisor is not giving you the direction you need to do your job correctly.

    _____

    _____

    _____

5. A coworker refuses to let you use tools you need and your boss is angry the job is not completed.

    _____

    _____

    _____

6. Your supervisor keeps giving you more work and you cannot catch up.

    _____

    _____

    _____

7. You are a supervisor and your employee takes frequent breaks to have a cigarette.

    _____

    _____

    _____

8. The Chief Custodian informs you that Ginger's work area is messy beyond belief—rotten food and leftovers are all over and her desk is covered with personal items.

_____

_____

_____

9. Your supervisor has been procrastinating in signing your family leave request and you have to travel 3,000 miles to see your dying Mother.

_____

_____

_____

10. You are an overweight employee and are offended by the letters, posters, and other weight-loss materials left by coworkers at your locker and workstation. You have approached your supervisor about this twice before and no change has occurred in the employees' behaviors.

_____

_____

_____

internet

Activity 11-6

Challenges for Supervisors

Surf Internet newsgroups and chat rooms for discussions dealing with supervisors. Write a synopsis of the problems covered, how were they handled, and the consequences of how they were handled.

Activity 11-7

The Team Approach

team

Return to the employee manual your team is developing. Discuss what interpersonal relationship issues and considerations should be included. Ask team members to write documents discussing the issues and add them to the manual.

Dealing Successfully with Stress on the Job

After reading this chapter, you will be able to:

1. Provide definitions of stress, frustration, and anger.

2. Describe how stress can cause physical problems.

3. Develop a list of appropriate ways to cope with stress.

4. Understand the consequences of using inappropriate coping skills.

Smart **T I P**

Stress is always present in some form.

Gerard, an auto repair technician, was having one of those days when everything he did went wrong. He had a hard time finding the problem in the car engine that had to be repaired within two hours. He discovered the parts he needed were not in stock, and he had to go to the supply house to purchase them; Sam, his coworker, borrowed his favorite screwdriver and didn't return it; his boss kept reminding him of the time; and his girlfriend called and wanted him to go to the movies with her instead of his usual basketball game. Then, just as he finished the job, he stumbled against a table causing it to collapse. When his boss stepped into the garage and asked whether the job was finished, Gerard yelled, "How can I get my work done with you constantly nagging me?" Gerard was experiencing stress and frustration, which caused him to get angry.

Although you often hear people say, "I am very stressed-out at work," "It's hard for me to drag myself to work each day," or "I can't deal with this stress anymore," stress is only part of the picture. In this chapter, we will discuss job stress, frustration, and anger—what causes you to experience them, and constructive ways to handle them.

Stress Explained

Stress is a catch-all word involving many different feelings—happiness, anticipation, frustration, or anger. You can experience them one at a time or all at once.

Understanding Job Stress

Stress is the pressure many people experience every day. It can help them face challenges, resolve conflicts, and make decisions. Stress is an internal response to outside stimuli. These stimuli are called stressors. Stressors can affect your digestive, circulatory, or respiratory systems. Stressors can be pleasant, such as getting a new car, a raise, a promotion, or recognition at work; or unpleasant, like oversleeping, spilling your morning coffee on your new suit, or missing a deadline at work. Some stress is minor, like misplacing your pen or dropping your keys when you are in a hurry; some is major, such as being in a car accident, forgetting an appointment, or having a disagreement with your supervisor.

Responding to Stress. People react to stress in a number of ways. A reaction can be external, where you act out, often on a person or object that is not causing the stress. You are probably aware of people who become verbally or physically aggressive when under stress. They yell and shout, verbally abuse others, throw things, and get into fights. Also, they have been known to punch walls.

In our modern society, most people internalize stress, keeping it inside and not expressing their feelings. Knowing that being physically or verbally aggressive is unacceptable, they keep everything bottled up inside. They react by blaming themselves or ignoring their feelings. When stress builds up, it can cause a variety of physical and emotional ailments.

Results of Stress. Stress is your body's physical, mental, or chemical response to something that has frightened, excited, confused, endangered, or upset your well-being. Prolonged exposure to stress—that is, being under stress for a long period of time with no relief—can cause a number of physical problems. These are your body's way of saying it needs a rest.

Smart **T I P**

Ask yourself: "How do I respond to stress?"

Some Physical Symptoms that Stress Can Cause:

- Headaches
- Backaches
- Ulcers, stomach upset
- Eating disorders
- High blood pressure
- Irregular heartbeat
- Heart attacks
- Insomnia
- Skin rashes
- Dermatological problems
- Extreme fatigue
- Lack of energy
- Asthma attacks
- Emotional problems
- Nervousness
- Anxiety
- Lack of concentration

When you become overwhelmed by unrelieved stress, your work most likely will suffer. Ultimately, you can experience burnout. This means you are completely used up by your job. You have no more energy left, cannot give anything more to the job tasks, and are unable to function efficiently or effectively.

On The Job, Stress Can Cause You To:

- Have poor attendance and punctuality.
- Develop poor work habits.
- Be unable to concentrate.
- Develop poor work attitudes.
- Decrease work productivity.
- Produce low-quality work.
- Have accidents.
- Withdraw from others.
- Have poor working relationships.

Martin is working long hours as a salesman in a large appliance store. He wants to earn enough money in commissions to buy a new car he needs very badly. Business is slow, however, especially with competition from the new discount store on the highway. The other sales associates also want to make sales, so they compete with Martin for the customers who do come in. Martin is affected by these stressors, and is suffering from headaches and stomach pains. He dreads going into work each day, but knows he must. Now, his doctor has told him to take it easy and rest more.

Understanding Job Frustration

Frustration is the disheartening feeling you experience when you cannot reach your goal. You think everything is useless because your efforts have not yielded the desired results. This is something everyone experiences now and then to some degree. Whether you find the store is out of your favorite cookies, a social engagement is canceled, your air-conditioner is broken in 90-degree weather, or your supervisor is not giving you sufficient instructions to do a task, the end result is you are frustrated.

The greater your desire to achieve a goal, the greater the frustration you can experience when something goes wrong. Frustration can make you want to lash out, cry, run away, or just quit.

Seng Yee is a chef at a fancy restaurant. He works long hours, starting early in the morning when he goes to the markets to order his produce and ingredients. Then he returns to the restaurant to start planning the menu and cooking the sauces and soups. This afternoon he discovered he did not buy the right vegetables for a dish he was preparing, the sauces did not turn out right, the soup had too much salt in it, and the bakery was late in delivering the bread and cakes. Seng Yee felt like quitting, just walking away, or doing something else for a living.

Understanding Job-Related Anger

Anger is a strong feeling of unhappiness or displeasure with something or someone. You might get angry when people do not do what you want. Situations that are harmful to you or someone close to you, or cause you frustration or stress can create angry feelings. You might become angry when you are confronted by the prospect of physical harm, embarrassment, or displeasure.

People react differently to feelings of anger. Some people want to strike out or scream at the person or situation causing them distress; others react by running away from the source of their anger. Your emotions are internalized when you run away, and can cause you to overreact. You might consider yourself personally to blame for getting into such a situation, for not being smart enough to see what was coming, or for just being foolish.

ACTIVITY I

Understanding Yourself

Understanding what makes you feel the way you do is important. When you are on the job, you need to be able to handle stressful situations. Everyone has experienced these feelings at one time or another. Think about situations in which you felt this way. What happened to cause you discomfort? The more you think about this, the more you will remember, so keep updating the following list:

1. I get angry because of these things:

   a. _____   g. _____
   b. _____   h. _____
   c. _____   i. _____
   d. _____   j. _____
   e. _____   k. _____
   f. _____   l. _____

2. I was frustrated when:

   a. _____   f. _____
   b. _____   g. _____
   c. _____   h. _____
   d. _____   i. _____
   e. _____   j. _____

3. I experience stress when:

   a. _____   g. _____
   b. _____   h. _____
   c. _____   i. _____
   d. _____   j. _____
   e. _____   k. _____
   f. _____   l. _____

Causes Of Job-Related Stress

Smart TIP

All jobs entail stress, but the causes are different.

Frame Art is a medium-sized company framing artwork, posters, and photographs for interior design firms that decorate hotels, offices, and other large buildings. Most of the work must be completed by a contract deadline. If Frame Art doesn't meet the deadline, the order can be canceled by the customer. Overtime is common and the employees seem to work at breakneck speed all the time. Accuracy is critical. Jonathan works as hard as everyone else, but he thinks he never catches up with his work. He thinks, "Management should plan these jobs more carefully. We aren't given enough time to do the job right, and we're all making too many mistakes." Just like Jonathan, you can experience stress at work from a variety of causes.

Task-Related Stress

Smart TIP

Analyze what causes your stress.

Some of the stress we experience results from specific job tasks or demands of the business. Likewise, some businesses and public-sector agencies are stressful by the very nature of their work. For example, stress is often high for police officers, firefighters, cappers of oil-well fires, neurosurgeons, nuclear-plant technicians, prison guards, and skyscraper crane operators. Many of the workers in these jobs actually thrive on the stress. In fact, a nine-to-five office job might cause them more stress than their own high-risk jobs.

Missed Deadlines. Stress increases when employees fall behind in their work and do not meet their deadlines. Frequent, unexpected, and unreasonable deadlines are major causes of stress. For example, Robby's supervisor scheduled deadlines for four new projects close together. Robby was also expected to meet interim deadlines for a long-term, ongoing project for which he was solely responsible, as well as to attend product development meetings. No wonder Robby started to develop severe headaches by the middle of the day, always had an upset stomach, and barked at everyone around him. Although he could ordinarily do the work with ease, the stress of meeting all these deadlines was too much for him.

Heavy Workload. A common complaint from today's workers is too much work and not enough people to do it. As companies downsize—reduce the number of employees or departments to make the company more efficient—the workers who remain are expected to also do the work done by those who were let go. Work that is repetitive or extremely detailed will add to task-related stress.

Long Hours. Increased workloads mean longer workdays and more overtime for employees. Overtime can be a good thing, but only in moderation. Stress increases when overtime means too many long workdays in a row or too many weeks of 60-plus hours. If you are going to night school, have to care for your children, or have other re-

Figure 12-1 Spending long hours on the job does not necessarily relieve the stress of a heavy workload.

sponsibilities, the pressure to work overtime can be a major stressor. In cases like these, you will probably experience stress whether you choose to work the overtime or not.

Inadequate Pay In the United States today, people are working longer and harder than ever before. Yet some believe they are not being paid fairly for the work they are doing, and others cannot meet their basic needs on the money they are making.

Lack of Recognition All of us need to be told we are doing a worthwhile job and our work is appreciated. Studies have shown people will continue to work difficult jobs if they and their work receive recognition, approval, and acceptance. If your supervisor never tells you, "Thank you for doing such a terrific job," you might feel unappreciated. Of course, you cannot reasonably expect supervisors to pat you on the back or give you *strokes* if you are only doing the minimal amount of work necessary. Generally, recognition is given for "going the extra mile," giving more than was requested, and realizing more of your potential.

Inadequate Equipment Employees are sometimes required to work with inadequate, obsolete, or broken equipment. Stress mounts as you try to do an acceptable job without the proper equipment. No matter how hard you try, your efforts are wasted when you truly need more or better equipment. No baseball-team owner ever expected his baseball team to win if his players were given ill-fitting cleats.

Poor Working Conditions People are happier and more productive when they work in pleasant surroundings. If you are used to working in a nice place, you might come to expect that level of quality in your work environment. Even so, environments can deteriorate—lighting dims, noise levels rise, noxious fumes creep in, or dirt accumulates—creating a less pleasant and more stressful situation for you.

People-Related Stress

Working with some coworkers can cause you to experience stress. Even in the best work situations, interpersonal relations will not be perfect. No matter how hard you try to develop good interpersonal relations, you might discover someone at work with whom you cannot get along.

Trying to get along with a subordinate or superior is difficult when you don't like each other. Coexistence, which is peacefully occupying the same space with other such people, is even more difficult. Little habits and disagreements start to build into major problems causing a great deal of stress. You could even feel discrimination or experience harassment, to the point where you don't want to go to work.

*S*mart **T I P**

People-related stress is frequently hard to perceive.

Smart **T I P**

Stress from sources outside the workplace affects you in the workplace.

Smart **T I P**

Everyone copes with stress differently. Find your own effective methods.

Outside Stress

Your coworkers have lives outside the company, and they can bring stresses from their personal lives to the workplace. These stressors can include:

1. Issues with significant others
2. Other problems with family members, especially children or parents
3. Home life
4. Daily chores and responsibilities
5. Community issues
6. Excessive involvement in outside activities

Coping Skills

Sam and Julie are hairstylists at New Styles. Their responsibilities and hours are the same. When appointments get backed up and clients are waiting, Sam works faster, gets very quiet, and nibbles on candy. By the end of the day, Sam's heart is pounding, he has a headache, and his face is flushed. He's too tired to go out for dinner with the other hairstylists. Julie works fast under pressure, but, between clients, she asks the receptionist, "Please telephone the rest of my clients, tell them I'm running late, and ask them to come in a little later or reschedule their appointments." At the end of the day, Julie looks forward to going out with her coworkers. You can see that Sam internalizes stress while Julie handles it in a constructive manner.

No matter how hard everyone tries to develop good work attitudes and interpersonal relations, no job is free from stress, frustration, and anger. How you handle this stress is important.

Coping with Stress

How you handle feelings and problems at work affects your working relationships with your coworkers and management. Mishandling them can jeopardize your job. When you have problems coping with negative feelings, be aware of what is causing them. Take a break when you need to and collect your energies so you can cope better. If you work in a setting with a great deal of stress and pressure, you must learn to relax. A break will help you perform better and handle the stress better.

✔ **Effective Coping Techniques**   **Checklist 12-1**

- Talk things over with someone you trust and respect.
- Exercise, play, use up excess energy.
- Meditate, practice yoga.
- Do breathing exercises.
- Write your feelings down on paper.

- Take a break from your daily routine.
- Do something different.
- Do something for others, like volunteering.
- Listen to your body, especially pay attention to its need for food or rest.

Handling Your Feelings

Everyone experiences anger, frustration, or stress at some time. When you experience these feelings, how do you handle them? Answer the following questions honestly. Share your answers with your classmates to explore similarities and differences in your responses.

1. When someone shouts at me in anger, I _____
   _____
   _____
   _____
   _____

2. When I realize I have made a mistake, I tell myself _____
   _____
   _____
   _____
   _____

3. When I have many important things to think about at the same time, I usually _____
   _____
   _____
   _____
   _____

4. When I am criticized, I _____
   _____
   _____
   _____
   _____

5. When nothing I do seems to be right, I _____
   _____
   _____
   _____
   _____

How to Deal with Stress and Emotions

You can more easily deal with stress once you have identified the stressors.

Confront the Problem or Situation.

Understand what is causing you to feel the way you do. Learn to recognize the little irritations bothering you. Often, your reaction to small annoyances is caused by a bigger problem you have not dealt with. For example, let's say Janet works at the next desk. When she talks on the phone to customers, her voice gets loud. This never bothered you before, but lately you have been doing a lot of detail work and hearing her voice so loud makes concentrating hard for you. Are you sure it is Janet's voice that's causing you problems?

Maybe you have more work than you can handle right now and that is the real cause of your stress. Get control of the situation by evaluating each and every aspect. Decide what is important and what is not. Usually, when viewed this way, the entire problem does not seem so bad. Some situations call for you to change your attitude and take things less seriously. Maintain your sense of humor.

Remember Your Human Relations.

At work you are rarely alone when having to deal with feelings of stress, frustration, and anger. When you are around coworkers, if you act out these feelings, you can damage your relationships with them. You can hurt the feelings of others, even if they are not the cause of your bad mood. Avoid embarrassing yourself and others by your words or actions. Most importantly, consider the consequences of your actions.

 ## Ways to Deal with Stress

Checklist 12-2

Do

- Confront the situation
- Discuss the situation calmly
- Maintain your dignity
- Exercise
- Produce quality work on time
- Re-evaluate your goals
- Accept responsibility for your actions
- Meditate

Don't

- Run away
- Make threats or physically abuse others
- Use verbal aggression, such as yelling, cursing, or name calling
- Cry, whine, or complain
- Use the "silent treatment"
- Stall and not do your work properly or on time
- Blame others
- Quit the job
- Abuse alcohol
- Use drugs

Try to Strike a Balance Between Your Work Life and Social Life. So many people carry their work problems with them everywhere. Somehow they just can't let go. Here's a worst-case scenario: Chester is a high-school teacher; he eats, sleeps, and breathes his students, the lessons, tests, discipline problems, disgruntled parents, irate supervisors, and a hundred other things teachers have to deal with each day. These thoughts are in his mind when he's eating and sleeping (Chester even dreams about them!) He has stopped participating in family events and seeing friends because "lesson plans have to be developed," "a test must be marked," "grades have to be entered" or "letters of recommendation have to be written."

Think of what you want the outcome to be when you decide how to handle stress and negative emotions. Work toward an acceptable solution by following some of the tips above. Take action to remedy the stressor situation by speaking to your supervisor about the issues. You could, for example, request fewer hours, the advancing of a project deadline, a lessening of your workload, or budgeting more money for temp workers.

Smart **T I P**

Set your priorities.

ACTIVITY 3

Cammy likes her job very much. Sometimes, though, she is under pressure to work against a deadline. She must be accurate and work quickly. She suffers from headaches, rashes, and fatigue. What can Cammy do?

_____

_____

_____

_____

_____

_____

_____

_____

_____

_____

_____

_____

_____

_____

_____

_____

_____

_____

_____

Activity 12-1

Using Important Words and Information

A. **Important Words.** Your instructor will assign various projects to help you achieve the goal of adding these words to your business vocabulary.

1. Anger	5. Downsize	9. Recognition
2. Burnout	6. External response	10. Repetitive
3. Coping	7. Frustration	11. Stress
4. Deadline	8. Internalize	12. Stressors

B. **Learning Log.** Using your word processing program, summarize what you have learned from the material in this chapter and what it means to you. How could you apply this information and gain personal insight about yourself?

_____

_____

_____

_____

_____

_____

_____

_____

_____

_____

_____

_____

_____

_____

_____

_____

_____

_____

_____

_____

_____

_____

Activity 12-2

Write complete answers to the questions in this section. Explain your answers completely, using examples to illustrate your answer. Be prepared to discuss your responses with the class.

1. Explain how stress can be internalized.

_____

_____

_____

2. List five effects stress can have on your physical well-being.

_____   _____

_____   _____

_____

3. List five effects stress can have on your performance at work.

_____   _____

_____   _____

_____

4. Describe how people respond to frustration.

_____

_____

_____

5. When people externalize their response to anger, how do they generally behave?

_____

_____

_____

6. List six causes of job-related stress.

_____   _____

_____   _____

_____   _____

7. List five effective coping techniques.

_____   _____

_____   _____

_____

8. Explain why this statement, "If I ignore it, the stress will go away by itself," is false.

_____

_____

_____

Activity 12-3

Case Studies

Write complete answers to the questions posed in the case studies below. Be prepared to discuss and explain your responses with your classmates.

CASE 1: Dirk and Gabrielle work in a hospital billing department. Mrs. MacTeague, their supervisor, sets unrealistic goals for them each day. Dirk tries to do all the work assigned and gets fatigued, angry, and irritable. Gabrielle goofs off, talks with friends on the phone, and takes extended breaks. How can they handle this situation more effectively?

_____

_____

_____

_____

_____

_____

_____

CASE 2: Lynn is always busy. She works two jobs and goes to college two nights a week to get her degree. With two children and a husband who need her attention, Lynn has little time for hobbies or socializing with friends. At her full-time job, coworkers are friendly, but very serious, overly conscientious, and do not like changes made to their routines. They do not take breaks, they talk business over lunch, and take work home each night. When not discussing work, they talk mainly about their children. Lynn has headaches, is always tired, thinks everything she does is useless, and is envious of people who have "interesting conversations." She gets angry with her children for silly reasons, complains about both jobs, and is sad because nothing seems to go right. She has also started taking days off from her full-time job just to sleep.

1. What are Lynn's problems? What clues help you to know this?

   _____

   _____

   _____

2. Describe how Lynn is coping with her situation.

   _____

   _____

   _____

3. Using the exact words you would say, explain to Lynn what she might do to better alleviate stress and cope with her situation.

   _____

   _____

   _____

CASE 3: Manolo works for an upholsterer as a carpenter. He dislikes deadlines and believes they apply to everyone but him. For the last two weeks he has been working on an antique sofa for a client. Josie, the owner of the shop, is getting increasingly upset because Manolo is taking a long time to complete his part of the job. Josie knows the client's daughter is getting married and needs the sofa for her home by next Wednesday. What should Josie do?

_____

_____

_____

_____

_____

_____

_____

_____

_____

_____

_____

_____

_____

Activity 12-4

Taking Time to Think About Yourself

A. Analyze what causes you stress and frustration

1. What are some of the things causing you stress at home? At work? In school?

_____

_____

_____

_____

_____

2. How do you know these situations caused you stress? Describe the physical and emotional symptoms.

_____

_____

_____

_____

_____

B. Listed in the chart below are some of the ways you can handle stress on or off the job. Consider how you handle stress. For each method you have used, place an **X** in the columns **On the Job** and **Off the Job.** If you have never used a specific method, write **Never** in the columns.

Method	On the Job	Off the Job
1. Take a walk		
2. Talk things over with someone		
3. Pound your fist on a table or wall		
4. Listen to some music		
5. Take a break		
6. Eat everything in sight		
7. Get into a fight		
8. Exercise		
9. Watch television		
10. Write your thoughts down		
11. Scream and yell		
12. Do volunteer work		
13. Try to forget about the problem		
14. Do nothing		
15. Go to a party		
16. Do breathing exercises		
17. Drink soft drinks or coffee		
18. Go to the restroom		
19. Talk on the telephone		
20. Use drugs		
21. Engage in a hobby		

C. Analyze the methods you have used in the inventory above. Which of them have been effective for you? Which have not helped situations and perhaps made them worse? Discuss your responses fully.

_____
_____
_____
_____
_____
_____
_____
_____
_____
_____

D. Develop a plan of action. What methods of coping should you begin to use to help you handle stress and frustration more effectively? Why?

_____

_____

_____

_____

_____

_____

_____

_____

_____

_____

_____

_____

Activity 12-5

Practicing *I Statements*

Write *I statements* to tell the following people about the stress you are experiencing.

1. Your supervisor

   _____

   _____

   _____

2. A coworker

   _____

   _____

   _____

3. A friend

   _____

   _____

   _____

4. A family member

   _____

   _____

   _____

5. A salesperson who is serving you

_____

_____

_____

6. A customer

_____

_____

_____

7. A team member

_____

_____

_____

8. Your significant other (if you have one)

_____

_____

_____

internet

Activity 12-6

Tackling Stress

Search the Internet for articles, books, discussions, bulletin boards, and chat rooms dealing with the subject of *coping with stress at work*. Report your findings according to the directions given by your instructor.

Activity 12-7

The Team Approach

team

Much has been written about the subject of this chapter, stress and coping on the job. Research this subject and develop a presentation using pictures, graphs, demonstrations, and role-playing activities for the class.

Developing Your Career Portfolio

You are now beginning to assemble your portfolio. It is beginning to take shape as a portrait of you. You want prospective employers to know you through the work you do. Therefore you should continue collecting samples of your work that are illustrative of your abilities and best efforts. Remember, your portfolio can include tests, reports, projects, teachers' evaluations, and other assessments.

Employers are interested in people who can think critically, write clearly, and make appropriate decisions. To show you have these skills, write an essay on one of the following topics:

a. Proper business decorum

b. Dealing with coworkers on the job

c. Romance on the job

d. The difficult boss—who that person is and what to do when confronted with this kind of nightmare

Research: Employers want to know their employees can use their resources, have critical thinking skills, know how to make decisions, and work well with others. All these abilities can be demonstrated with a research project. Research one of the following topics and write a report:

a. Corporate culture and how it influences you, the employee

b. Different management styles and your ideal boss

c. New trends in managerial organization

The time is 8:50 on a warm spring morning and the employees at Melbrook Sporting Goods, Inc. are coming in from the parking lot and bus stop. Miguel, Timothy, Kiesha, and Ellen have been working at Melbrook for two months now. Let's visit and see how things are going.

Miguel Garcia comes in promptly and goes to his work space, nodding to his coworkers. They, in response, say "Good morning" and turn away, ignoring him. He turns on his computer and starts working on the assignment he was given the day before. When he is finished with this job, Miguel sits quietly at his machine exploring what else he can do with it, sending e-mail and communicating with chat-room friends while waiting to be given a new assignment.

Miguel thinks his coworkers do not understand him. Nor do they know how hard he had to work to get the education for this type of job. To him, they seem very silly and immature, chatting in the morning over coffee. He muses, "They should have their coffee before they come to work." Miguel thinks this job is "just a breeze." He cannot understand why everyone takes so long to do simple tasks and why they have problems with the more complex ones. He has made his attitude known in the office. He thinks, "If they can't do the work, then maybe they should do something else. If they don't want to be friends with me, well, that's okay too."

Miguel believes Mrs. Black, his supervisor and head of the Accounts Receivable Department, is satisfied with his work. He is always prompt, does the work assigned to him accurately and quickly, knows his job well, and asks questions when necessary. He makes a point of keeping his work area very neat and tidy, plus he is always well groomed and feels good about the way he looks. Therefore, he cannot understand why Mrs. Black always seems so annoyed with him.

To tell the truth, he finds Mrs. Black very hard to understand. He also questions why the company officers gave a woman a managerial position. Miguel has noticed Mrs. Black rarely comes out of her office to talk with her staff and does not talk with anyone unless that person goes to her office, and then she mostly sits at her desk and frowns. "Just like a woman," he thinks. She is there when he arrives in the morning and is still there when he leaves in the evening.

Mrs. Black gives very detailed instructions and always has each job well-defined with all the materials ready. Employees in the Accounting Department are expected to do their jobs to her specifications with no questions asked. If a mistake is made, Mrs. Black does not yell, but she will make embarrassing comments about a person's ability, intelligence, or personality. He is thankful this rarely happens to him. Miguel would never talk back to her like some of the other staff members do. He just nods, ignores her rudeness, and then quietly redoes the work.

Miguel has always dreamed about a job like this one and he has worked hard to get here. He has always found computers interesting and is confident of having a successful career. His family and friends are impressed with his position at Melbrook. He is earning a good salary, and is saving money and planning for the future. Then why does he feel so bad, so anxious? Miguel has discovered that a few drinks during lunch help him get through the rest of the day and ease some of his anxiety.

Kiesha Is Adjusting

Arriving at work, **Kiesha Brown** greets everyone warmly as she joins her coworkers for coffee. She has a smile and a friendly word for everyone. Marilyn, the coworker with whom she trained when she began in this position, is on maternity leave and Kiesha finds she really misses her. Kiesha realizes that with Marilyn's help she got a good start in this job. When she tells her coworkers about her feelings, they all say they feel the same way. Marilyn really ran the department, because Mrs. Sadar-Wright, the Customer Relations Supervisor, delegated most of her authority to Marilyn as she was always busy with other issues and did not take an active interest in what was happening in their section.

Mrs. Sadar-Wright seemed to like Marilyn the best of all the employees in her department. The others didn't mind because Marilyn never took advantage of the situation. She worked just as hard or even harder than everyone else. Marilyn was pleasant, friendly, warm, and very businesslike in her dealings with her colleagues, the customers, and those in authority. Kiesha hopes to be like Marilyn and has started to dress like her, wearing simple suits and dresses, low-heeled shoes, and only a little jewelry. She found she was even beginning to talk like Marilyn, using the same words and expressions, the same tone of voice.

She and Marilyn used to have long talks about the best way to do the job and how to handle her paperwork accurately. Kiesha believes she still has to work on this aspect of the job and wonders, "Would it be all right to call Marilyn at home for advice? Did our friendship go that far?" She really got upset and started to cry one time when Mrs. Sadar-Wright criticized her because of her lack of accuracy. Mr. Sampson, the head of Marketing, even came into the office and accused her of not being dependable. She just did not see what the fuss was all about. She was sure if Marilyn were still around, none of this would have happened.

Timothy's Working Style

In the metalworking shop, **Timothy Landers** is busy welding small parts together. He has discovered he can do very small, delicate, and intricate work particularly well. The other people in the department are glad to have him do this type of work because it takes patience, a steady hand, deep concentration, and great skill. Timothy likes the challenge. Mr. Jones, his supervisor, is impressed with the quality of Timothy's work, his dependability and reliability. He has said so in front of Timothy's coworkers.

Timothy likes his job, is pleasant, friendly, and enjoys the humor of his fellow employees. When they tease him about his preference for doing the delicate work, he teases them in return. He and his coworkers enjoy taking their breaks and eating lunch together. They are all members of a bowling team in a local league that plays every Monday evening. Timothy is respectful to the others in his department. When he first began working at Melbrook, he asked questions about the job assignments, how to do the work and use the equipment. He made an effort to learn as much as he possibly could about the type of work the department did.

Despite his easygoing attitude, Timothy does not like to be told about mistakes he might have made. At such times, he becomes angry and claims he did not do the work or makes other unlikely excuses. When this occurs, everyone wonders what Mr. Jones will do, or whether Timothy will ever learn and grow up. Mr. Jones lets Timothy cool down, then calls him into his office for a meeting on proper business behavior. Also, he has warned Timothy that acting in this manner is inappropriate and can be cause for dismissal.

Ellen Copes

Ellen Post, the clerk in the Shipping Department, is unhappy because she does not like her coworkers. She considers everyone unfriendly. They never stop to chat about what they do on weekends or about their families. They always seem too busy to pay any attention to her. She feels she has never really liked this job and keeps telling herself, "Maybe it's time to change. Two months is a long time to stay where you are not wanted."

Ellen is also frustrated by not being able to wear her nice business clothes to work; she has to wear work pants, boots, and frequently, a hard hat. She always dreamed about working in a place were everyone dresses nicely and saved a long time for business clothes. Now her clothes are going to waste. "Just look at me, I'm wearing work boots!" she sighs.

Her immediate supervisor, Mr. Constantine, usually walks around and watches the staff as they work. Sometimes he stands at a tall table near the entrance to the storage area doing his paperwork and giving orders. He expects everyone to jump when he says the word, and everyone does. Ellen gets angry when he checks the orders she has filled because she thinks he does not trust her.

Ellen believes she does her job well. The work is not difficult and she works very quickly and efficiently. After several weeks on the job, Ellen discovered easier ways to accomplish some of her tasks. She suggested to Mr. Constantine that her ideas could save time, money, and people power. He was unwilling to listen, telling her, "This is the way the job has always been done."

Mr. Constantine doesn't smile or ask the employees how they feel in the morning. He yells at Ellen in front of other employees, embarrassing her especially when she is late, which seems to be happening often lately. He doesn't want to listen to her reasons, even though Ellen thinks they are valid. Ellen believes he doesn't understand her problems or like her. When she gets very upset about Mr. Constantine's attitude, Ellen goes to the restroom for a long rest. On the way back, she stops in the lounge to chat with whoever is there at the moment. She has met some very interesting people at Melbrook and wishes she could work in one of their departments.

Ellen has begun to feel very tired lately. She seems to have constant problems with her stomach, and has developed headaches; at home she likes to sleep all the time. She dreams of what she would like to do to Mr. Constantine and what he can do with this job. Her family and friends cannot understand why she is ill all the time or why she feels the way she does about her job. After all, she is making good money working for a large prestigious company.

Timothy, Kiesha, Ellen, and Miguel have been working for two months now. Let's examine how they are doing.

Progress Report

1. A person's attitude on the job is very important. A positive attitude is an asset in getting ahead and being a success on the job. A negative attitude can be a hindrance and work against you. Respond to the following statements about each employee. Substantiate your answer by describing each employee's attitudes and citing examples to support your responses.

Miguel:

a. Miguel has good attitudes toward his job.

_____

_____

_____

b. Miguel is accepting of his fellow coworkers.

_____

_____

_____

c. Which attitudes must Miguel improve? Why?

_____

_____

_____

Kiesha:

a. Kiesha has good work attitudes.

_____

_____

_____

b. She is working to improve her attitudes.

_____

_____

_____

c. Which attitudes must Kiesha improve? Why?

_____

_____

_____

Ellen:

a. Ellen has good work attitudes.

_____

_____

_____

b. Her attitudes do not affect her work.

_____

_____

_____

c. Ellen's attitudes are the result of her current job, and working in general.

_____

_____

_____

Timothy:

a. Timothy has good work attitudes.

_____

_____

_____

b. His attitudes toward his work are apparent.

_____

_____

_____

c. Which attitudes must Timothy improve? Why?

_____

_____

_____

2. People spend a large part of each day at work with coworkers. Therefore, interpersonal relations with coworkers and supervisors are important. Your answers to the following questions may vary from those of fellow classmates. Give detailed reasons and specific examples to substantiate your responses. Be prepared to discuss your answers with your classmates.

a. Which of the four employees, in your opinion, has the best interpersonal relations?

_____

b. Which of the four do you believe has the worst interpersonal relations?

_____

c. Which of the four do you believe is aware of the need to improve his or her interpersonal relations?

_____

d. How are their relations with their coworkers affecting their work? Explain your answers.

EMPLOYEE	
Miguel	
Keisha	
Ellen	
Timothy	

e. Which of the four has the best understanding of his or her supervisor? Explain.

_____
_____
_____
_____

f. Which of the four has the most difficulty dealing with the supervisor? Explain.

_____
_____
_____
_____

3. Stress is part of everyday life and is found on every job. It tends to build up, one thing after another, until the body reacts. Anger and frustration are also found in daily life. How one handles these emotions is very important. Complete the following chart illustrating how each person is experiencing stress and coping with it. Also write a brief paragraph discussing 1) whether each individual's way of coping with stress is successful, and 2) the consequences of their actions as it affects their jobs.

	Stressors	Symptoms of Stress	Ways of Coping
Miguel:			

Discussion: _____

_____

_____

Kiesha:			

Discussion: _____

_____

_____

Ellen:			

Discussion: _____

_____

_____

Timothy:			

Discussion: _____

_____

_____

Ah! The Supervisor

Each supervisor has his or her own management style. Within one company you will find many different styles.

1. Complete the following chart describing the management style (authoritarian, laissez-faire, participative, or a combination) of each of the four supervisors you have met. Give examples to support your descriptions.

	SUPERVISION STYLE	SUPPORTING EXAMPLES
Mrs. Sadar-Wright (Customer Relations)		
Mr. Jones (Metalworking)		
Mrs. Black (Accounting)		
Mr. Constantine (Shipping)		

2. Do you think Ellen, Kiesha, Timothy, and Miguel understand and work well with their respective supervisors? Give your reasons.

EMPLOYEE	
Miguel	
Keisha	
Ellen	
Timothy	

Using Tact

Each of the new employees has had to make a statement, ask for something, or react to a fellow employee or a supervisor. Pick an instance where this occurred for the Melbrook quartet. Describe the situation and write a tactful way for each of the employees to express themselves. Write the exact words they will speak.

EMPLOYEE	
Miguel	
Keisha	
Ellen	
Timothy	

Unit *4*

Smart Moves
on the Job

Chapter 13

Measuring Your Success on the Job

Skills

O B J E C T I V E S

After reading this chapter, you will be able to:

1. Verbalize the personal attributes a company deems important for promoting an employee.

2. Know the issues an individual must consider when choosing to remain in a job or seek another position.

3. Discuss the need for performance evaluations and how they are conducted.

4. Understand the proper employee attitudes to a performance interview.

Smart TIP

Plan for the future.

Zoraida Castro has been working as a receptionist at the Breckenridge Drapery Corporation for a year. Her job is interesting and she has met many nice people by being out front in the reception area. Zoraida's communication skills have improved and she is well-versed about the company and its operations. A friendly, sincere, hard-working, and cooperative person, Zoraida is liked by just about everyone at Breckenridge. But recently she has been thinking, "I don't want to be a receptionist forever. I could move up into one of the art and design areas. After all, I'm creative and I would like to do something more exciting and fulfilling."

Zoraida is beginning to think about her future at Breckenridge. Where else can she work in the company? Should she stay at the same company or move to another company? She is evaluating her career. To plan her future, Zoraida will need to evaluate her current job and the opportunities it can offer her.

Evaluating Your Job

Sooner or later everyone who works has to examine his or her future with their current job. Do you want to stay at your present job, work for a promotion within your company, move to a different company, or perhaps change fields altogether? Some days even the best job in the world is awful and you wish you could quit and start all over with a different job for a new company. The next day, however, could be exciting and terrific, and you might think you would not want to leave this job ever.

By evaluating your employment situation, you can determine whether you like the job enough to stay. Consider the following questions when contemplating your future with a particular job. If your answer to most of them is *yes*, you are probably happy at your current job.

Consider the People

Are your coworkers nice, cooperative, and friendly? Have you made friends with your coworkers? Do you enjoy socializing with them? Do your coworkers help each other or do they compete and back-stab?

Is your supervisor pleasant and considerate? Do you have a good working relationship with him or her? Does your supervisor treat you fairly? Does your supervisor give you positive feedback? And, when criticism is warranted, is it constructive criticism?

Consider the Company

Is this a good company to work for? Do you like working for the company? Are you proud to work here? Does the company treat employees well? Does the company have a good reputation in the community and in its industry? Do your values and those of the company agree? Does the company care about the environment and well-being of its city?

Does the company provide a good benefits package? Are you receiving benefits similar to those offered by other companies in your area? Do you need benefits your company does not provide? Would you be able to get these benefits at another company?

Do you like the working conditions at your job? Is the work site pleasant and safe? Are the hours reasonable? Are the offices, buildings, and facilities adequate for the work being done and are they attractive? Is transportation to and from work easy, safe, and affordable?

Does the company offer a good product or service? Are you happy to be associated with its product or service? Does the company ask a fair price for its product or service? Is the company technologically advanced and, thus, likely to remain in business?

Consider the Work You Do

Do you like the tasks involved with your work? Are you given reasonable assignments? Are you given enough time and resources to perform your job correctly? Are you told the level of performance expected of you? Are these expectations reasonable? Are you able to perform your job tasks properly? Are these tasks within the range of your abilities? Are you given respect and credit for your work? Are you acknowledged for the work you do?

Consider Opportunities for Growth

Does the company promote from within, providing opportunities for employee *advancement*? Can you be promoted if you continue to work for the company? If so, what are the policies and procedures for earning a promotion?

Does the company provide opportunities for training and education? Are you able to receive company-paid training on new machinery, technology systems, hardware, and software? Can you receive tuition reimbursement if you take courses at a college or technical institute to improve job-related skills? Does the company provide ongoing staff development and training?

Smart **T I P**

Analyze all aspects of your employment situation before making a move.

Consider How Long You Have Been on the Job

You need to stay on a job for at least a year before considering changing your position. As a matter of fact, a series of short periods of employment with a succession of companies generally keeps you from getting the experience you need to be an attractive job candidate. Your resume will begin to look like you have been *job-hopping*, frequently changing jobs held for short periods of time, and will not be viewed favorably by many businesses. Just as employers have an investment of time and money in you, you need to work at a job long enough to establish a reputation for stability and gain necessary experience.

What Do You Want to Do?

When you have taken a critical look at your job by answering the questions in the previous section, you should be able to decide whether to stay with your present job or do something else. The following are some key considerations:

"I want to keep my job." You like your job, company, people, and you want to stay. You want to continue to perform well on the job, and you do not want to go through the job-seeking process to look for another job like this one.

"I want to be promoted to a better job in the same company." You want to get ahead, advance further in this company, and increase your responsibilities. You desire the prestige, status, recognition, and sense of accomplishment a promotion brings.

"I want to leave this job because I am unhappy." You are unhappy with the people, company, tasks, or job environment and decide you should move to a similar position with another company. This is called making a *lateral move*.

"I need to make more money." If your current job cannot provide you with the income to meet your needs, you have to consider seeking a higher-paying job within the company or moving to another company where you can earn enough money. You will need to determine whether you have enough experience and the appropriate skills to accomplish this.

"I cannot move up in this company, so I must leave." You have received all the raises and promotions you can in this company. To advance your career, you should consider seeking a position with more opportunities.

You have decided to stay with your current company, perhaps determining to get a promotion. Now you must consider how to achieve your goals. Employers usually consider employees for promotion on the basis of job performance and personal attributes.

Smart **T I P**

Evaluate your choices and opt for the one most beneficial to you.

Preston has been working as an office assistant at Frigid Foods, a frozen-food processing company, for almost two years. He started in the mailroom and was promoted to his present position nine months ago. He is now eligible to join the pension plan and begin saving for his retirement. Preston likes the people at Frigid Foods and most things about the company. He's beginning to get bored with the daily tasks of his job, but sees opportunities for advancement if he learns management techniques and acquires computer skills.

1. Why should Preston analyze his future on the job?

_____

_____

_____

_____

2. What three things must Preston consider in evaluating his job?

_____

_____

_____

_____

3. What goals should Preston set for himself at Frigid Foods?

_____

_____

_____

_____

Job Performance Evaluation

A *job performance evaluation* is a formal written assessment of your job performance. A copy will probably be given to you after a discussion with your supervisor. This evaluation reviews work you have done, your progress, and attitudes.

Many companies have their own ways of evaluating job performance. In some companies, both the employee and the supervisor complete an evaluation form and then meet to discuss the employee's performance. An employee's assessment of his or her own performance is called a *self-assessment*.

Each company has a different policy concerning job performance evaluations. Your company might review employees every six months (semiannually) or once a year (annually). You should discuss the job review process during your initial job interview and orientation.

The job evaluation form can be a checklist like the one shown in Figure 13-1, or a document like a letter or report.

Your Job Performance Review Evaluates:

- The work you have done during the evaluation period.
- Your interpersonal relationships with your coworkers, supervisor, and other people in positions of authority.
- Your level of cooperation with others.
- Your attitudes at work.
- Whether you have the necessary job skills.
- Your ability to complete a job.
- Your attendance and punctuality.

Probationary Job Performance Evaluation

Employee: _____   Supervisor: _____

Position: _____   Title: _____

Start of employment: _____   Date of evaluation: _____

RATING:	Excellent	Good	Fair	Needs Improvement
Attendance	❑	❑	❑	❑
Reliability	❑	❑	❑	❑
Dependability	❑	❑	❑	❑
Interest in job	❑	❑	❑	❑
Quality of work	❑	❑	❑	❑
Ability to follow instructions	❑	❑	❑	❑
Attitude towards supervisor	❑	❑	❑	❑
Attitude towards employees	❑	❑	❑	❑
Job skills	❑	❑	❑	❑
Initiative	❑	❑	❑	❑
Honesty	❑	❑	❑	❑
Interpersonal relations	❑	❑	❑	❑

Comments _____

_____

_____

_____   _____
Employee Signature   Supervisor Signature

Figure 13-1 Job Performance Evaluation Checklist

Job Evaluation Procedures

An evaluation is an opportunity for you to receive feedback on your job performance. *Feedback* gives you information about your actions. For example, Belinda, a word-processing operator, finished a legal brief ahead of schedule yesterday. Her supervisor remarked, "You did a terrific job getting that brief done so quickly. Keep up the good work." This is immediate oral feedback. The job performance evaluation, however, consists of written feedback.

When you receive your performance review, you will probably have an interview with your supervisor. Give all your attention to the evaluation process. This is the company's way to tell you how you are doing and how it expects you to improve. This can be an appropriate time for you to discuss your feelings about your job, coworkers, or supervisor—especially if they are adversely affecting your job performance.

Your Supervisor Evaluates You. Your immediate supervisor prepares for your job performance evaluation in advance. He or she is the best person to evaluate you because he or she is responsible for giving you work and judging it. As mentioned earlier, you might be asked to complete an evaluation form as well. If you work for more than one person, the highest-ranking person might conduct the evaluation interview, or you could have a group interview.

Your evaluation should be private and confidential. Performance evaluations should be conducted by you and your supervisor in a private office. Everyone should respect the confidentiality of job performance evaluations and not discuss them with coworkers. Administrative assistants, secretaries, or others who have access to job evaluation reports should also respect this confidentiality.

Your job performance evaluation should be specific. The evaluation should be comprehensive, and note your strengths and positive attributes along with your weaknesses. Much of the evaluation will be devoted to specific areas you need to improve. During the review, you and your supervisor should come to an agreement as to the ways you will improve and the time period in which the improvements will be made.

Smart **T I P**

Know the aspects on which you will be evaluated on when you start your job.

Smart **T I P**

Confidentiality must be respected.

A Complete Job Evaluation Should Answer These Questions: Checklist 13-2

- What successes have you had on the job?
- What failures have you had?
- What are your areas of strength?
- What are your weaknesses?
- How can you improve your performance?

Ways to Achieve Needed Improvements

Depending on your specific job description and the policies of the company, you and your supervisor might plan to use one or more of the following approaches to help you meet your improvement goals:

1. Get training in areas where improvement is needed.

2. Use the *buddy system*. Your supervisor assigns you to work with another employee, who knows how to do the specific tasks you need to learn. That employee helps you to master the tasks.

3. Get more supervision from your boss. This could involve your supervisor's written approval of all your work before it is sent to another department or company.

4. Obtain detailed instructions for all tasks. These should be written and available for easy reference.

5. Correct problems using your own initiative and effort. For example, if your attendance needs to be improved, devise ways to make sure you get to work on time every day. Enlist the help of family and friends if necessary. Should your skills need improvement, attend a training program. If interpersonal relations are your downfall, look for ways to improve and opportunities to socialize.

A supervisor ideally gives feedback—positive and negative—on an ongoing basis. The fact is, however, many supervisors are not comfortable doing this, especially when negative feedback is involved. Consequently, many employees are truly surprised when they receive unfavorable comments during a performance review. You should therefore be prepared to hear some negative feedback. Be honest with yourself in your self-assessment, and try to anticipate areas where you might be criticized.

Major Reasons For Negative Comments In A Job Performance Review

- Poor work attitudes
- Poor work habits
- Poor skills
- Poor attendance

- Excessive lateness
- Poor relationships with coworkers
- Dishonesty
- Failure to take responsibility

What to Do If You Get an Unfair Review

A fair review contains positive, as well as negative, comments about your performance. And it should detail how you can improve in the areas where improvements are needed. If you disagree with and want to challenge any of the negative statements made in your review, follow the company grievance procedure. A *grievance* is a formal complaint made by an employee who feels he or she has been treated unfairly by an employer.

American businesses are under pressure to provide well-documented performance reviews that are fair and unbiased. If you believe you have been treated unfairly, discuss the situation *calmly* with your supervisor. If your supervisor is the problem, you should report the situation to someone else, perhaps the person in Human Resources who handles employee complaints. Most companies designate a specific person to help employees with grievances. If all else fails, you may submit a formal complaint to your state's Department of Labor. If you belong to a union, the grievance procedure is written into your contract.

Documentation is important in handling a grievance. Keep your reviews and all other pertinent documents in a folder at home. Also, keep all letters of recommendation.

Smart **TIP**

Understand your company's grievance procedures.

The Importance of Evaluations

Your evaluation is like the report card you receive in school. Your evaluation affects your continued success with the firm. Positive evaluations lead to ongoing employment with the firm, raises, bonuses, and promotions.

If you fail to improve enough within the agreed-upon time period or you receive further negative evaluations, you will likely be terminated. *Termination* means you no longer have a job with this company—the company has fired you. You yourself can terminate your employment, by quitting, or resigning. If business is slow, the company can let you go through a *layoff*. This means the company lets you go, through no fault of your own. In some industries, being laid off means you will be called back to your job when business improves. In today's business environment, though, layoffs are often permanent. You should keep current about your company, its industry, and the nation's economy so you are not surprised by these and other employment changes.

ACTIVITY 2

Mr. Sebastian, Marlene's supervisor, sat on the edge of Marlene's desk and re-marked loud enough for everyone to hear, "You are doing a great job here, Marlene. Here's your job performance evaluation. Look it over when you have a chance, sign it to prove you received it, and return it to me before the end of the day. Oh, and you're not getting a raise right now because the company is in a slump."

1. How do you think Marlene felt during this encounter with her supervisor? Why?

_____

_____

2. How could Mr. Sebastian have conducted Marlene's job performance evaluation better?

_____

_____

3. What should Marlene say to Mr. Sebastian to let him know she is not happy with the outcome of her evaluation? Write the exact words.

_____

_____

$\boldsymbol{P}$romotions

Smart TIP

Ask about the company's promotion policy during your job interview.

A *promotion* is a rise in rank or position, an advancement to a more prestigious and better-paying job within the company. For example, if you have been working as a sales assistant in a clothing store, you could be promoted to floor supervisor, sales manager, or store manager. A mailroom courier could become the mailroom supervisor or be promoted into another department.

Being Promoted Within the Company

Most companies try to promote people within the company when a high-ranking position becomes available, but each company is different. You first heard about your company's promotion policy during your job interview and employee orientation. Many firms have written handbooks detailing how they promote. Be familiar with these policies so you can take advantage of opportunities for advancement.

When Do Promotions Happen?

A promotion can be made at any time of the year. The following common scenarios often result in a company offering one or more promotions.

Smart TIP

Set your sights on your next promotion.

Job openings arise in the company. An opening can occur because an employee left, retired, or was promoted. For example, Joanna is a machine tool operator for an airplane manufacturer. Barry, the assistant supervisor, has been promoted to the supervisor's position. Now, the company has an opening for the assistant supervisor's position. Joanna can apply for this position, and if she gets it, she will have been promoted.

The company is reorganizing. Promotions are offered when a new job is created within the company. Consider this scenario: Paul has been a data processing clerk with Serge, Inc., a men's suit manufacturer, for five years. Company sales are rising and two new data processing clerks have been hired. Because the department workload has increased, the company creates a new job with a new title, Assistant Supervisor of Data Processing. Paul, a valued employee, is promoted to fill this new job.

Companies also expand by creating a new division. Let's look at Serge, Inc. again. Because the women's suit market is growing, a new division called Silk, Inc. is created to manufacture ladies' suits. All the job openings in this new division are created by *expansion*, growth within the company. In an expansion, Paul could be offered a further promotion, perhaps to Supervisor of Data Processing at his company.

Other reorganizations occur when companies *downsize* and combine divisions, branches, or departments work more efficiently at lower costs. Some employees will be encouraged to take early retirement, while others can be dismissed. When this happens, the remaining staff members could be moved to new positions within the company. These are generally *lateral promotions*, horizontal moves within a company that do not represent a move upwards or lead to more prestigious positions.

Why Do Companies Promote Employees?

Your employer spends time and money training you to do your job. Once you are familiar with it and company routines, you are valuable to the firm. If the company chooses people from the outside to fill job openings, it faces the time and expense of training these new workers. The company, therefore, would prefer to train you and offer you the advancement opportunity.

Employees Are Promoted Within A Company Because They: **Checklist 13-3**

- Know the corporate routines.
- Understand company policy.
- Are already trained.

- Are proven workers with good track records.
- Are valuable to the company.

ACTIVITY 3

Sandy Ruiz has worked as a video editor for Daytime TV Clips Inc. for 10 months. She reviews videotapes of daytime television programs. Her job is to isolate and edit the commercials run during a specific show. She splices the videotape and creates a new tape containing only commercials. The company then sells the tape with the commercials to the advertising agencies who ran the ads. Sandy is very meticulous and pays attention to minute details on the videotape. Because she is so good at her job, Daytime just offered her a promotion to a new position as Senior Editor.

1. Why did Daytime TV Clips Inc. promote Sandy Ruiz?

   _____

   _____

2. Explain how Sandy is an asset to her employer.

   _____

   _____

3. Why is Daytime well served by promoting Sandy?

   _____

   _____

Personal Attributes Needed for Promotion

Lars Nelson is a relatively new employee at the Market Systems Credit Agency. A recent community college graduate, Lars is self-confident and wants to get ahead in business. Mr. Kingman, his supervisor, is watching this bright, energetic, intelligent, hard-working employee to see how well he fits in the company. If he works out as well as Mr. Kingman thinks he will, Lars will be considered for promotion next year. Lars has the personal characteristics needed for promotion at the agency.

Personal attributes are the qualities and characteristics of a person. They include one's personal ethics and all the things that make one employee stand apart from the others. In the example above, Lars is described as being "bright, energetic, intelligent, hard-working." These are Lars' personal attributes.

Take the initiative. Let your employer know you want to be promoted. Many people assume a promotion has to be *offered* to them. In fact, you may *ask* for a promotion if an opening occurs. Here is a perfect situation to be assertive, as someone less qualified could get the promotion because he or she was assertive and you were not.

Figure 13-2 You have learned your organization's routines; you understand its policies; you have acquired the needed, special work skills; you have a record of successes; and you believe you are valuable to the organization. Is it time to consider seeking a promotion?

One employee stands out from all the others. Company officials and supervisors observe employees all the time to spot the people who *excel*, who are better than the others. One of your supervisor's tasks is to evaluate and judge you and your coworkers to see who is the best, because only the best get promoted.

$\mathcal{S}$mart **T I P**

Be the employee your company wants to promote.

The Employee Who Stands Out From The Others:

- Presents a positive image to everyone.
- Is someone who wants to get ahead.
- Is someone supervisors would like to have in their departments.
- Is someone supervisors consider a strong candidate for promotion.

The employee is an asset to the company.

Promotable employees are assets to a company. An *asset* is a person, place, or thing having monetary value to a company. For example, the machinery in a dairy is an asset. Employees in a company are likewise assets. A company without valued employees cannot stay in business for very long.

An employee who is an asset is an employee the company wants to keep. He or she helps the company meet its goals by completing work accurately and on time. Additionally, the company usually is willing to invest more time and money in training a valued employee. For example, Charlie is a crane operator for a construction company. Matthew, his supervisor, is sending Charlie for training on a new computerized crane the company has just purchased. The construction company pays a fee for Charlie's training plus his salary while he is at crane operator's school because management believes Charlie's training is an investment in the future.

✔ **Employees Are In Control When They:** **Checklist 13-4**

- Make good impressions.
- Show dedication to their jobs.
- Show a willingness to improve and grow.
- Show knowledge of company policies.
- Show they have what it takes to get ahead.
- Show they know how to get ahead.

Turning Down an Offer of Promotion

As stated earlier, when you think you are ready for promotion, you should let your supervisor know. When a higher-level position opens up, you do not have to sit back and wait for it to be offered to you. Still, situations arise where you will be offered a promotion you did not request. Of course, you can turn down such an offer; you do not have to accept every one. The offer might include certain conditions you are not ready or willing to handle, such as relocating to a different geographical area or working nights.

Do you have enough self-confidence? You might not think you can handle more responsibility, even though you really want a promotion. Discuss this with the person making the offer. Remember, your employer believes you can handle this new job, or it would not have been offered to you. You must believe in yourself, too.

Does the new position meet your career goals? The promotion offered to you could fall short of meeting your own career goals. If a move does not help you further your goals, you should decline. For example, Adam is working as a customer service representative at Ball Auto Service while attending college. He has just been offered a promotion to be supervisor of Customer Service. But, Adam just earned his degree in accounting and is now a licensed Certified Public Accountant (CPA). In declining the offer, Adam says, "I appreciate your confidence in me, but I am interested in a position in which I can use my accounting skills and CPA license. I hope we can discuss a possible move in that direction soon."

Is the promotion a disguised lateral move? You can be offered a promotion, with a small pay increase, to a position exactly like your current one, but in a different department or division. The new job might be very similar to your old one. In fact, this is not a move upwards at all, but simply a *lateral move* within the company, and you must decide whether this is acceptable.

What are the consequences of not accepting a promotion. You probably will not be fired if you decline a promotion. However, you might have to face some consequences if you decline. You could be perceived as lacking ambition or not being a team player. This perception could lead to your being passed over for future advancement or additional training within the company. Your supervisor could interpret your refusal to accept a promotion as a personal affront or even an act of disloyalty or betrayal. If you decline a promotion, try to head off these possible negative reactions by making your reasons clear and rational. Express sincere appreciation for the offer and continue to perform at a high level despite any tensions that might arise.

Activity 13-1

Using Important Words and Information

A. **Important Words.** Your instructor will assign various projects to help you add these words to your business vocabulary.

1. Advancement	7. Feedback	12. Lateral promotion
2. Asset	8. Grievance	13. Layoff
3. Buddy system	9. Job-hopping	14. Personal attribute
4. Downsize	10. Job performance evaluation	15. Promotion
5. Excel		16. Self-assessment
6. Expansion	11. Lateral move	17. Termination

B. **Learning Log.** Summarize what you have learned from material in this chapter and what it means to you. How could you apply this information to gaining personal insights about yourself or your employment situation?

_____

_____

_____

_____

_____

_____

_____

_____

_____

_____

_____

_____

_____

_____

_____

_____

_____

_____

_____

_____

_____

Activity 13-2

Write complete answers to the questions in this section. Explain your answers using specific examples. Be prepared to discuss your answers with the class.

1. How should you evaluate your present job and your future at that job?

   _____

   _____

2. Why would someone want to be promoted?

   _____

   _____

   _____

3. List and explain four things evaluated on a job performance review.

   _____

   _____

   _____

4. What questions should be answered in a job performance interview?

   _____

   _____

   _____

5. Describe the ideal job performance evaluation interview with your supervisor.

   _____

   _____

6. List the eight reasons for negative comments in a job performance review.

   _____

   _____

   _____

7. What can you do when you receive an unfair evaluation?

   _____

   _____

8. What does a good evaluation mean to an employee?

   _____

   _____

9. What does a bad evaluation mean to an employee?

   _____

   _____

Activity 13-3

Employment Situations

Write complete answers to the questions posed in the case studies in this section. Be prepared to discuss and explain your responses with your classmates.

CASE 1: Françoise, an accountant, receives a mixed job performance evaluation from Isabelle Macintosh, Vice President of the Accounting Division. Françoise has excellent technical skills and gets along well with her coworkers. Françoise had been excessively absent, however, has poor telephone manners, and does not meet job deadlines. Françoise is asked to take a communication skills course through the company training program and remedies for her absenteeism and missed deadlines are also suggested. A timetable is drawn up noting dates where improvement is expected.

1. List the things Ms. Macintosh did properly during the review.

   _____   _____

   _____   _____

2. Describe the effects of the evaluation for Françoise.

   _____

   _____

3. Why was developing a timetable important in Françoise's review?

   _____

   _____

   _____

CASE 2: Milan, an administrative assistant at Stoner and Chung, a private investment banking company, works for Rose Kiernan, a vice president of the company. Six weeks after her annual job performance review, Mrs. Boyd, the Operations Manager, offers Milan a job as administrative assistant to Whitney Gould, another vice president.

1. Is this an upward or lateral move? Why?

   _____

   _____

2. If you were Milan, how would you react to this offer? Why?

   _____

   _____

   _____

3. Suppose Milan were promoted to be the administrative assistant to Stu Stoner, one of the founding partners of the company. How would this position be different for her?

   _____

   _____

   _____

Activity 13-4

Communicating in a Job Performance Interview

Write complete answers to the questions below. Be prepared to discuss and explain your responses.

A. Damien is having his semiannual job performance interview with his supervisor, Mr. Ross. Write a response for Damien to each of Mr. Ross' comments.

Mr. Ross Says: **Damien Could Respond:**

1. "Your overall job performance is very good. You have mastered the technical aspects and your output is excellent. Would you like to be trained to operate the new X1460 machinery?"

_____

_____

_____

_____

_____

2. "Damien, you do your own work well, but you seem to be unhappy when asked to help others do their jobs."

_____

_____

_____

_____

3. "You have been late six times in the last month. What steps will you take to make sure you get to work on time from now on?"

_____

_____

_____

_____

B. Rewrite each of the following inappropriate comments made by employees during a job performance interview.

1. "Sure, I talk a lot while I'm working—doesn't everybody?"

_____

_____

_____

_____

2. "I'm a single working parent and I can't help being late every morning. It's just not easy getting everything done and getting my child over to daycare each day."

_____

_____

_____

_____

3. "I can't afford to buy a new wardrobe for this job. I don't think my clothes are too casual to work here."

_____

_____

_____

_____

4. "Yeah, I like working here. But I'm getting bored because my job's too easy."

_____

_____

_____

5. "I like to smoke. I mean, I just have to have a cigarette. I can't help it if there are flammable things around here. I can't leave my workstation, you know."

_____

_____

_____

_____

internet

Activity 13-5

Courses for Self-Improvement

Search the Internet for courses you can take to update and enhance your job and career-management skills. Make a list of these courses with their Web addresses.

Activity 13-6

The Team Approach

team

Team members are to choose people having different types of jobs and employed in different industries to interview about their employer's job performance evaluation procedures. During these interviews, probe to find out exactly *how* each is evaluated on his or her respective jobs.

Chapter 14

Planning Your Career

Skills

OBJECTIVES

After you have worked through this chapter, you will be able to:

1. Recognize the importance of setting goals.

2. Evaluate considerations important to setting goals.

3. Enumerate the steps in decision making.

4. Apply the decision-making steps to solve a specific problem.

5. Discuss the roles of mentors and role models in one's career.

6. Understand the concept of networking

When Lynne was in high school, she thought she wanted to be a secretary in a large, expensively decorated office, working for an executive high up in the corporate hierarchy. She wanted the glamour and prestige of the world of big business. The first job she had after graduation was a disappointment. Lynne found secretarial work boring and discovered she did not like being stuck at a desk in an office every day. She realized being a secretary was not what she wanted after all. Rather than waste her skills, she decided to go to college to become a business education teacher. Lynne liked teaching. She enjoyed working with the students, helping them develop their skills, and then seeing them enter the work force. While teaching, Lynne discovered she had a talent for working with students who were having personal and family problems. The counselors at her school encouraged her to go to graduate school to earn a degree in counseling.

As Lynne's career progressed, she learned even though her original decision did not work out, nonetheless, she was able to leverage her secretarial skills to get bigger and better jobs. Through her experiences, she also learned what she really wanted from a job. Lynne changed, her goals changed, and her career changed. During her career, Lynne had to make numerous decisions concerning the direction her career was taking.

Decision Making

How many times have you been asked, "What are you going to be when you grow up?" The answer could be, "A brain surgeon," "A teacher," "An artist," "A model," or "I don't know." When you are young, the future looms as one enormous stretch of time, and you frequently don't give it much thought; the present is enough. As you get older, though, the future becomes more clear, and your dreams and hopes change accordingly. Decisions you make as a teenager might not work out, times and circumstances change, and you will change as a person as you experience new things. The decisions you make, therefore, will have to change as new opportunities present themselves. As you develop new interests, learn new skills, and circumstances in your life change, you will probably make an ever-stronger commitment to grow personally, realizing its importance to the decision-making process.

Figure 14-1 Your career will probably change paths and direction during your working lifetime.

Decision making is the act of choosing from a number of alternatives to solve a problem.

We make decisions all the time, whether we realize it or not. Even by choosing to delay or postpone a decision, or by trying to avoid making one at all, you are, in fact, making a decision—you are deciding *not* to act. We all know someone who acts before thinking, who does something and then gets angry at the result. That individual has not considered the consequences of his or her decisions.

Every decision we make involves an element of **risk**, the chance of loss, the possibility we might lose out. What would happen if you decided you had another 10 minutes before you had to get up this morning? Another 20 minutes? What if you decided not to get up at all?

Smart **TIP**

You are in control of making your own decisions.

Educated Decisions

You want to make educated decisions, so you can minimize the risks and the consequences involved. Educated decisions are those you make after considering all important information and projecting all possible outcomes. In the working world, making educated decisions is vital because:

1. You make wiser decisions bringing you the results you desire.
2. Educated decisions lead to more and better opportunities in the future.
3. You take control of events instead of letting events control you.
4. Issues of importance to you are not left to chance.

ACTIVITY 1

You have been making decisions all day today, from the moment you woke up. The first one might have been, "Do I have to get up yet? Can I sleep another 10 minutes?" From that point on, list all the decisions you have made today.

_____

_____

_____

_____

How Decisions Are Made

As shown in Figure 14-2, making decisions is a multiple-step process. The following five steps describe the way most people make the majority of decisions:

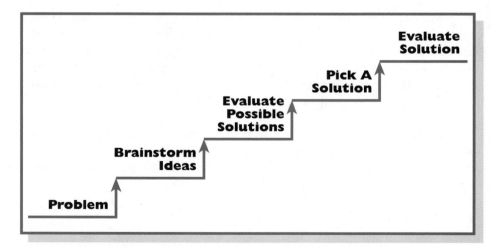

Figure 14-2 The decision-making process consists of five steps.

Step One: *Evaluate the problem* and examine all the facts. You should be able to state the problem, making sure you've identified it correctly.

Step Two: *Brainstorm,* think of all possible issues, solutions, and contingencies. At this time, you do not have to think of the best solutions. List not only all rational solutions, but also unusual, emotional, outlandish, crazy, silly, stupid, and creative solutions too.

Step Three: *Consider the consequences,* the probable outcomes of each idea. Outcomes are results that, being realistic, you think are likely to happen if you follow a specific course of action. Examine all outcomes, weighing the pros and cons of each, and ask yourself whether you can live with them. Discard the ideas you do not like, that do not solve the problem, or that are impractical.

Step Four: *Choose* a solution and apply it to the problem.

Step Five: *Evaluate the outcome.* Did it solve the problem, was the outcome desirable, were the consequences of the decision acceptable? If you did not like a solution, consider another one, rethink all possible solutions, or reevaluate the problem to make sure you defined it correctly. Examine the original description of the problem. Did it contain all the details to be considered? If you like the solution, act—repeat steps 4 and 5.

ACTIVITY 2

Allen works 15 hours a week at Oil Changes. His friend, Cherokee, tells him of a job opening where he works, at Quickie Lube. The work is similar and pays $1.50 more per hour than Allen is making now, but the work schedule does not appear to be as convenient. Long-term prospects for advancement appear to be better at Oil Changes. Allen is seriously thinking of changing jobs. Let's help Allen make his decision.

1. What is Allen's problem? _____

2. List the possible solutions to Allen's problem. _____
_____
_____

3. What is the probable outcome of each solution? _____
_____
_____
_____

4. Make Allen's decision by choosing one of the solutions. How well does it solve the problem?
_____
_____
_____

Setting Goals for the Future

As Lynne learned, you should be able to take control of the events affecting your life and pursue what you want to do. You are responsible for your career. Your career is the progression of all your jobs in your profession. Some people have only one career in their lifetime; others change careers frequently. Reviewing Lynne's careers, one sees they included her working as a secretary, teacher, and counselor. Each career is usually made up of a series of jobs, one leading to another, forming what is known as a career path.

The Importance of Setting Goals

To grow within a given career, you must make the best use of opportunities as they arise, dare to take risks, and seek out new opportunities. To make career changes advantageous to you, you must consider many things. Your career goal is what you hope to achieve in your career. Make educated decisions when deciding on career choices so you have a direction that is realistic for you and that you believe will meet your needs.

When setting career goals, you must know yourself and what is important to you. What are your ambitions and dreams? Each individual is unique, and therefore each individual's goals will be different. Yet, many common issues must be addressed when setting your goals.

People Make Changes In Their Jobs And Careers To:

- Achieve growth and gain responsibility.
- Acquire more authority.
- Satisfy personal needs, such as relocating to a better city or getting a better salary.
- Escape problems, such as incompatibility with a supervisor.
- Leave an unethical business environment.
- Experience greater job satisfaction in a field more compatible with talents and interests.
- Get out of a dead-end job, one lacking opportunity for growth.
- Find new employment when terminated from a job.
- Find employment when laid off from a job.

Self-Assessment

Following is a list of factors for your consideration. Fill in the blanks on the right side of the page. Your answers should be honest and pertain to you as you are at the present time.

Self-Assessment Form

Date Completed: _____

Part I. The Assessment

A. Lifestyle:

1. Where do you want to live? Urban environment, suburban, or rural?

   _____
   _____

2. What region of the country do you want to live in? Would you consider relocating now? In the future?

   _____
   _____
   _____

3. Do you want to live in a house? How large? Or would you prefer a condo, co-op, or apartment?

   _____
   _____
   _____

4. What possessions do you wish to own (cars, computers, property, stereos, jewelry)? How important are they to you?

   _____
   _____
   _____

5. What are your hobbies?

   _____
   _____

6. What do you do in your leisure time? Common activities include sports, music, dining out, theater, movies, dancing, reading, attending lectures.

   _____
   _____
   _____
   _____

7. Do you volunteer in your community? At a local hospital, school, homeless shelter, or church? How important is this work to you?

   _____
   _____
   _____

B. Family Commitments:

1. What is the size of your family? Who lives with you? For whom are you responsible?

   _____
   _____

2. Are you bound by a family commitment (spouse works and cannot move, parents need care)?

   _____
   _____
   _____

3. Are you responsible for shelter, food, health care, tuition, or other expenses for yourself, children, or other family members?

   _____
   _____
   _____

C. Personal Commitments:

1. Are you enrolled in any school or college? _____

2. What social obligations do you have? _____

3. To what civic organizations do you belong? _____

4. What other commitments do you have? _____
   _____

D. Abilities and Interests:

1. What can you do well? What are your skills, talents, abilities? _____
   _____
   _____

2. What training and education have you received? _____
   _____
   _____

3. What do you like to do? Work with people. solitary work, scientific pursuits, art interests, work with your hands, athletics? _____
   _____
   _____
   _____

E. Values: Values are things of importance, of *worth*, to you and essential to your happiness.

1. What are your career values? Consider salary, degree of supervision and security; working with people or alone; working with your hands or your mind; working with machinery; working in a creative environment. _____
   _____
   _____
   _____

2. What are your personal values? Consider types of people you like and what makes you happy—surroundings, keeping busy, books, music, food, socializing, religious activities, competition, humor. _____
   _____
   _____
   _____
   _____

F. Ambitions:

1. What would you like to see yourself doing in five years? Ten years? _____
   _____

2. Where would you like to be in your career in five years? Ten years? Twenty years? _____
   _____

3. What are your career goals? _____

ACTIVITY 3 (continued)

Part II. Evaluation

1. Your answers give you a profile of how you see yourself, your future, your job, and your career. To get the whole picture, write a description of the person who completed the Self-Assessment Form above. Step back and look at what this person is like. What direction do you think this person should take in planning life and career?

_____

_____

_____

_____

_____

2. If you are currently working, look at your work situation. Are you satisfied with what you see? Do you want to stay where you are? Do you want to make any changes? Do you want to make any changes to the course you believe will lead to your goals?

_____

_____

_____

_____

_____

3. List all the things you need to do to reach your career goals. Prioritize this list and identify the short-term and long-term goals. Short-term goals are those needing to be met immediately.

_____   _____

_____   _____

_____   _____

_____   _____

_____   _____

Preparing For Advancement

As you are enhancing your skills and furthering your education by attending school or a training program, you must prepare for career advancement. You cannot expect a promotion or change of profession before you are ready to meet their challenges. Start preparing for advancement now by considering options available to you.

Training and Professional Courses

Ellen and Peter work for Prime Cable, a local cable TV provider, as installers of cable TV systems in homes and businesses. They have been working with standard hard-wire analog systems for a long time. In the

Smart T I P

Education opens many career doors.

field of cable, however, much discussion has taken place regarding the change from analog to digital technology. Prime Cable's management has decided to switch to a digital network because of its improved reception and potential for increasing its customer base. As soon as Ellen heard about this, she inquired about and enrolled in digital technology courses at the local technology training center. Now she holds an edge over Peter, who thought he knew enough to *get by* at his job. When Prime Cable supervisors look for employees who know digital, Ellen's foresight will pay off.

Many who want to advance in their chosen careers find their way blocked because they have not had the necessary education. Still, you might think education is not necessary for your present position. Remember, even as education and training take time, so do advances in careers. Because of rapid changes in the technology used in the average workplace, you should be competent on the computer and the application programs used in your profession. Be proficient in the newest versions of these programs and generally stay on the cutting edge of the technology used in your field of work.

Solid Work Record

Katlyn is absent from school four times each month. Her teachers have begged and pleaded with Katlyn to improve her attendance and her guidance counselor is concerned because her academic record is suffering. Katlyn is likely to take this problem with her when she enters college or the job market. Because she does not have a good attendance record in school, she probably will not have a good one at work.

Building a Good Work Record Throughout this text, we have discussed the work habits and personal attributes helping you succeed on the job. These are reflected in your job performance evaluation (see Chapter 13) and become part of your work record. Your work record will provide the information needed if your employer is asked to write a job recommendation for you.

Some Items Included In Your Work Record

- Personal information (address, phone, date of birth)
- Job information, including job title, responsibilities, and salary

- Attendance and lateness
- Participation in company activities
- Job Performance Evaluations
- Promotions and raises

Building a Good Record of Work Experience Every time you accept more responsibility on the job, you add to your experience. By declining offers of promotion without good reason, you indicate an unwillingness to advance. Participation in outside activities, such as professional organizations, also enhances your work record and increases your value to the company.

Role Models and Mentors

You are already showing good work attitudes and getting the needed training. You also have to dress and behave appropriately for the position you want. Study someone who is already in the position and use him or her as a role model, someone you admire and look to for guidance. Examine the way the person dresses and start to build a similar wardrobe for that job. This means you have to buy the clothes, shoes, and accessories appropriate for your *desired* job, if they differ from what you wear for your *present* job. Watch how people in this position walk, talk, and behave. Be aware of how they communicate with each other. Emulate them, which means imitate, model, and copy what they do.

Relationships with mentors, trusted persons who can guide you through your career, have become important in today's society. In the academic environment, teachers were often thought of as mentors because they helped mold people as they went through school. You might find you have rapport, a special relationship or affinity for, your supervisor or other person in a position to help guide you in your career. Choose your mentor wisely. Be sure the person really wants to help you and is able to do so without any strings attached. For your part, be willing to cooperate and make changes.

Terrence, whom we met before, notices all the male managers in his company wear dark suits or slacks and a jacket, solid or striped shirts, and conservative ties. Terrence has observed these managers walk straight, hold their heads high, and acknowledge everyone they pass with a nod. He is trying to do the same—that is, emulate them.

Networking

If you are interested in a promotion, no one will know about it unless you let it be known. Speak with your supervisor, the personnel department, and other coworkers to let them know you are interested in a promotion. You have to be alert for job openings as they arise, so you can apply for them. You also want those in authority to know you are competent and capable of handling other, more challenging positions. In effect, you are mounting a sales campaign to sell management on the idea you are a good employee to promote.

Arnold is a technician in the blood bank at Community Hospital. He is interested in medical research and wants to find a job as a technician in the hospital's medical research lab. Arnold asks his friend Morris, who works there, to tell him about job openings as they appear.

Caroline is the assistant office manager at College Signs, Inc., a small business. She is looking for a position with more responsibility in a company similar to and perhaps larger than College Signs. Active in the local Network for Business and Professional Women, Caroline has told members to alert her if they hear about suitable job openings.

All these people were networking. Networking is the process of working with other people to keep abreast of opportunities available to you. Colleagues, friend, and acquaintances form a network of people you can contact and work with as you advance in your career. This can be like a chain reaction, where you let others know your thoughts, ideas, or needs so they can help you accomplish your goals. Arnold told

Smart **TIP**

Find positive role models.

Smart **TIP**

Choose your mentor carefully; do not copy the wrong person.

Smart **TIP**

A mentor can be your personal on-the-job trainer, coach, or guru.

Smart **TIP**

Network! You never know where your next opportunity will come from.

his friend he wanted to work in medical research lab; Caroline told members of a community networking organization she was looking for a new job, and the kind of job she wanted.

People Network for a Variety of Reasons

- To stimulate professional growth and gain experience.
- To gather information—to find out what something is or how something is done
- To help others gather information.

- To connect "buyers" and "sellers."
- To learn about new opportunities.
- To share experiences.
- To aid problem-solving.

Networking is an important ingredient in getting ahead on the job. In your company, networking can help you become more visible, especially as others learn of your goals and abilities. You learn about expansion and new opportunities as they arise, and find out how coworkers got their positions. You discover the training programs to help you achieve your goals, and what you can do to improve your current work output. As you network outside your company, you will learn of job opportunities in other firms.

You Can Network Professionally By:

- Joining professional organizations and attending their meetings.
- Opening channels of communication with other professionals with whom you come in contact by exchanging addresses, phone numbers, and business cards.
- Becoming an active member in social and civic organizations to which you belong and cultivating friendships there.
- Keeping current by reading professional journals.
- Using computer bulletin boards to make new contacts.
- Attending conferences and workshops sponsored by professional organizations.

Letting Your Desire for Promotion Be Known

When you are networking with others, how should you mention your desire for a change?

Try some of these statements:

1. "What kinds of knowledge and skills did you have to achieve your position?"

2. "Keep me in mind for future openings."

$Smart$ T I P

You must advertise your goals to get ahead.

3. "I'll send you my resume."

4. "Please give me other ideas about where I can look."

After you have made contact with others, you need to *follow-up* to show continued interest in both them and your goal. To do this, you will have to:

1. Make an appointment to see the person again.

2. If the person gets a new position, send a *letter* (not e-mail) of con-gratulations.

3. Telephone to see whether the person received your resume.

4. Thank him or her for taking the time to speak with you.

Taking Risks

To reach your goal, you will have to take risks, meaning you will have to invest time, money, and energy —make a move, go for special train-ing, take a job for which you are not fully qualified, work on a special project—with no guarantee of success. Do not, however, take risks without considering the consequences involved. You might need the support of family and friends to take on a monetary risk, or if you take a position at a lower salary with hopes of earning more as you advance. To minimize your risks, you should network with those who have al-ready taken the step you are considering. Gather as much information as possible, especially about the risk factors. If possible, make the change on a provisional basis to see whether it is suitable, and consider fallback options should you not be successful.

Smart **TIP**

Take risks when you are ready to make a move.

ACTIVITY 4

Margarita wants to own her own word processing service. At present, she is working for a tempo-rary agency. Margarita knows she likes working on various types of reports and projects for differ-ent clients. She likes the hours because she can work at her own pace, as long as the work is done on time. Right now she is paid by the page, which means she earns a specified amount of money for each page of a document she completes. She knows her boss charges the client a lot more per page than she earns.

1. List the risks Margarita will have to take to set up her own word processing service.

_____   _____
_____   _____

2. What do you think Margarita will have to do to minimize her risks?

_____
_____

3. If you were Margarita, would you take the risk? Why? Why not?

_____
_____

Activity 14-1

Using Important Words and Information

A. **Important Words.** Your instructor will assign various projects to help you add these words to your business vocabulary.

1. Brainstorm	6. Educated decision	11. Outcome
2. Career goal	7. Emulate	12. Rapport
3. Career path	8. Evaluate	13. Risk
4. Dead-end job	9. Mentor	14. Role model
5. Decision making	10. Networking	15. Values

B. **Learning Log.** Using a word processing program, summarize what you have learned from the material in this chapter and what it means to you. How could you apply this information to gaining personal insights about yourself?

_____

_____

_____

_____

_____

_____

_____

_____

_____

_____

_____

_____

_____

_____

_____

_____

_____

_____

_____

Activity 14-2

Write complete answers to the questions in this section. Explain your answers using specific examples. Be prepared to discuss your answers with the class.

1. Explain the statement, "Future goals are achieved by planning, not by chance."

   _____

   _____

2. List all the steps in the decision-making process.

   _____   _____

   _____   _____

   _____   _____

3. "By not making a decision, you are actually making one." Explain this statement.

   _____

   _____

   _____

4. List and explain three things influencing the lifestyle you might wish to live.

   _____

   _____

   _____

5. List five things you might have to do to achieve your goals.

   _____   _____

   _____   _____

   _____

6. Define networking and explain why it is important in getting ahead on the job.

   _____

   _____

   _____

7. Describe four ways you can network.

   _____

   _____

   _____

   _____

8. Why will you have to take risks to get ahead?

   _____

   _____

   _____

Activity 14-3

Employment Situations

Consider the following situations. In each, a person has to take an action, and that means making decisions. Put yourself in each person's position and make a decision. Be prepared to discuss and explain your responses with your classmates.

SITUATION 1: Felicity works for a large data processing firm as an administrative assistant. The company is planning to move from Chicago to Atlanta and has offered Felicity a promotion and pay raise if she will move with the company. Felicity has lived in Chicago all her life and has a lot of friends there. Her parents are in good health, and moved to Florida two years ago when they retired.

1. What should Felicity do?

   _____

   _____

2. What are her considerations?

   _____

   _____

   _____

3. Using the decision-making process, what would you decide? Why?

   _____

   _____

   _____

SITUATION 2: Phillipa, the single mother of two high-school girls, has always dreamed of being the manager of the dress department of Lowell's Department Store, where she has worked for the past five years. She thinks now that her daughters are older, she can work the hours required, and she could use the extra money the job would bring.

1. What steps should Phillipa take to achieve the goal of becoming the manager?

   _____   _____

   _____   _____

   _____   _____

2. Prioritize these steps.

   _____   _____

   _____   _____

   _____   _____

3. What should Phillipa do to achieve these steps?

   _____

   _____

   _____

SITUATION 3: Simon has worked in the shipping department at the Ajax Carrier Company, located in Ohio, for more than 20 years, working his way up from freight handler to assistant manager. He has just been told the company is going out of business and he will be out of a job at the end of the month. Simon has always wanted to own a fleet of fishing boats that could be chartered by fishermen sailing from a southern port. He figures now is the time to do it.

1. What things should Simon consider in making such a move?

   _____
   _____
   _____

2. What risks are involved?

   _____
   _____
   _____

3. What problems must be solved?

   _____
   _____

Activity 14-4

Dream sheet

Take a moment to dream about your ideal job.

1. Write down your dream. _____

   _____
   _____

   a. Where you will be working? _____

      _____

   b. What will the work site look like? _____

      _____
      _____

   c. What kinds of people will be your coworkers? ___

      _____
      _____

   d. What will you be doing? _____

      _____

2. What do you have to do to make your dreams a reality? _____

_____

_____

_____

3. Set goals for making your dreams a reality for yourself. _____

_____

_____

_____

internet

Activity 14-5

Career Information

Do a career search. First, find a career field of interest to you and download all the information you can find about it. Then do a job search and download five or more job listings in this field for which you would like to apply.

Activity 14-6

The Team Approach

team

Each team member should pick a field of interest to a wide variety of people. These may include medicine, sports, business, entertainment, education, the arts, and the sciences. Research many types of jobs within each field. Include the job descriptions, requirements, and salaries, and investigate both public and private job opportunities. Assemble your findings into a career handbook, poster, or bulletin board presentation.

*D*eveloping Your Career Portfolio

In completing this activity, remember the purpose is to collect examples of your best work and place them in a binder. Thereafter, this can then be brought to job interviews as a demonstration of the type of work you do.

1. Review each of the items you have collected and decide whether it presents you and your abilities in a good light. Be selective, as too many items in your portfolio will make it overly large and cumbersome. When applying for a job, you will have to carry it with you and prospective employers will have a limited amount of time to view it.

2. Employers will want to know more about you and your career plans, and so you will want to prepare the following:

   a. A document detailing your future career plans including all milestones necessary to achieve your goal.

   b. A short essay describing what you would like to achieve in your life. Include your family, job, residence, activities, and lifestyle. (Refer to the Self-Assessment Form in Chapter 13.)

3. Arrange your materials in the optimal order. You might, for example, decide to keep all the same types of documents together, like papers, awards, tests, or reports. You might decide to group the materials by subject matter. Whatever approach you choose, the reader should understand why you have grouped the materials as you did.

4. Place your name, address, telephone number, and e-mail address (if you have one) on the front of your portfolio. Keep the presentation simple, as you want to make a good impression and the cover is the first thing a reader will see.

Three months have passed since that eventful day when Timothy Landers, Kiesha Brown, Miguel Garcia, and Ellen Post first met in Ms. Weber's office. That was their first day on the job at Melbrook Sporting Goods. Now, each feels like a seasoned employee.

Melbrook Sporting Goods, Inc. has a policy, as explained during orientation, whereby all new employees are put on probation for the first three months of employment. At the end of three months, employees will have a job performance evaluation, including a written report completed by their supervisors. Reports are discussed privately in the supervisors' offices. Should employees have any grievances, they can ask for an appointment to discuss the matter with the appropriate person in the Personnel Department.

Kiesha is very happy on the job. She considers that, after a shaky start, she is doing well. The company manufactures so many items that she took a long time to learn about them, but now she is confident she can answer any question she might be asked about any product. Kiesha realizes she still has a problem with accuracy on the telephone and, even now, paperwork continues to challenge her. She sees no good reason for so much paperwork, but Marilyn, her coworker who helped train her, said "Do it." So she is making an effort, even though, as she admits, it is half-hearted.

She has observed other successful employees and has started to emulate them—how they dress, act, and talk. After three months on the job, Kiesha is content. She considers herself fortunate to have found a job she likes so much.

Ellen, on the other hand, is extremely unhappy. She cannot understand why she is still at this job, except for the fact "the pay is so good." She is angry to find herself in this situation but has made no effort to change it. Ellen thinks her skills are not being used at this job and does not see a future for herself in her department. She does not like her coworkers, who are all men, and is beginning to believe her problems are based on gender, and not her specifically.

Timothy is happy and excited. He never believed he would find a job that would meet his needs so well. He has an opportunity to use his welding skills and he receives satisfaction and approval for the fine work he does on delicate pieces. He likes the people he works with and thinks that his supervisor, Jack Jones, is great. Except, that is, when he makes him call customers about problems with the current welding job. Timothy understands the need for this, but customers intimidate him. Timothy thinks he could do this job forever and be satisfied.

Miguel is bored. He has worked very hard to have a successful career and loves working with computers. His dream is to oversee a computer department where he could develop new programs. He has come to the conclusion he never found this job very difficult, nor has it challenged his skills. He thinks to himself, "Accounts Receivable in a known company seemed like a step in the right direction." Now he is not so sure; where does he go from here?

Melbrook Sporting Goods, Inc.
Probationary Job Performance Evaluation

Employee: _Ellen Post_

Position: _Order Processor_

Start of employment: _____

Supervisor: _Mr. Constantine_

Title: _Shipping Supervisor_

Date of evaluation: _____

Rating:	Excellent	Good	Fair	Needs Improvement
Attendance	☐	☐	☒	☐
Reliability	☐	☐	☒	☐
Dependability	☐	☐	☐	☒
Interest in job	☐	☐	☐	☒
Quality of work	☐	☐	☐	☒
Ability to follow instructions	☐	☐	☐	☒
Job skills	☐	☒	☐	☐
Initiative	☐	☒	☐	☐
Honesty	☐	☒	☐	☐
Interpersonal relations	☐	☐	☐	☒

Comments _Can do the work well, attitude towards job and people needs improvement. At this point, continued employment is in doubt._

Employee Signature _____

Supervisor Signature _____

Melbrook Sporting Goods, Inc.
Probationary Job Performance Evaluation

Employee: _Keisha Brown_

Position: _Customer Rep._

Start of employment: _____

Supervisor: _Ms. Sadar-Wright_

Title: _Manager, Customer Relations_

Date of evaluation: _____

Rating:	Excellent	Good	Fair	Needs Improvement
Attendance	☒	☐	☐	☐
Reliability	☐	☐	☒	☐
Dependability	☐	☒	☐	☐
Interest in job	☒	☐	☐	☐
Quality of work	☐	☐	☒	☐
Ability to follow instructions	☐	☒	☐	☐
Job skills	☒	☐	☐	☐
Initiative	☐	☒	☐	☐
Honesty	☐	☐	☒	☐
Interpersonal relations	☐	☒	☐	☐

Comments _Making an effort to improve accuracy and reliability. Is learning to become a good Customer Relations person. Can do well._

Employee Signature _____

Supervisor Signature _____

Melbrook Sporting Goods, Inc.
Probationary Job Performance Evaluation

Employee: _Miguel Garcia_   Supervisor: _Carmen Black_

Position: _Computer Operator_   Title: _Manager, Accounts Receivable_

Start of employment: _____   Date of evaluation: _____

Rating:	Excellent	Good	Fair	Needs Improvement
Attendance	☒	☐	☐	☐
Reliability	☒	☐	☐	☐
Dependability	☒	☐	☐	☐
Interest in job	☐	☒	☐	☐
Quality of work	☒	☐	☐	☐
Ability to follow instructions	☒	☐	☐	☐
Job skills	☒	☐	☐	☐
Initiative	☐	☐	☒	☐
Honesty	☒	☐	☐	☐
Interpersonal relations	☐	☐	☐	☒

Comments _Excellent employee, excellent skills. Needs to show more initiative when he has finished jobs, come get more work. Must develop relations with people in the department._

_____   _____
Employee Signature   Supervisor Signature

Melbrook Sporting Goods, Inc.
Probationary Job Performance Evaluation

Employee: _Timothy Landers_   Supervisor: _Jack Jones_

Position: _Metalworking, Welder_   Title: _Manager, Metalworking_

Start of employment: _____   Date of evaluation: _____

Rating:	Excellent	Good	Fair	Needs Improvement
Attendance	☒	☐	☐	☐
Reliability	☒	☐	☐	☐
Dependability	☒	☐	☐	☐
Interest in job	☒	☐	☐	☐
Quality of work	☒	☐	☐	☐
Ability to follow instructions	☒	☐	☐	☐
Job skills	☒	☐	☐	☐
Initiative	☒	☐	☐	☐
Honesty	☐	☒	☐	☐
Interpersonal relations	☐	☐	☒	☐

Comments _A very valuable employee. His temper gets in the way of his work and that of the department. Must learn to control it or we may have to let him go._

_____   _____
Employee Signature   Supervisor Signature

1. Job evaluations give you feedback as to how well you are doing. You learn how your supervisor perceives you and your strengths and weaknesses. Our four friends have just received their Probationary Evaluations after three months on the job. Analyze their strengths, their weaknesses, and list what they can do to improve their performances.

Timothy
Strengths:
Weaknesses:
Can improve by:

Ellen
Strengths:
Weaknesses:
Can improve by:

Keisha
Strengths:
Weaknesses:
Can improve by:

Miguel
Strengths:
Weaknesses:
Can improve by:

2. This also can be the time for the employees to evaluate their jobs. Using a word processing program, write an essay, for presentation, discussing specifically how Timothy, Kiesha, Miguel, and Ellen feel about their jobs, their coworkers, their supervisors, and what they consider the company has to offer them. Be ready to discuss this essay in small groups of classmates.

3. At the end of this three-month probationary period, each employee has to make some decisions about his or her job and future. To do this, each will have use decision-making skills to analyze what they think about the job and what they have learned from their evaluations. Writing this down will be helpful.

A. List the decision-making steps that should be followed in making a good decision.

_____

_____

_____

_____

_____

B. Each must make a decision. What is the issue for:

EMPLOYEE
Keisha
Timothy
Ellen
Miguel

C. Applying the decision-making steps you listed in section A above, outline how each employee makes a decision to help solve his or her problem. Use the worksheet at the end of this exercise to help you. On separate sheet of paper, detail your decision-making process, including the following information.

Decision Making Process
Worksheet

Name:

Problem:

Step 1:

Step 2:

Step 3:

Step 4:

Step 5:

Decision:

D. What is the decision each has made?

EMPLOYEE	
Keisha	
Timothy	
Ellen	
Miguel	

4. Each of our friends has now made a decision regarding their career or job. How can they act on these decisions? What should they do to reach their goals? To do this, they must develop a plan of action.

Ellen
Her decision:
Her goal:
To reach her goal, she should:

Keisha
Her decision:
Her goal:
To reach her goal, she should:

Miguel
His decision:
His goal:
To reach his goal, he should:

Timothy
His decision:
His goal:
To reach his goal, he should:

Glossary

Accessory extra item worn or carried to enhance one's appearance.

Advancement move to a better job.

Aggressive extreme form of **assertive** behavior where one uses aggression, hostility, rudeness, or violence.

Anger strong feelings of displeasure and hostility toward something or someone.

Assertive standing up for one's self by expressing to others one's true feelings, thoughts, and desires.

Asset person, place, or thing having monetary value to a company.

Attendance being present at the job site.

Attire clothes.

Attitude overall state of mind with regard to a person, place, or thing.

Attitude, negative excessive focusing on negative people, places, and things.

Attitude, positive focusing on positive people, places, things.

Attribute, personal qualities and characteristics of a person.

Audit eliminating by a sender words, gestures, or actions he or she thinks any concerned receivers will find offensive.

Authority one's responsibility, accountability, and power to command in a company.

Authority, line of path through which authority flows in a company.

Barrier, communication impediment to communication.

Benefit non-salary monetary contribution made to an employee by an employer.

Bond, fidelity *see* **bond, security.**

Bond, security insurance policy reimbursing the employee's company if the employee loses data, documents, or steals from the company. Also known as **fidelity bond.**

Boss *see* **supervisor.**

Burnout state of being completely depleted by too much work or stress.

Career path series of jobs in a employee's career, with each successive job ideally being in the same field, more prestigious, and better-paying than the previous one.

Chain of command series of individuals in a company, each having greater power to command than the previous individual.

Chart, org *see* **chart, organizational.**

Chart, organizational flowchart detailing a company's structure and its line of authority. Also known as **org chart.**

Clarify to make a message more clear.

Client name by which a professional firm calls a customer.

Collective bargaining process by which conditions of employment are negotiated with management by a union.

College tuition reimbursement refund of tuition or textbook expenses given to an employee when he or she successfully completes a college course.

Communication process by which information is exchanged among people and machines.

Communication, horizontal communication among individuals or departments at the same level in the company hierarchy.

Communication, line of path through which information flows in a company.

Communication, oral communication using spoken words.

Communication, system of formal collection of guidelines and procedures by which employees in a company communicate.

Communication, vertical communication among individuals or departments at different levels in the company hierarchy.

Communication, visual communication using a non-verbal, visual method.

Communication, written communication using written words.

Compliment praise.

Consensus high degree of agreement by members of a group.

Consumer person who uses a company's products or services.

Content information or facts of a message; the "what."

Courtesy politeness and consideration for others.

Criticism judgment made by others expressing disapproval of a person's attitude, behavior, or work.

Criticism, constructive respectful criticism of a person's attitude, behavior, or work that includes ideas for how improvements should be made.

Criticism, destructive disrespectful criticism of a person's attitude, behavior, or work that does not include ideas for how improvements should be made.

Culture beliefs, values, and customs held by a group of individuals.

Culture, corporate personality and style of a company.

Customer person who purchases a company's products or services.

Decision making act of reaching a conclusion.

Decode to get a message from a coded form or language.

Deductible initial amount of money an employee pays for an expense before being reimbursed by the employer's insurance company.

Department group of people in a company who have specific duties and work together closely.

Dependent someone who relies on another person for most of his or her financial support.

Discrimination being denied an employment opportunity on the basis of ethnicity, religion, gender, or physical disability.

Dock to deduct money from an employee's paycheck as a penalty for an absence or other reason.

Downsize to terminate a significant number of employees at one time to reduce company costs.

Empathize to relate to another person's thoughts or feelings.

Employment record file containing an employee's history with a company.

Emulate to imitate what one considers the good qualities of another person.

Encode to put a message into a coded form or language.

Excel to be more skilled than average or others at a given task.

Expansion growth of a company, especially into a new area.

Expression sum total of all facial movements. Also called **facial expression.**

Expression, facial *see* **expression.**

Feedback reaction, usually verbal or written, by a person in response to an action or communication by another person.

Feedback response to a message.

Filter to process information through the "sieve" of one's own beliefs, values, knowledge, and experiences.

Fire to dismiss an employee from a job. Also known as **terminate.**

Firing the dismissing of an employee from a job. Also known as **termination.**

Flex-time business practice whereby an employee is given the flexibility to work non-standard hours.

Form way in which a message is presented; the "how."

Frustration disheartening feeling of being blocked from reaching a goal.

Gesture movement of the body, head, or hands when communicating.

Goal, career ultimate outcome desired by an employee as the culmination of his or her work efforts.

Gossip to speak of people's personal matters and propagate rumors.

Gossip, office on-site employee who speaks of people's personal matters and propagates rumors.

Grapevine, the informal communication network through which information is conveyed by word of mouth – that is, by people talking with one another.

Grievance formal complaint made by an employee who considers he or she has been treated unfairly by an employer.

Grooming maintaining one's skin and hair.

Habit usual way of doing something.

Habit, bad usual way of doing something that is not beneficial to one's self or others.

Habit, good usual way of doing something that is beneficial to one's self or others.

Habit, work usual way of doing something at work.

Harassment being annoyed, bothered, pestered, teased, or tormented by coworkers.

Harassment, sexual unsolicited sexual advance considered offensive by the recipient.

Hardware, computer physical equipment making up a computer.

Hazing harassing of a new employee in specifically prescribed ways as a rite of passage.

Hearing passive process by which sounds are registered in the brain of a receiver.

Hierarchy, company vertical ranking of employees in a company according to their authority.

Hierarchy, unofficial company hierarchy reflecting unwritten rules and employee seniority, where the newer employees are expected to perform the more menial tasks.

Hygiene cleanliness of a person's body.

Image overall presentation of a person to the world.

Income money received by a business for the sale of its products or services.

Information, flow of path that information travels in a company.

In-house at a company site.

Instruction order given to an employee telling him or her what to do and usually how to do it.

Intent goal of the sender in conveying a message or taking an action.

Internalize technique of managing stress where a person keeps his or her thoughts and feelings inside, neither speaking of them nor acting out.

Job description list of all the duties of a given job.

Job performance review formal evaluation by an employer of an employee's job performance.

Job-hopping frequently changing jobs held for short periods of time.

Language, body communication of thoughts and feelings using posture, body movements, and facial expressions.

Layoff termination due to company downsizing.

Leave period of time that is neither vacation nor holiday that an employee spends away from his or her job.

Leave of absence, long-term long period of time an employee spends away from his or her job.

Leave, disability period of time an employee spends away from a job because of illness or injury.

Listening active process by which sounds are evaluated in the brain of a receiver.

Literacy, computer knowledge of and proficiency on the computer.

Loyalty faithfulness to a person, organization, or cause.

Mail hardcopy document delivered by a postal organization.

Mail, voice telephone system enabling the recording, saving, deleting, and forwarding of voice messages.

Manager *see* **supervisor.**

Mentor wise and knowledgeable person to whom one looks for training and guidance.

Menu list of choices of computer commands or voice-mail options.

Message content or meaning of information conveyed.

Message, mixed message containing contradictory elements.

Model, Role model person whom one wants to emulate.

Morale attitude and feeling an employee has for his or her work and workplace.

Move, lateral change to a new position comparable to the previous one, usually with a different company.

Networking communication among people to inform and take advantage of opportunities.

Networking, computer connecting two or more computers so they can share resources.

Noise activities or sounds distracting from, impeding, or preventing communication.

Nondirective management style characterized by much support for employees but little formal direction.

Off-site at a site other than a company site.

Organization, line of structure of a company detailing who is the manager of whom.

Orientation process by which an employee is informed about a range of company-related subjects, including benefits, safety rules, security regulations, and management philosophy.

Outcome result of one or more actions.

Output quantity and quality of work produced.

Passive not standing up for one's self and letting others dictate what they want without due consideration of one and one's life.

Patient name by which a medical firm calls a customer.

Pay *see* **salary.**

Pay, gross *see* **salary, gross.**

Pay, net *see* **salary, net.**

Pertinent relating directly to the subject or matter at hand.

Policy written and unwritten rules and procedures that management expects an employee to follow.

Posture way one carries one's body when standing, sitting, or walking. Also called **body posture.**

Posture, body *see* **posture.**

Pride feeling good about one's self and accomplishments.

Prioritize to assign a degree of importance to each task to be accomplished.

Privacy freedom from unauthorized intrusion or interference by others.

Probationary period introductory period of employment, typically three months, during which an employee has the status of a trainee.

Production generating goods or services.

Promotion advancement to a more prestigious and better-paying job in a company.

Promotion, lateral change to a new position comparable to the previous one in the same company.

Punctuality getting to one's workstation or other job site on or before a specified time.

Rapport good communication with, understanding of, and relationship with a person.

Reaction, external reaction to stress where a person acts out, perhaps abusing a person who is not causing the stress.

Reaction, internal body's response to the internalizing of stress, usually resulting in illness.

Receiver person who gets a message.

Record, employment file containing information about an employee's history with a company.

Reference testimonial from someone with whom a job candidate has worked regarding the candidate's job performance.

Relations, customer overall total of the quantity and quality of a company's interactions with its customers.

Relationship, interpersonal relationship between two people.

Reputation regard in which a person is held by others.

Respect acknowledging and honoring others by words and deeds.

Responsibility accountability.

Responsibility, line of path through which responsibility flows in a company.

Rights, territorial "ownership" by an employee of a company area, workstation, tools, or supplies.

Risk possibility of suffering loss or harm.

Rule, unwritten an unofficial rule, one that does not appear in company policies and procedures manuals but is nonetheless observed.

Salary amount of money an employee earns from a job. Also known as **pay** or **wage**.

Salary, gross amount of money an employee earns before deductions. Also known as **gross pay** or **gross wage**.

Salary, net amount of money an employee earns after deductions. Also known as **net pay** or **net wage**.

Salary, straight fixed amount of money an employee earns from a job regardless of the number of hours he or she has worked.

Self-assessment evaluation by an employee of his or her job performance.

Self-respect regard a person has for himself or herself.

Sender person who conveys information to another person.

Software, computer computer operating systems and application programs.

Space, body physical space claimed by a person in a social interaction. Also called **personal space**.

Space, personal *see* **space, body**.

Statement, I statement by person A telling person B what person A feels or thinks about something.

Statement, I, three-part statement by person A telling person B what person A feels or thinks about something, what person A believes is causing that feeling or thought, and what person A would like to happen as a result.

Statement, I, two-part statement by person A telling person B what person A feels or thinks about something and what person A would like to happen as a result.

Statement, you statement of blame where person A tells person B what person B is or should think, feel, or do.

Stress psychological pressure one feels, typically the result of certain people, events, and circumstances in one's life.

Stressor person, event, or circumstance causing stress.

Style, management way in which a manager manages.

Subordinate employee having a lower rank than a given employee.

Supervisor person who oversees employees at a job site and assigns the employees work. Also known as **manager** or **boss**.

Supplier company selling materials needed by another company.

System, buddy when two employees "join forces" unofficially to help each other.

Tact communicating in a polite, respectful, and graceful way.

Team group of people who perform related tasks and work together to achieve a common goal.

Telephone answering system, computerized telephone answering system controlled by a computer.

Tempo speed at which tasks are performed at a company.

Terminate *see* **fire**.

Termination *see* **firing**.

Tolerance acceptance of differences in other people.

Tools of the trade basic tools needed by essentially all members of a trade or profession.

Validity accuracy or truthfulness of a message.

Wage *see* **salary**.

Workstation company area where an employee performs his or her job.

Index